IMAGES
of America

SAYRE

On the Cover: This picture was taken on Main Street in Sayre by E.P. Hosmer Photography at the turn of the 20th century. These were busy times in the town, and people were allowed to park in the middle of Main Street. Note the Beckham County Courthouse at the end of the street. There are both Model-As and Model-Ts pictured. (Courtesy Blevins and Henderson.)

IMAGES
of America

SAYRE

Shirley Killian

ARCADIA
PUBLISHING

ISBN 978-0-7385-8252-8

Published by Arcadia Publishing
Charleston, South Carolina

Printed in the United States of America

Library of Congress Control Number: 2011928646

For all general information, please contact Arcadia Publishing:
Telephone 843-853-2070
Fax 843-853-0044
E-mail sales@arcadiapublishing.com
For customer service and orders:
Toll-Free 1-888-313-2665

Visit us on the Internet at www.arcadiapublishing.com

This book is dedicated to the Farmrail-Grainbelt Corporation.

Contents

Acknowledgments

I have many people to thank for help with this book: the Shortgrass County Museum for the loan of photographs to have scans made; the *Sayre Record* for printing many articles about early times in Sayre; the Farmrail-Grainbelt Corporation for letting us take pictures of their workers and trains to use in the book; the Carlton Cornels family for providing me information to use; Pam Jefferson at the Welcome Center for all her help; the citizens of Sayre, who allowed us to take photographs of homes and businesses; Ted Gerstle, for his patience and understanding; and to my husband, Ray Killian, who had faith that I could write a book and encouraged me to do so.

Unless otherwise noted, all images appear courtesy of the author.

INTRODUCTION

The town of Sayre, Oklahoma, was created in 1901, when the Choctaw, Oklahoma and Gulf Railroad extended its line through western Oklahoma, which was in Indian Territory at the time. The federal government wanted the railroad constructed to send supplies and troops. Until 1885, cattlemen used this land to graze their cattle on. There was always good water in the area supplied by creeks and the North Fork of the Red River. The area was settled during the Land Run of 1892 of Cheyenne and Arapaho territories. Settlers, nesters, and cattlemen alike found Sayre as an area of choice claims on which to construct homes and farm wheat, cotton, and corn.

The Choctaw, Oklahoma and Gulf Railroad, which later was taken over by the Chicago, Rock Island and Pacific Railroad (Rock Island Line), was constructed 24 miles west of El Reno, Oklahoma. About three years later, the Missouri-Kansas-Texas Railroad (or "Katy") was constructed. It was indeed fortunate that it came through Sayre, bringing prosperity to the town, which was called Riverton at the time. It was said that after the railroads came to Sayre, many small businesses came from all directions, causing it to grow by 1,000 people overnight. Locally, the Katy went from Leedy, Oklahoma, to Elk City, Merrit, Highway, Carter, Morave, Ocina, Willow, Brinkman, Mangum, and south to the Red River. There is a Katy Depot located in Elk City, Oklahoma.

Later, Riverton was named Sayre for Robert Heysham Sayre of Pennsylvania. He was a famous railroad man and chief engineer of the Lehigh Valley Railroad and was hired to run the railroad through Sayre. People here affectionately referred to him as "Doc" or "Captain." When he was working in town, he most likely stayed in the Old Hotel and ate at the Harvey House on the west end of town. Mr. Sayre agreed to give a silver cup to the first baby born in town; it happened to be a girl named Irene Sayre Roles, who was born in a dugout on the west side of Short Creek in Sayre. Her silver cup was destroyed by fire when her family was living in Mangum, Oklahoma. Irene lived to be 93 years of age.

Route 66 runs from Chicago through Oklahoma City to Amarillo, Texas, and on to California. It comes right down Fourth Street in Sayre. State Highway 152 also runs through town from Oklahoma City to Sayre to Dumas, Texas. State Highway 283 comes into town from Dodge City, Kansas, and then heads to Vernon, Texas. Interstate 40 runs from the East Coast to the West Coast within a half of a mile of the Beckham County Courthouse. Sayre used to be so busy with people on Friday and Saturday nights that one could hardly get through town because of the people and cars.

The author, her sister-in-law Gerry, her two kids, and the author's two daughters possibly rode the last passenger Rock Island train from Sayre to the depot in Elk City, Oklahoma, back in the 1970s. Of note, the old Rock Island Bridge that is west of Sayre has been washed out at least twice and has been reconstructed; it still stands today as railroad cars pass over it.

Although Rock Island left Sayre in 1979, another railroad company, Farmrail-Grainbelt, came to town in 1981. It has been the contract manager-lessee of the 89 miles of line between Hydro and Erick, Oklahoma. It was purchased from Chicago, Rock Island, and Pacific Railroad Company by the Oklahoma Department of Transportation. The state leased another 89 miles of track to Farmrail in 1992; the Atchison, Topeka and Santa Fe Railway Company previously operated it. Farmrail's affiliate, Grainbelt, owns 176 miles linking Enid and Frederick, acquired from the Burlington Northern Railroad Company in 1987. This 354 miles of coordinated regional network serves agricultural, manufacturing, and mineral interests in western Oklahoma.

The R.S. and K. Railroad Museum in Sayre, Oklahoma, is owned and operated by Ray and Shirley Killian. It contains over 300 toy trains, 400 toy cars, 200 lighted houses, and 250 pieces of railroad memorabilia. People from all 50 states, as well as 21 foreign countries, have visited the museum. One interesting occasion was when people from Pixar visited in 2001, which eventually led to the museum receiving a credit in the movie *Cars* that was released in 2005.

Of note, many of the old buildings on Main Street in Sayre are still standing. The Main Street Program has been very helpful in trying to get people to construct the buildings and help make Main Street look better.

One

Railroad

The first part of the railroad line that came through Sayre was built in Hot Springs, Arkansas. It was named the Diamond Joe Railroad because the owner and builder was said to have worn a vest that had diamonds for buttons. The Chicago, Rock Island and Pacific leased the line in 1901. The first part of the railroad, which is also currently part of the line now, served from Memphis, Tennessee, to Tucumcari, New Mexico. The Diamond Joe was sold to a syndicate that formed and constructed what was known as the Kali Inla Railroad, which operated from Memphis, Tennessee, to McAlester, Oklahoma. Almost as soon as the Kali Inla was completed, a wealthy man by the name of Henry Woods got control of it and organized the Choctaw, Oklahoma and Gulf Railroad. He built the line to Weatherford, which remained at the end of the railroad until July 1901. At this time, McCabe and Steen Contractors finished the grading of the roadbed, and the rails were laid from Weatherford to Texola. Around this time, the Rock Island leased the line and finished construction through Amarillo to Wildorado, Texas. It remained at the end of the line for about two years after. The line was finished from Tucumcari, and it connected with another part of the Rock Island.

Early Sayre engineers included B. Bowen, P.E. Easley, George Gage, "Si" Mecer, and Pat Kennem. The firemen were Frank Chapman, ? McKinney, Shorty Mateer, Dave Pope, Bill Burrow, and N.C. Hally. The conductors were M.J. Cain, E.J. McDevit, F.D. Geer, Edward Heap, and Gus Stanburg.

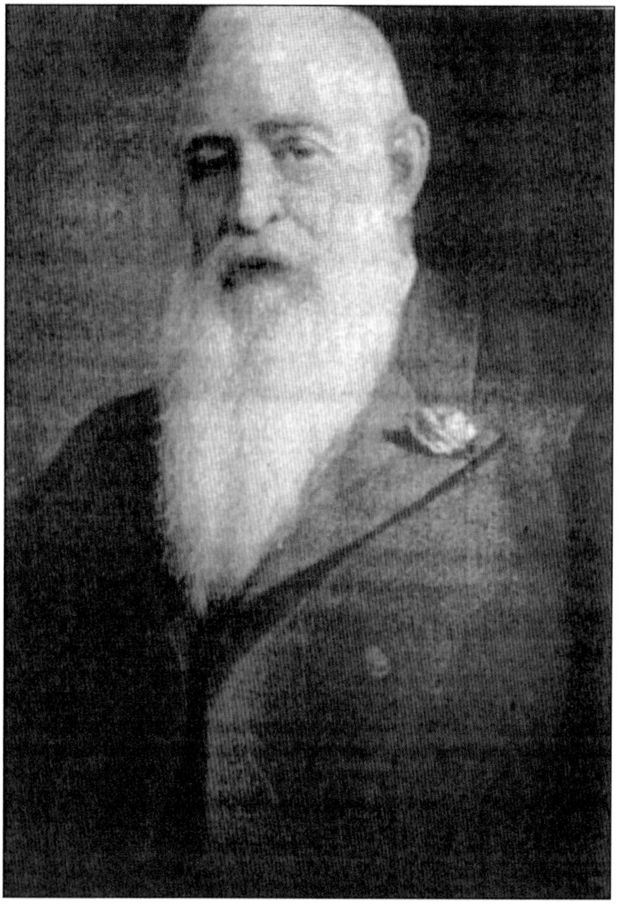

This is a picture of Robert Heysham Sayre, the stockholder for whom Sayre was named. People around town called him "Doc" or "Captain."

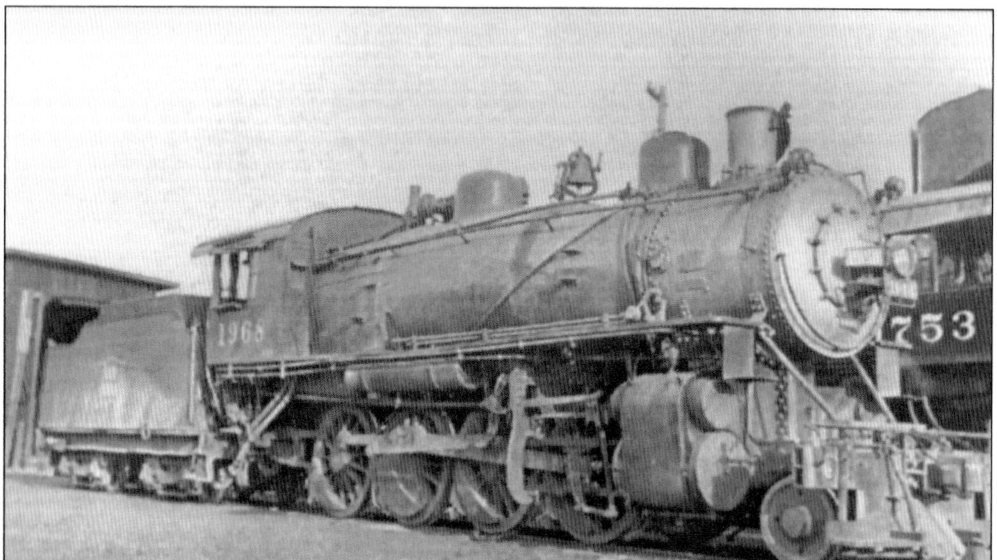

Rock Island engine no. 1968 is pictured here in 1939. It is a 2-8-0 because of the number of wheels it has.

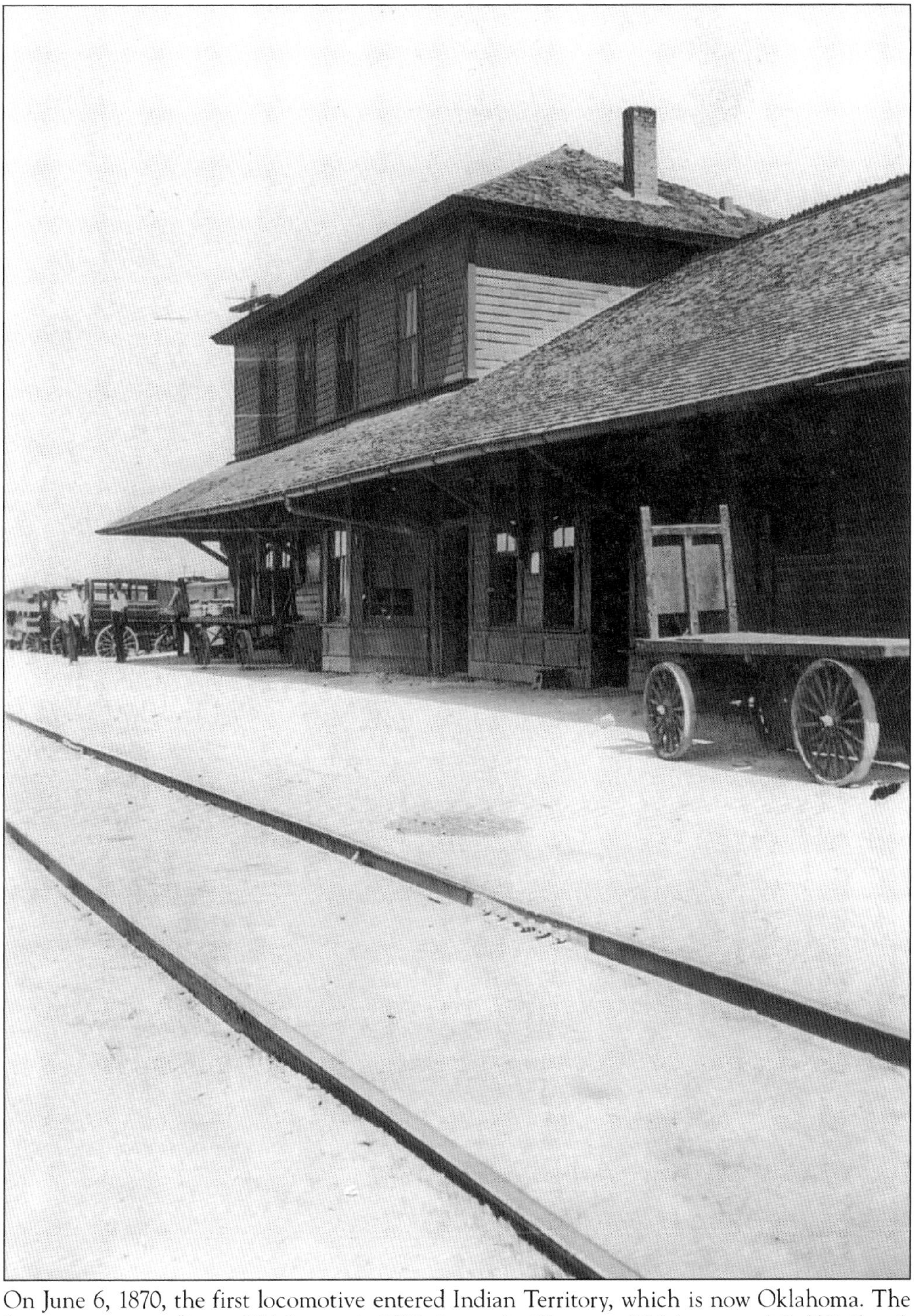

On June 6, 1870, the first locomotive entered Indian Territory, which is now Oklahoma. The first train came to Sayre, Oklahoma, in 1901. It was the Choctaw, Oklahoma and Gulf Railroad, which was later part of the Chicago, Rock Island and Pacific Railroad. Robert Heysham Sayre was a railroad man and chief engineer of construction of the Lehigh Valley Railroad. The last Rock Island train to leave Sayre was on September 26, 1979. The last steam engine was built in 1949.

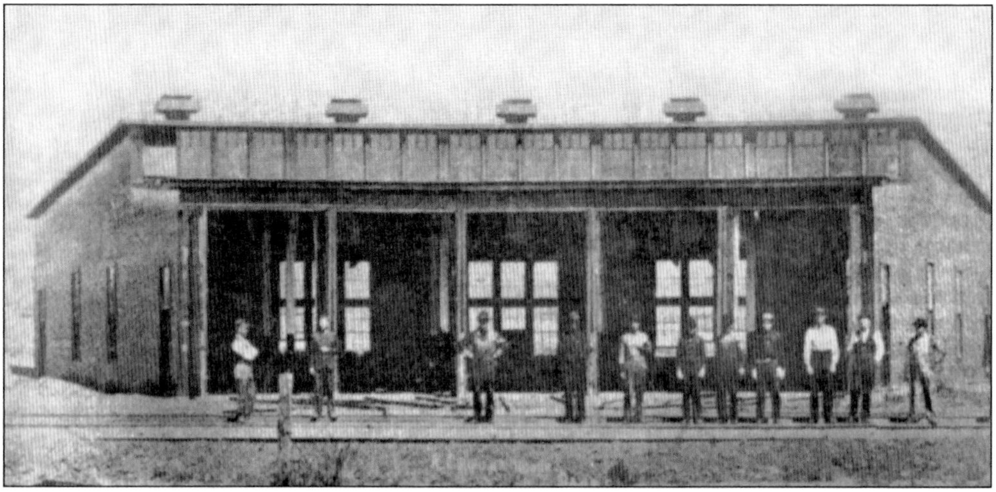

Here is the Rock Island Round House that used to be on the west end of town, around 1905, before it was completed.

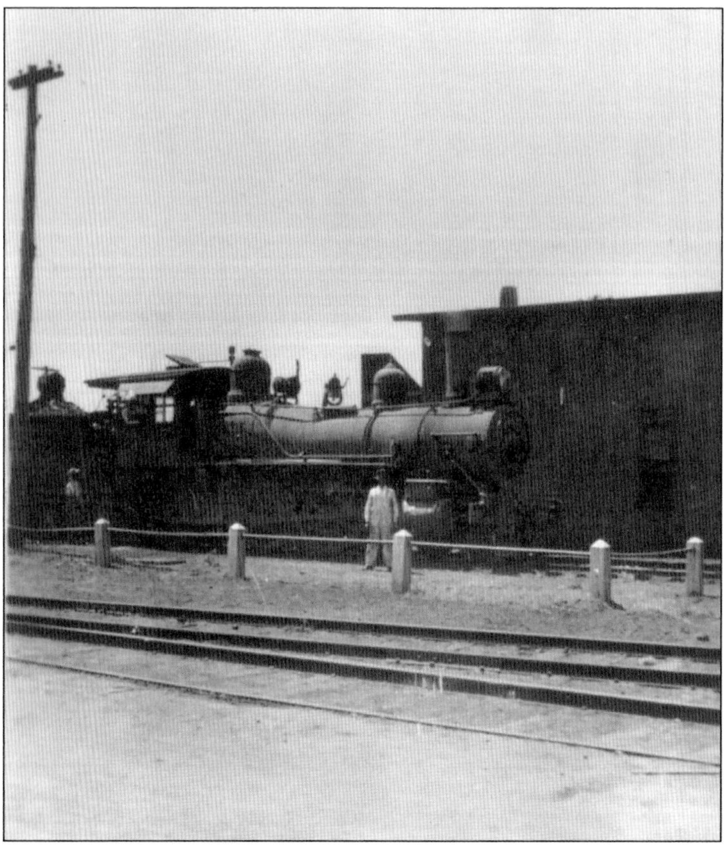

A Rock Island engine is parked near the roundhouse on the west end of Sayre.

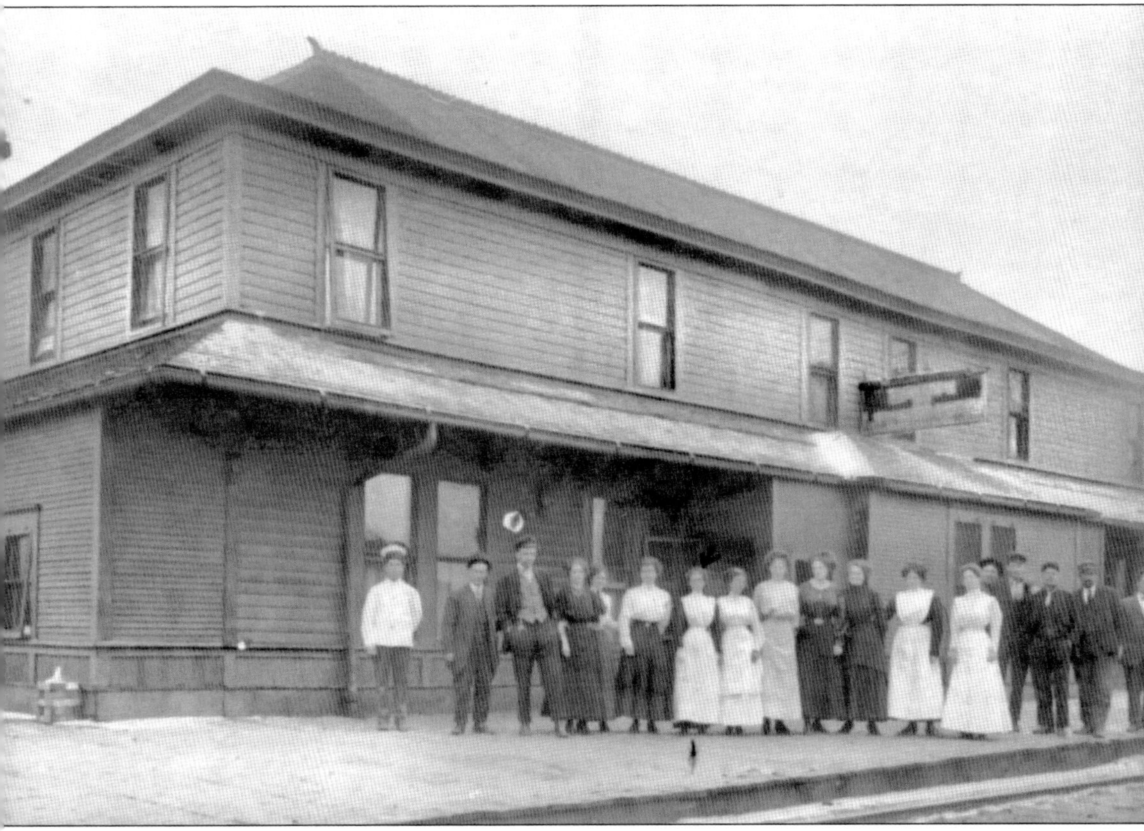

This is the Harvey House and Restaurant that was located on the west end of town in Sayre next to the Rock Island Depot. There are a number of Harvey girls out front. The one with the small arrow above her head (seventh from the left) is Josephine Schlieht Bohannon. The engineer would telegraph ahead and let them know how many people to prepare for. The Harvey Girls all wore starched black dresses with white pinafores over them and lived above the restaurant. (Courtesy of Nadine Bohannon.)

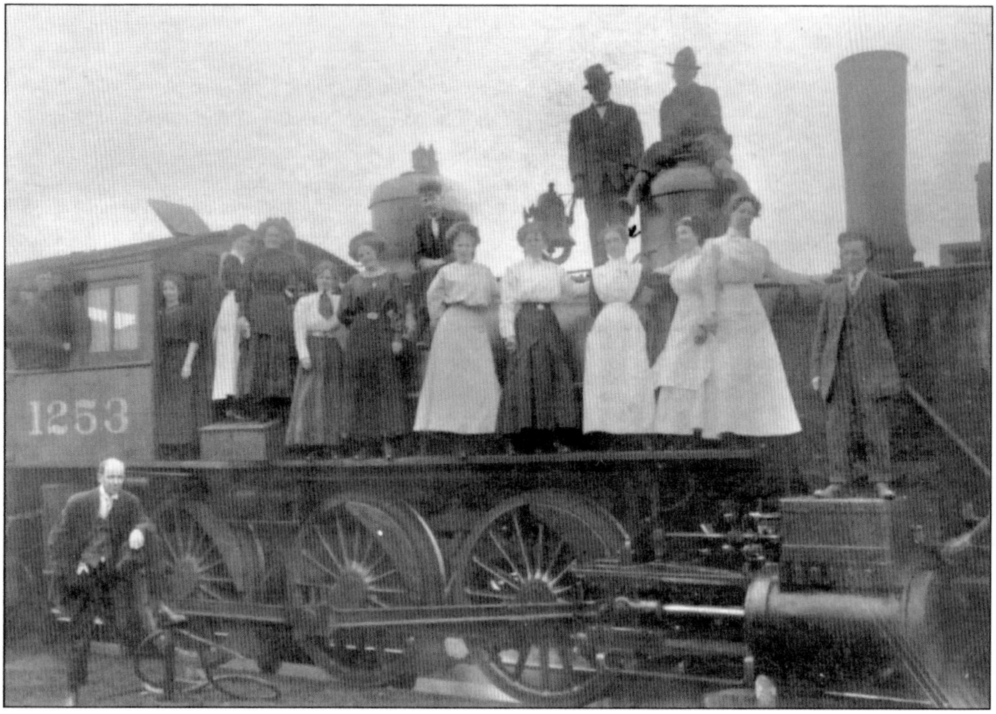

Rock Island engine no. 1253 is parked in front of the Harvey House and depot on the west end of town in Sayre. Note the people standing on the train engine, including the Harvey girls. (Courtesy of Nadine Bohannon.)

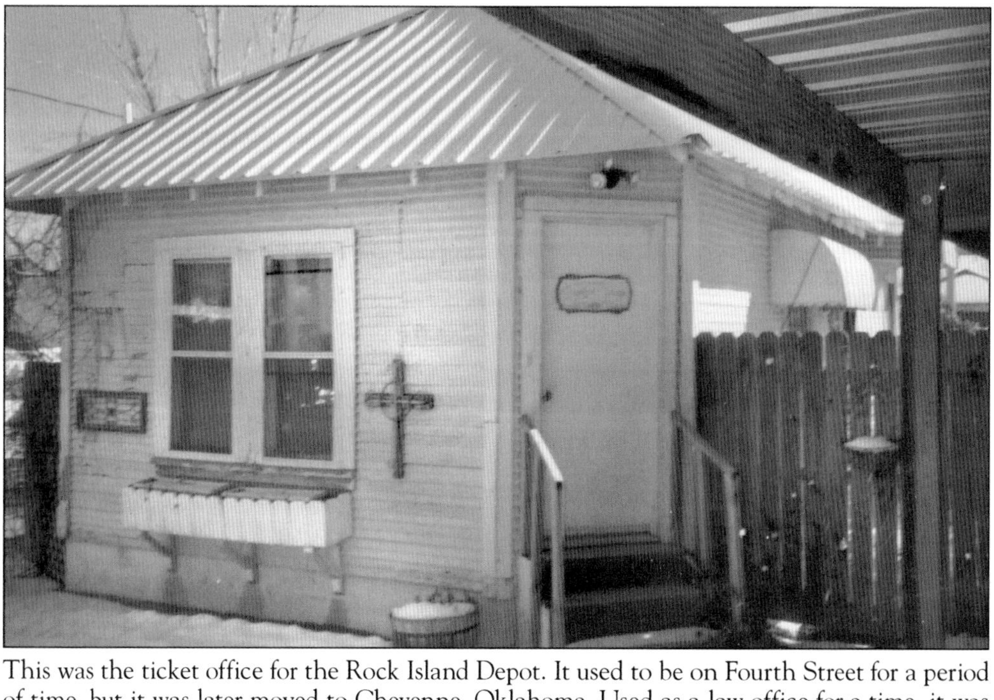

This was the ticket office for the Rock Island Depot. It used to be on Fourth Street for a period of time, but it was later moved to Cheyenne, Oklahoma. Used as a law office for a time, it was later moved back to Sayre behind the Rose Cottage to become a bed-and-breakfast.

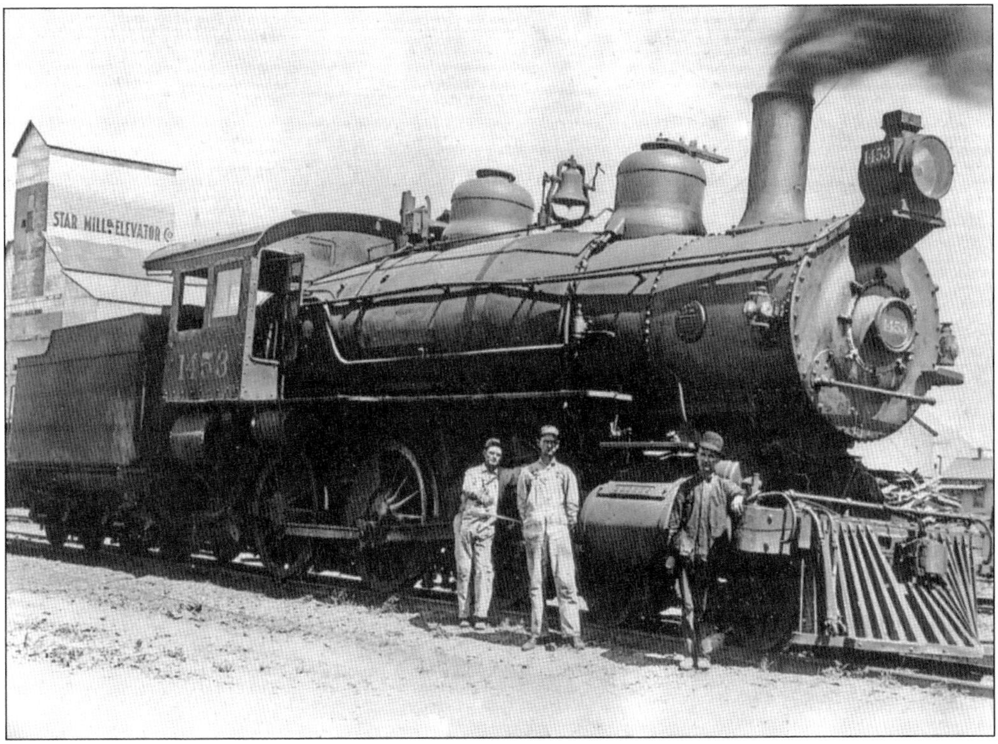

In 1901, the railroad had pushed west and had extended the line to Sayre. The town was named for railroad stockholder Robert H. Sayre. This is a 1910 picture of a locomotive, likely from Rock Island. The man in the center is Lawson G. Staples; the other two are unidentified.

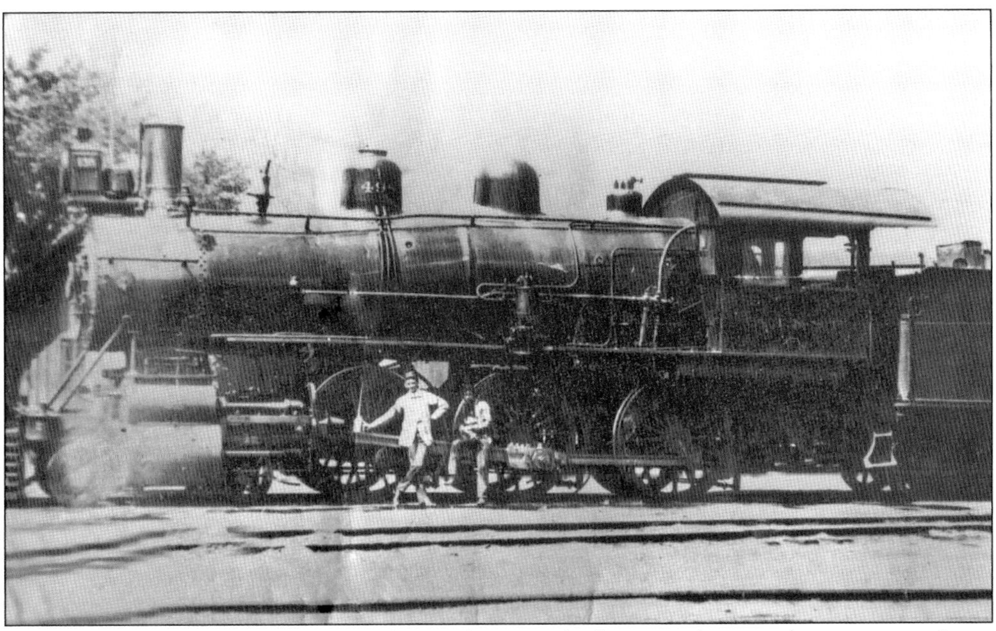

Pictured are a Rock Island engine, with a coal car attached to it, and two workers posing in front.

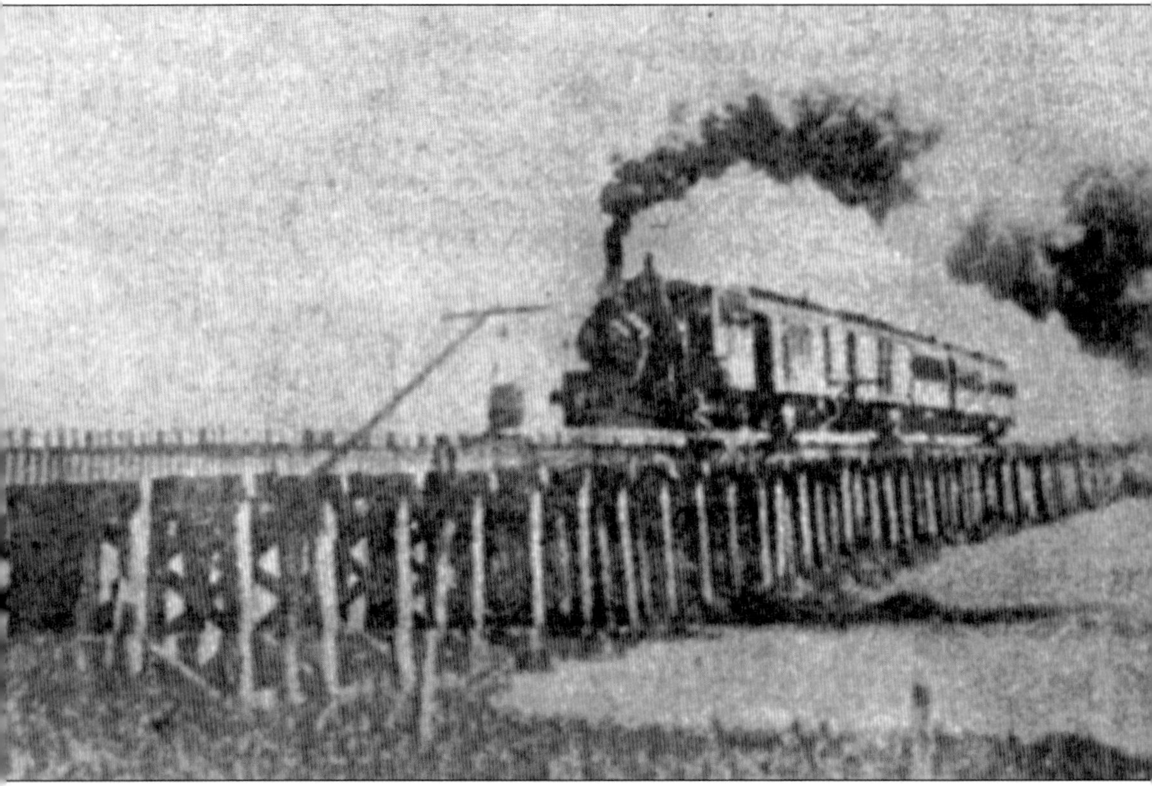

This is the Rock Island Bridge across the North Fork of the Red River in Sayre in the early 1900s. Parts of the old bridge still stand about a mile west of Butcher Boy Enterprises on the Fuch Farm near Long Creek. It is greatly responsible for the birth of Sayre. (Courtesy of the *Sayre Record*.)

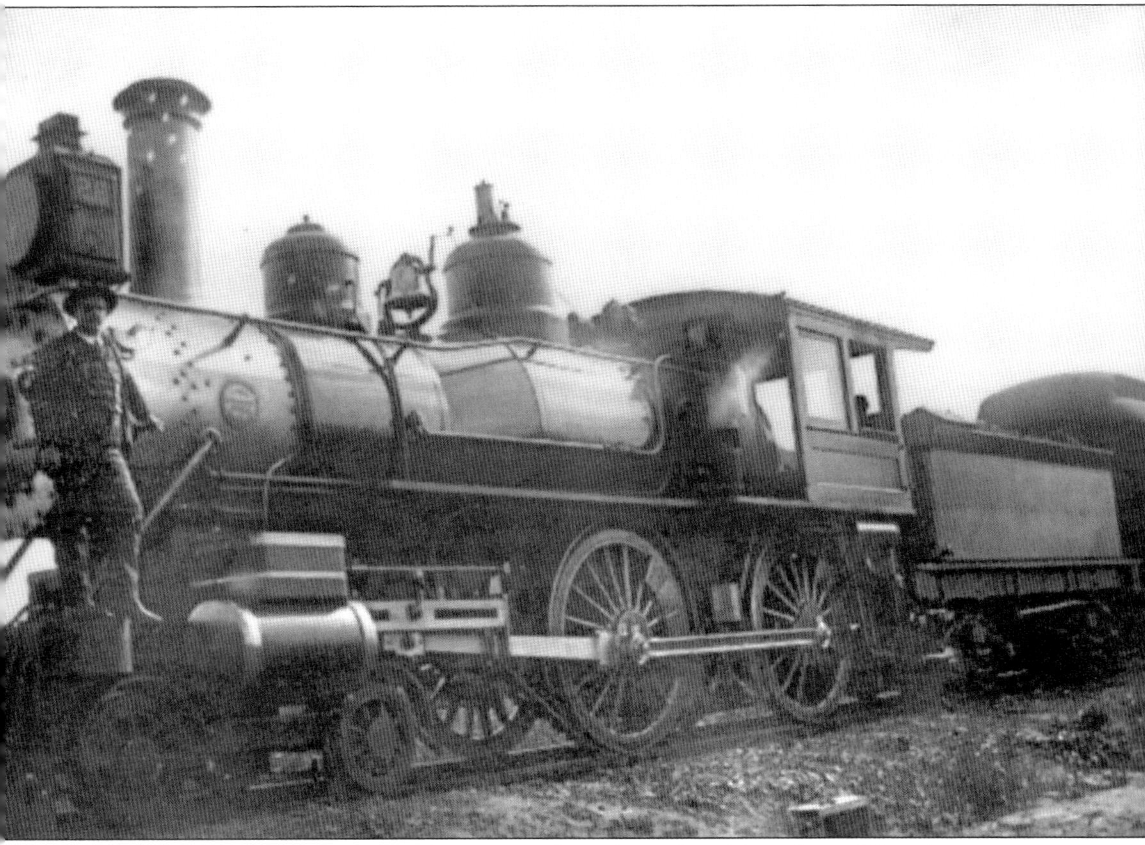

Pictured here is a Rock Island steam locomotive from the early 1900s in Sayre. These locomotives were used to pull both passenger and freight cars. It has a coal car and a boxcar hooked on to it. Note the man standing on the front of the engine. (Courtesy of David Brooks.)

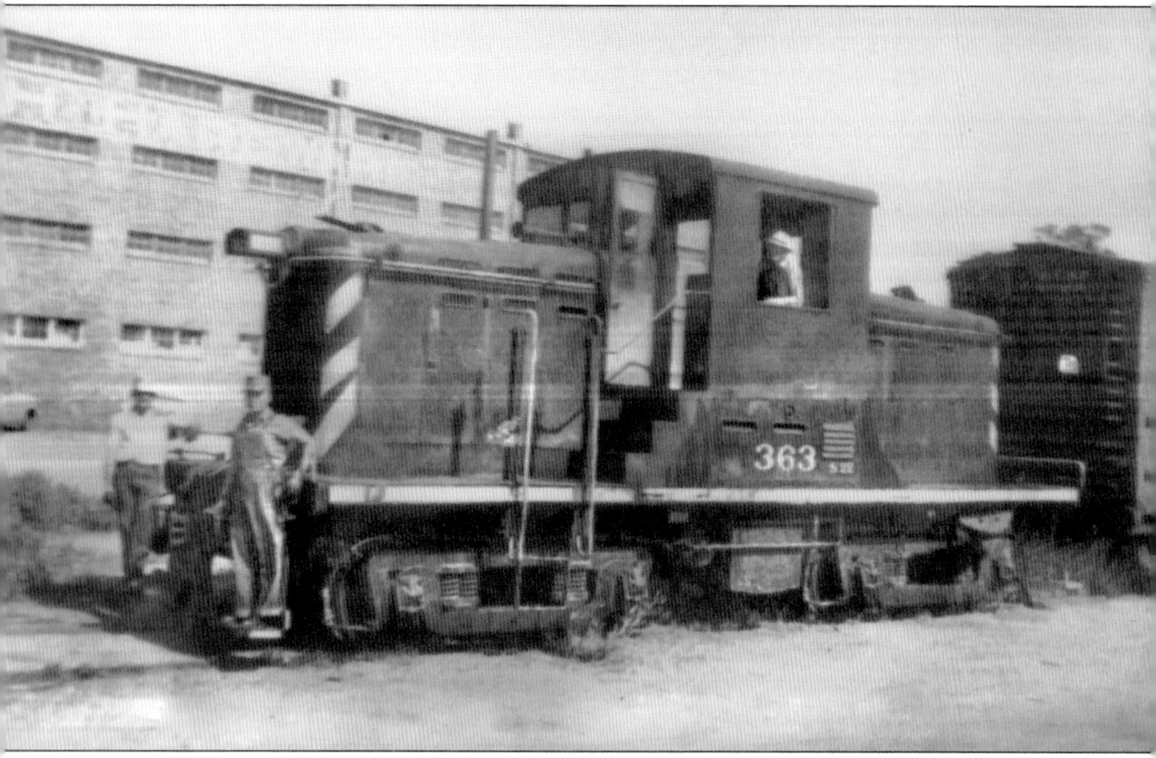

Roy Hildebrand went to work for Santa Fe in Winslow, Arizona, in 1952. He moved back to the farm in Delhi, Oklahoma, and started to work for Rock Island in Sayre. He worked for Frisco in Clinton for nine years, beginning in 1962. He and his family moved to Enid, where he worked for Burlington Northern, finishing out his 30-year career with the railroad. He and his wife still live in Enid. Roy is in the foreground at the front of the switch engine. He and his crew used to be switchers for railroads all around the world. His son Roy Gene Hildebrand went on to work for Burlington Northern after he graduated from high school in 1971. He is now an engineer for Burlington Northern-Santa Fe.

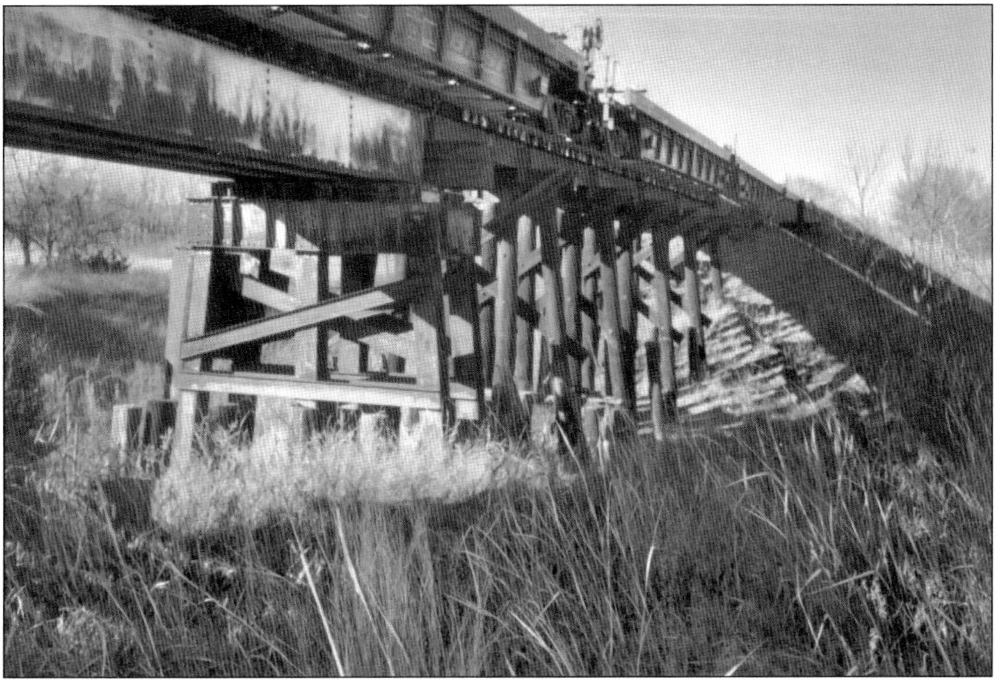

A Farmrail train is parked on the old wooden Red River Bridge two miles west of the stoplight in Sayre. The track is part of the Rock Island line.

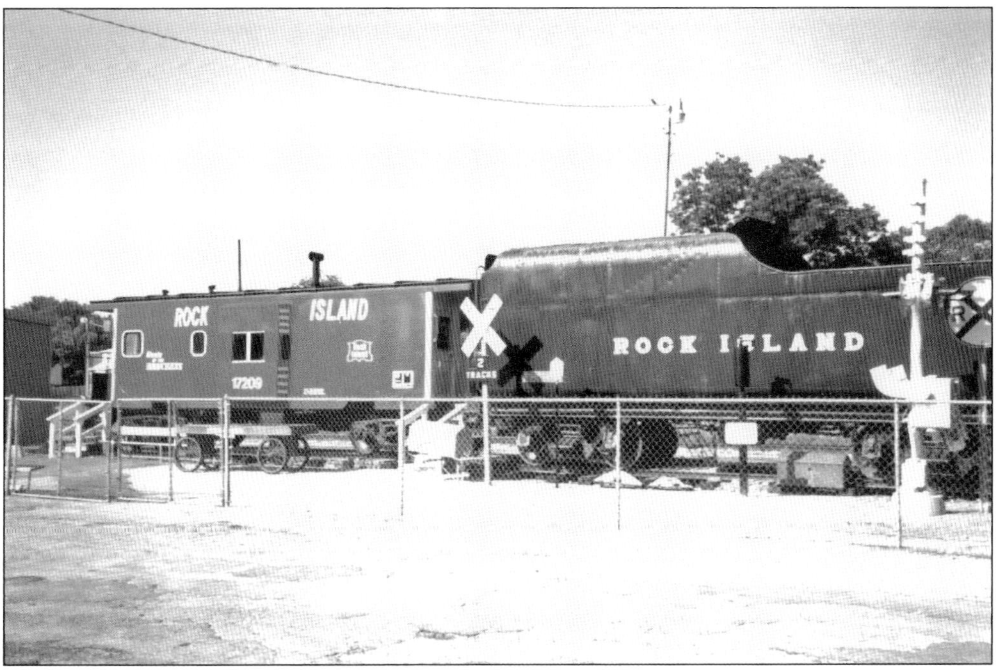

Pictured here is a Rock Island caboose and coal car tender. It is parked near the Rock Island Depot, which is now a museum in El Reno, Oklahoma.

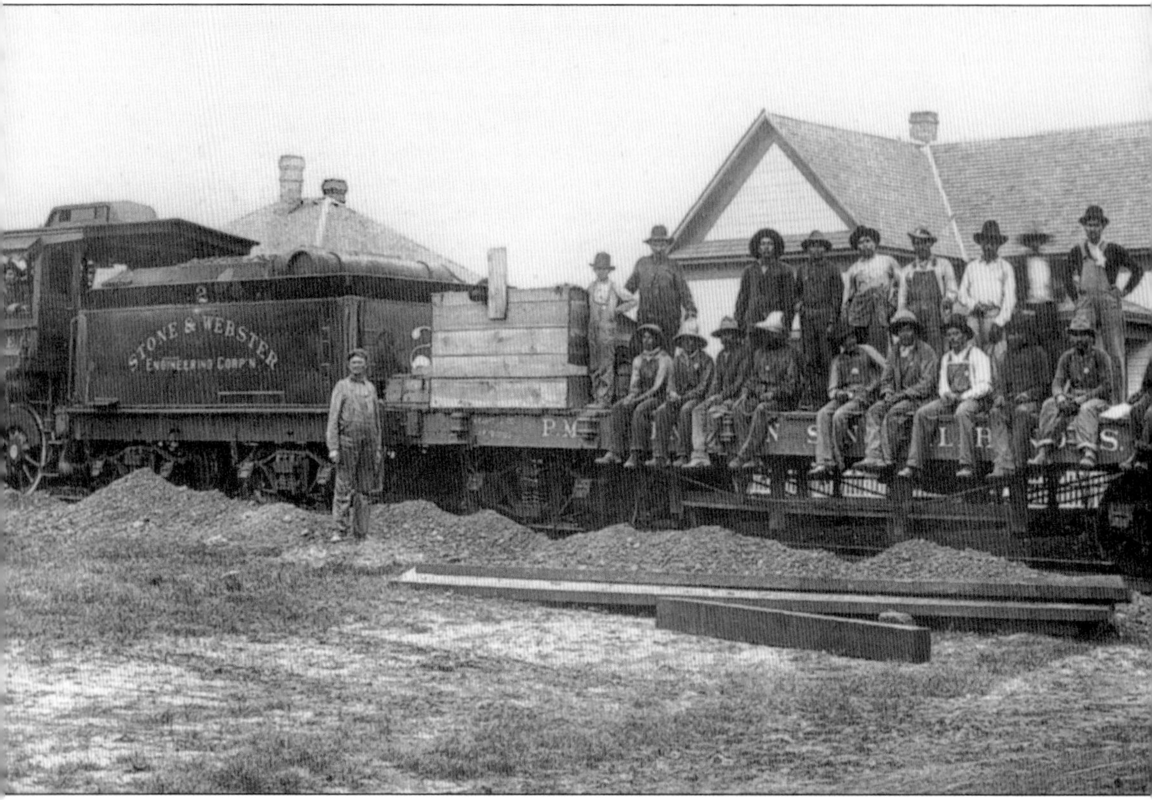

This is an early image of railroad workers in Sayre resting after a hard day on the line. The railroad arrived in the early 1900s.

Two

BIRTH OF A TOWN

Sayre was first called Riverton because it was located along the North Fork of the Red River. It was not until Robert Heysham Sayre came here to help build a railroad that the town was named Sayre after a famous railroad man. In July 1901, there was a Rock Island Depot, roundhouse, and a Harvey House built on the west end of town. In 1927, a new depot was constructed where it stands today, known as the Shortgrass County Museum. The courthouse was built in 1910 and serves as the county seat of Beckham County. At one time, Sayre had a mattress factory, six or seven lumber mills, four cotton gins, and a salt plant.

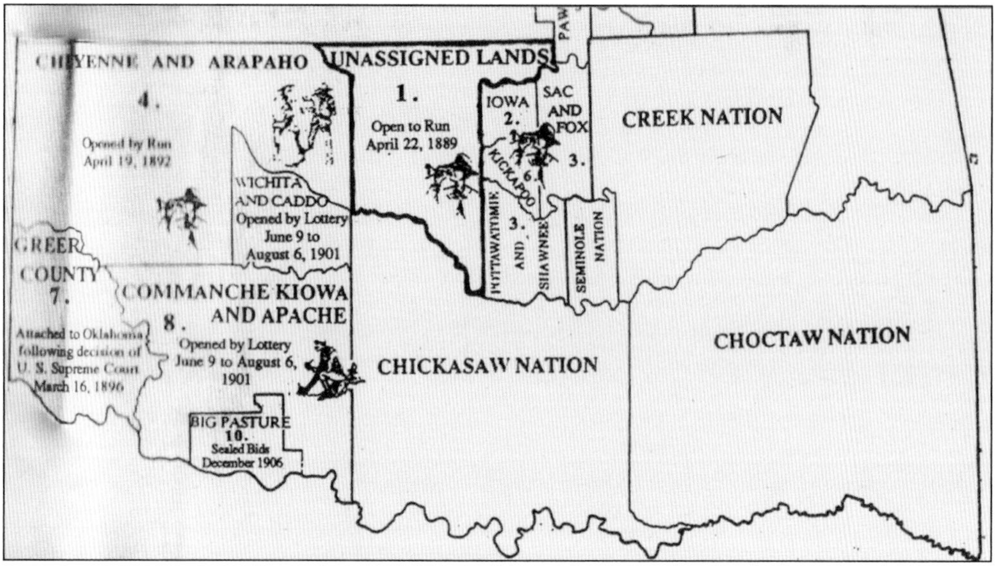

NO MAN'S LAND

Added to Oklahoma Territory by Organic Act May 2, 1890

2.

Land Openings In Oklahoma

1. "Old Oklahoma" or the Unassigned Lands: opened by run, April 12, 1889.
2. No Man's Land, Oklahoma Panhandle: opened by Organic Act of Congress on May 2, 1890.
3. Sac, Fox, Iowa, Pottawatomie and Shawnee Reservations: opened by run , Sept. 22, 1891.
4. Cheyenne and Arapaho reservation: opened by run on April 18, 1892.
5. Cherokee Outlet or "Strip," Pawnee and Tonkawa reservations: opened by run on September 16, 1893.
6. Kickapoo reservation: opened May 25, 1895.
7. Greer County: opened by County Homestead Act, January 1897.
8. Kiowa-Comanche-Apache and Wichita-Caddo reservations opened by lottery on August 6, 1901.
9. Ponca and Oto-Missouri Lands , by allotment, 1904.
10. The Big Pasture, 3 smaller pastures and Wood Reserve opened by sealed bids, late in 1906. Kaw Lands opened by Allotment, 1906.

The above map shows where Native American tribes were located in Oklahoma in the late 1800s and how it opened up for settlers in the early 1900s. This document at left explains the land openings in Oklahoma. At that time, before statehood, Sayre would have been considered to be in Greer County; now it is in Beckham County.

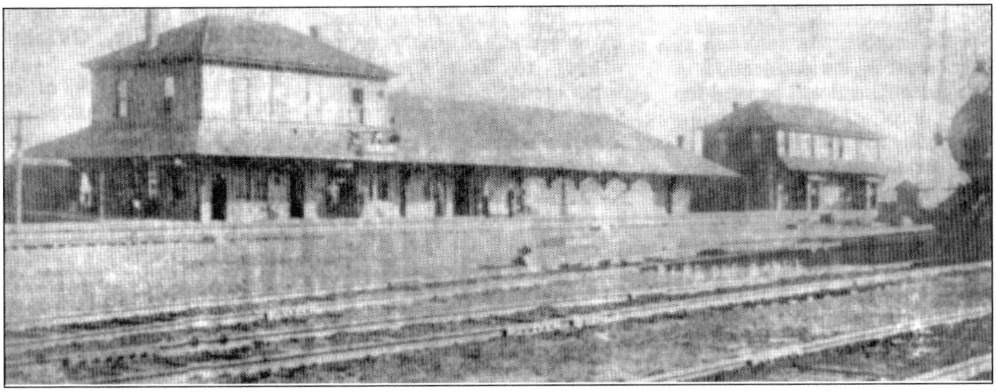

In this 1905 photograph is the old Rock Island Depot on the right and the Harvey House on the left. The Harvey Girls lived on the second floor of the building.

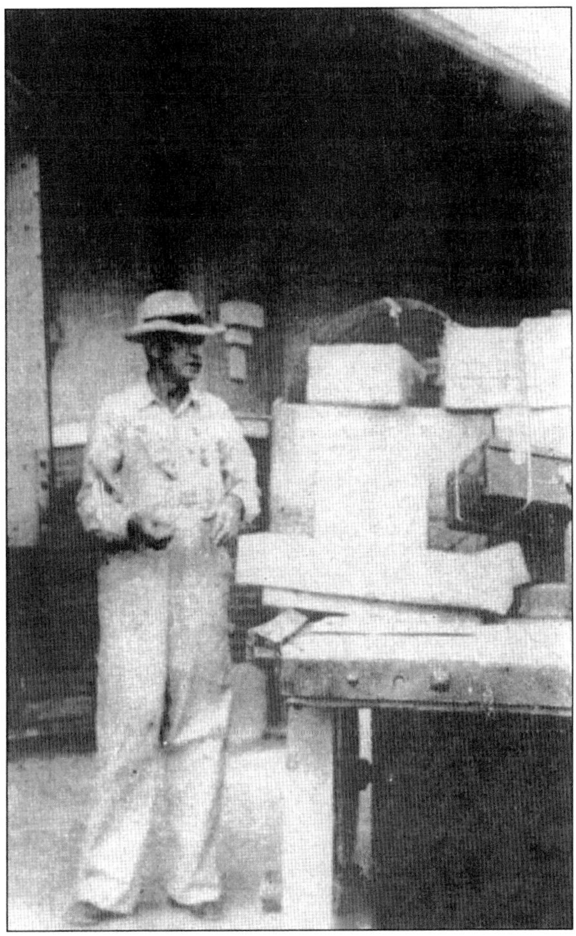

A.D. Flowers was the Railway Express agent in Sayre in the 1920s. He was responsible for unloading the mail and packages from the train at the depot. (Courtesy of the *Sayre Record*.)

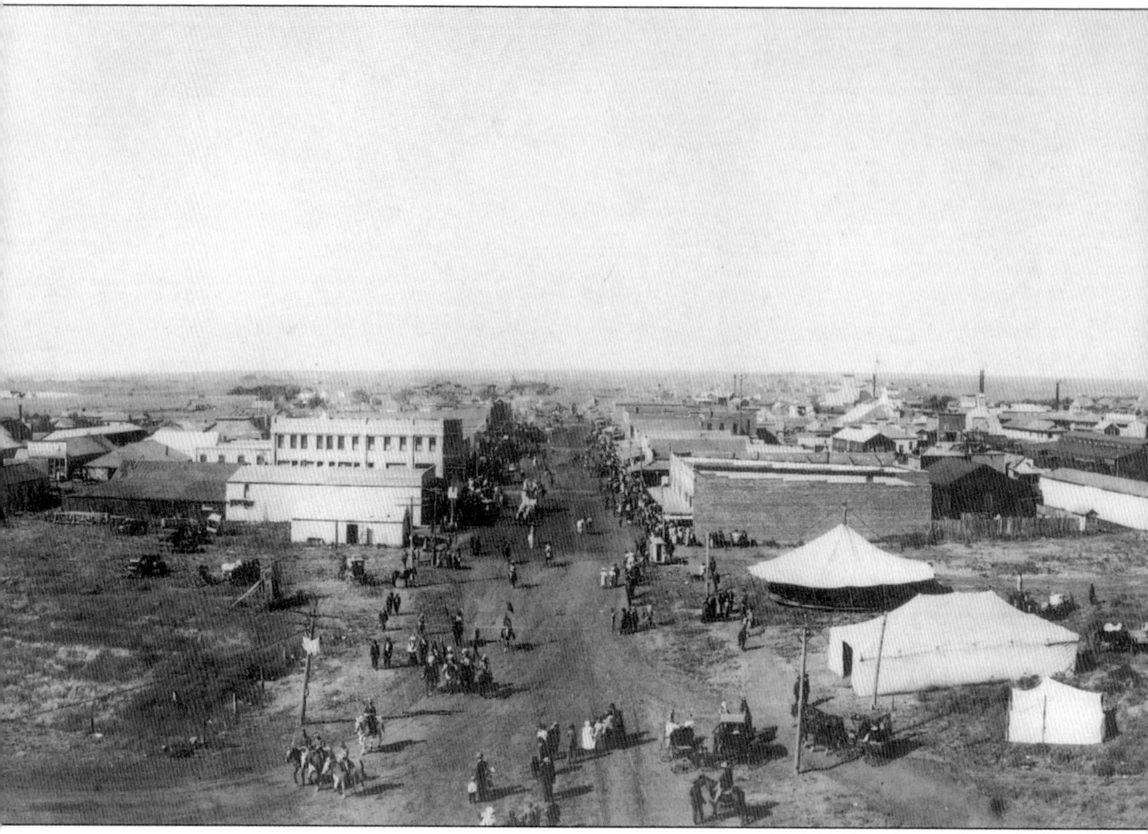

The railroad brought life and bustling energy to the city of Sayre. Pictured is a group of pioneers and workers that camped out near Sayre back in the early 1900s. As the background attests, Sayre has already begun to flourish.

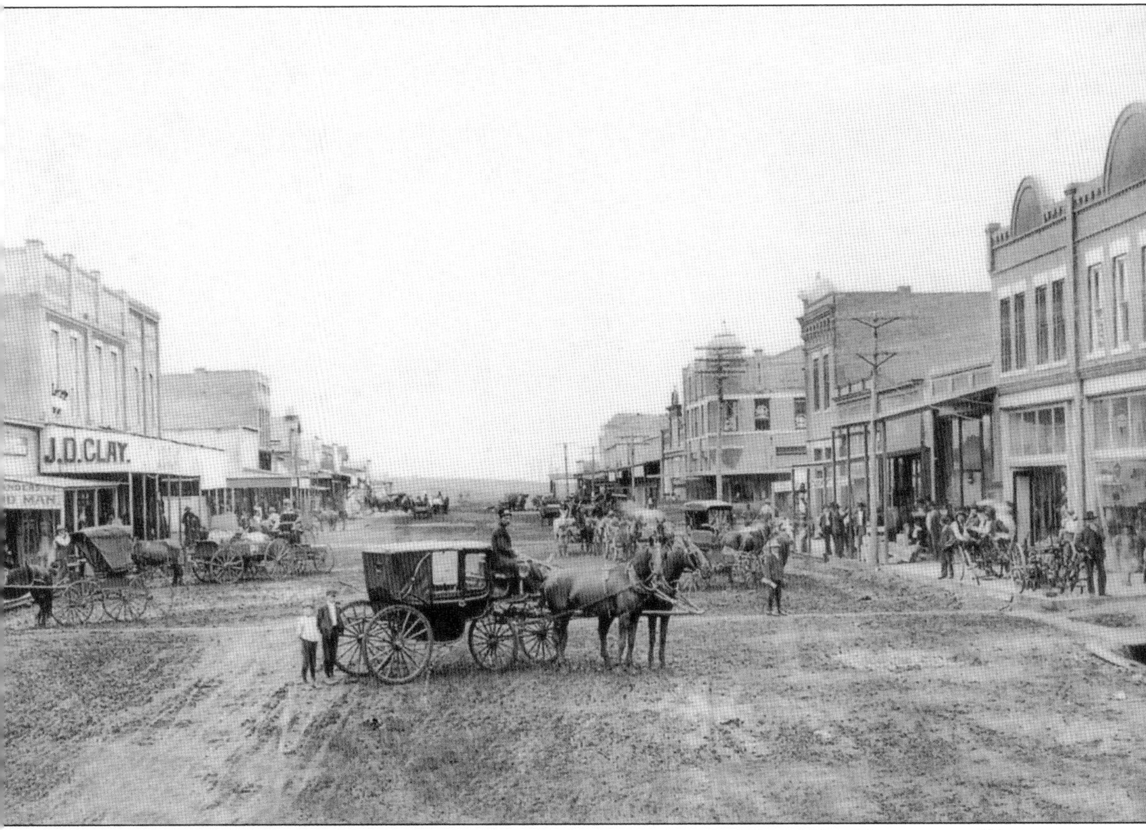

This is Main Street in Sayre, photographed from the west. Many of the old buildings are still here, such as Hullum Hardware on the left, which was constructed in the early 1900s. This image was taken before the courthouse was constructed.

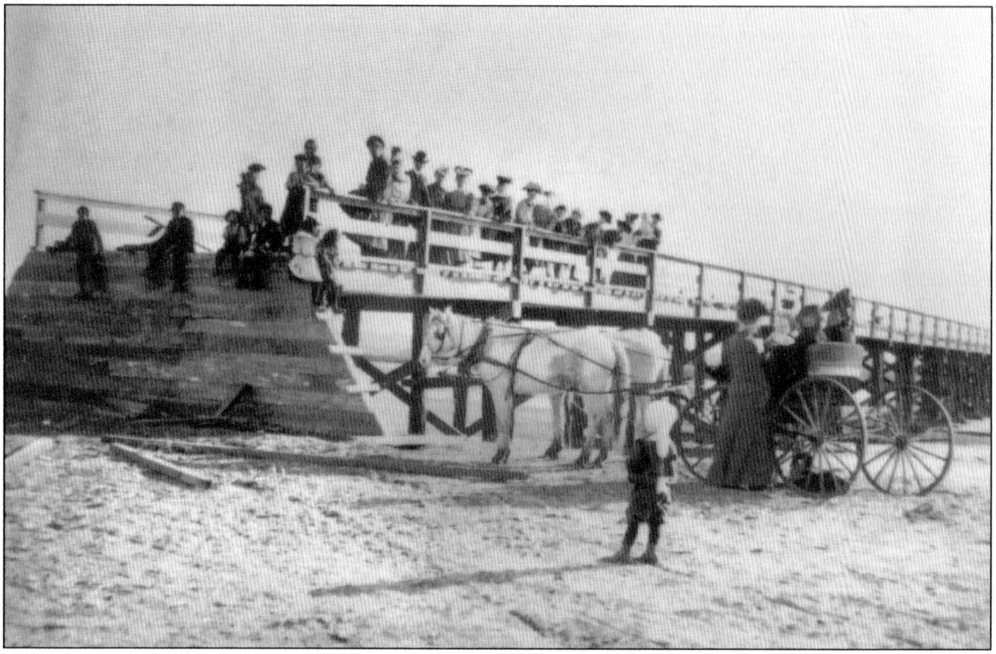

The old wooden bridge across the North Fork of the Red River is pictured here from Highway 283 and Route 66 on the south side of Sayre.

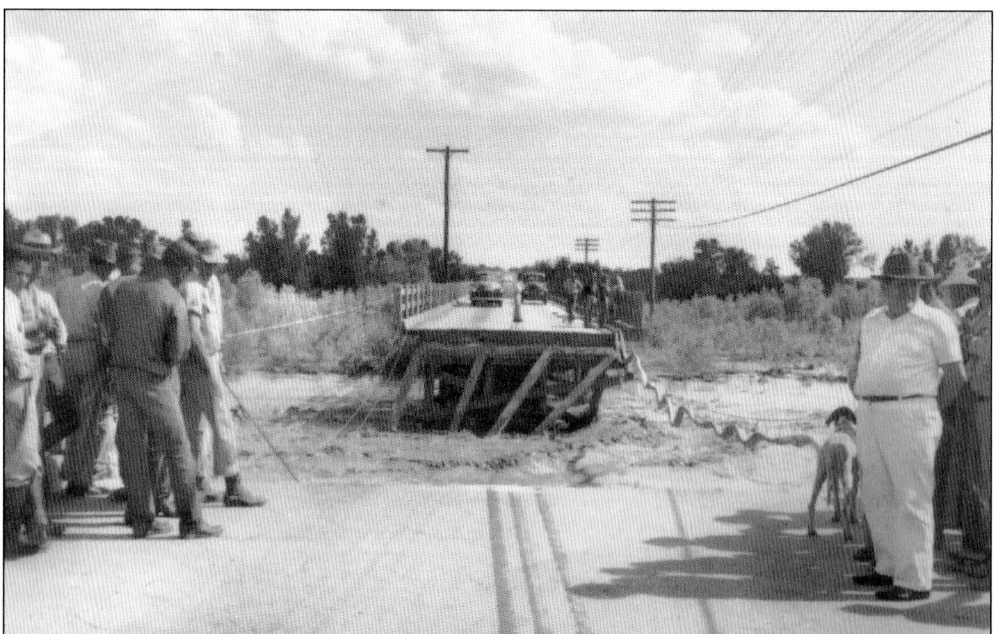

This was a cement bridge built across the North Fork of the Red River, which washed out in a flood. It was located on Highway 283 and Route 66 south of Sayre.

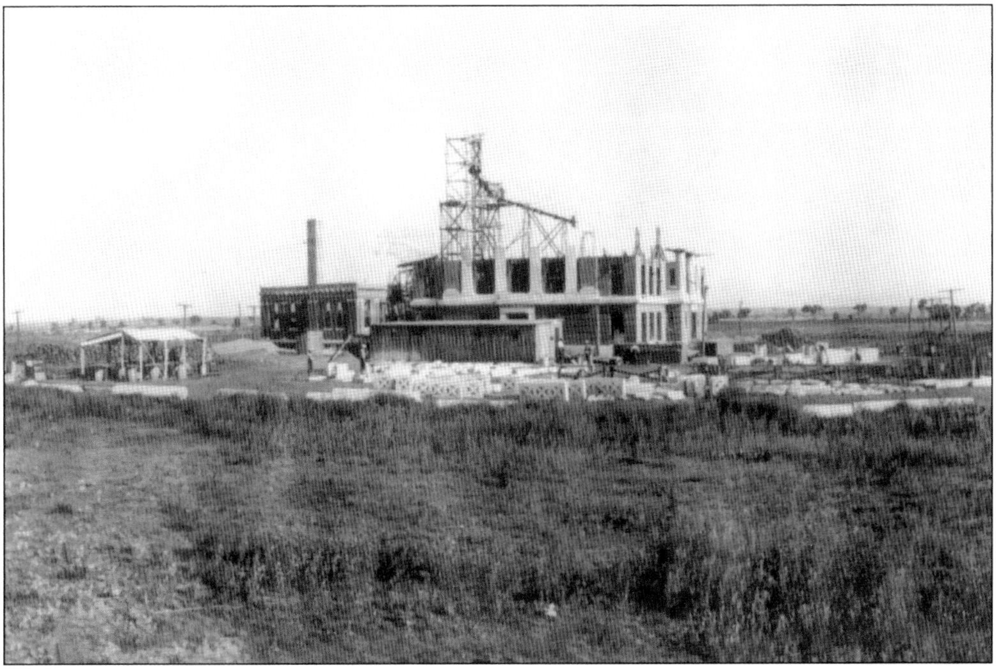

The construction of the courthouse is pictured here in 1911. It was featured in the 1940s movie *The Grapes of Wrath*, starring Henry Fonda. The building was only half complete when this photograph was taken.

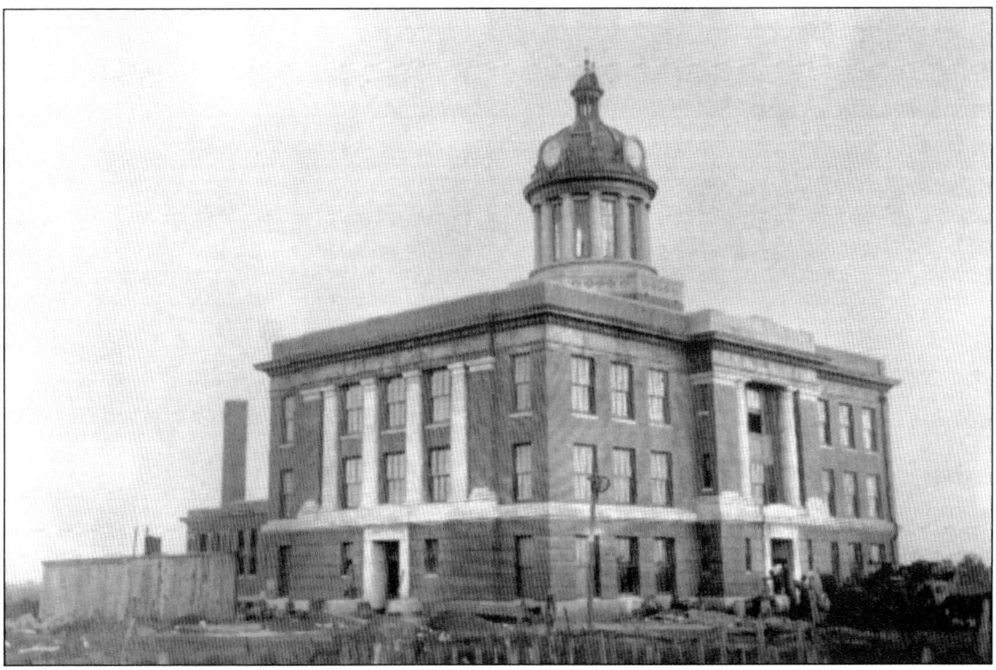

The courthouse in Sayre is seen here when it was nearing completion in 1911. The county jail is the building in the background.

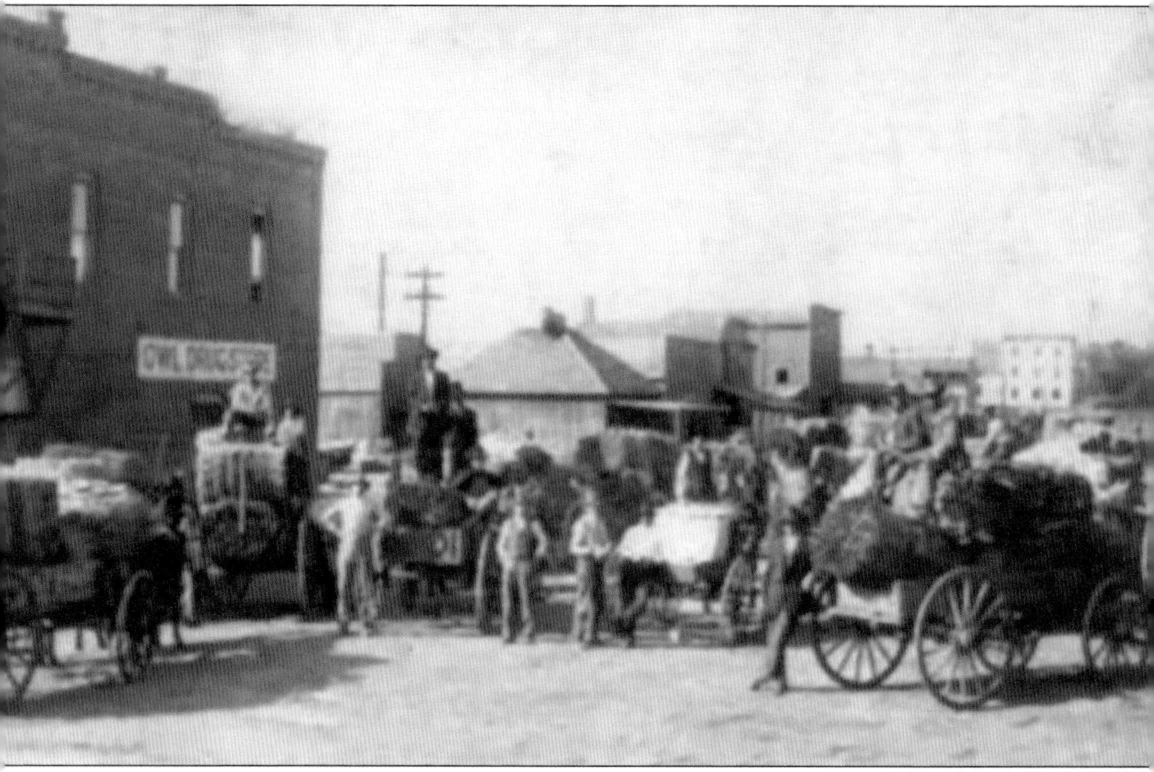

This photograph shows the Owl Drug Store and several other buildings along Main Street in Sayre. It was reportedly one of the first two-story brick buildings constructed and also one of the first 10 buildings present. It sits on what was one of the original sites purchased by the Choctaw Townsite and Improvement Company, which was responsible for the forming of the town.

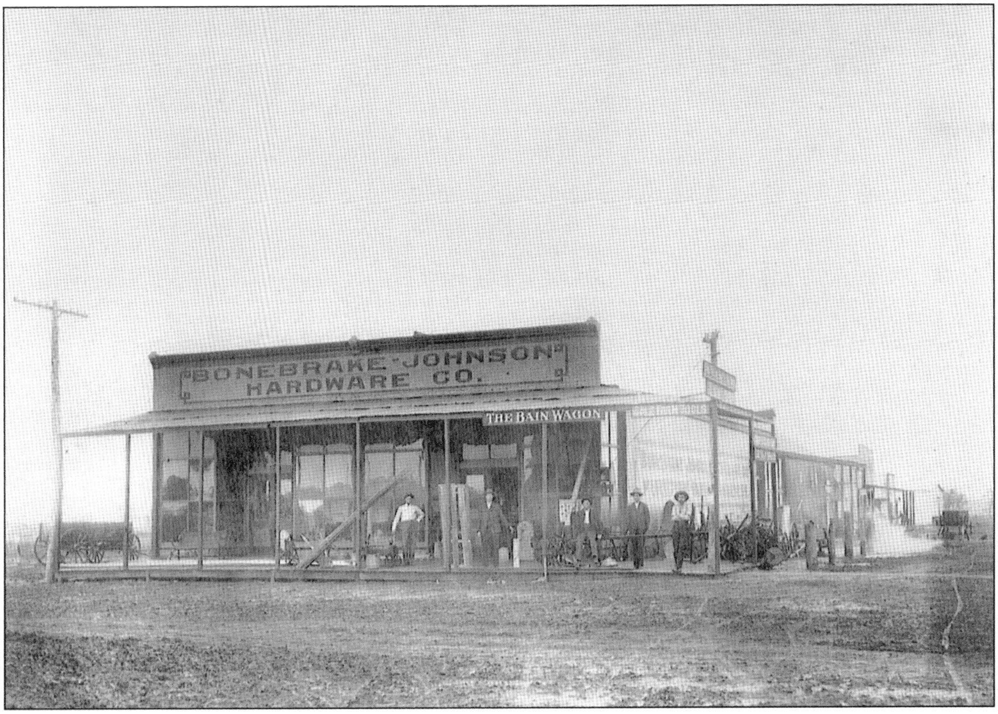

The Bonebrake and Johnson Hardware Company was a popular place for early settlers to shop and catch up on what was going on around town. It sold furniture and many other household items.

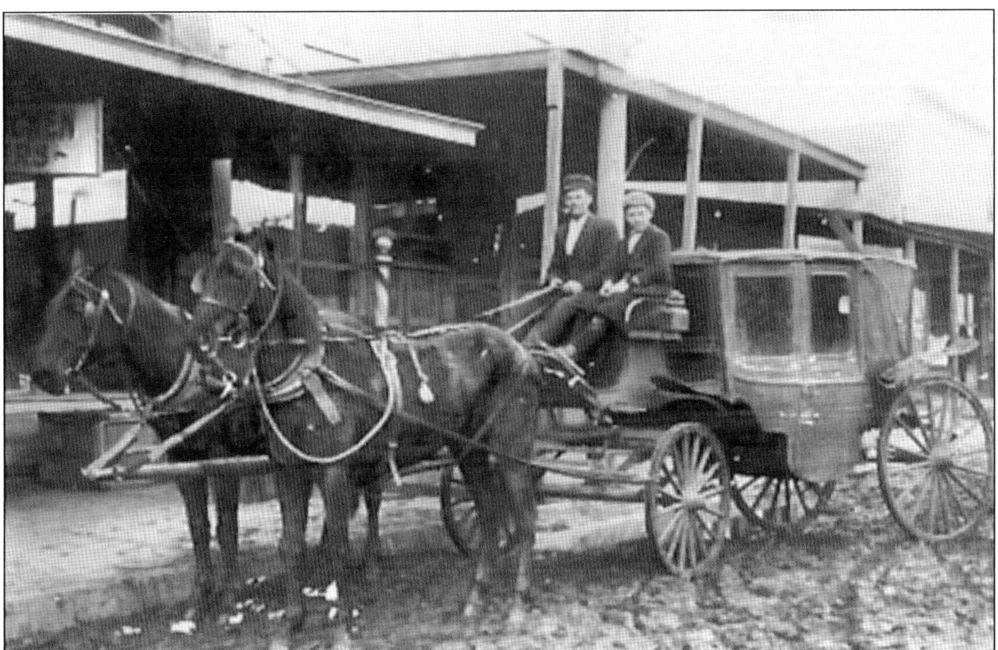

This photograph of horses and a stagecoach was taken in the early 1900s. It looks as if people were still working on a lot of the old buildings in Sayre at the time. (Courtesy of the *Sayre Record*.)

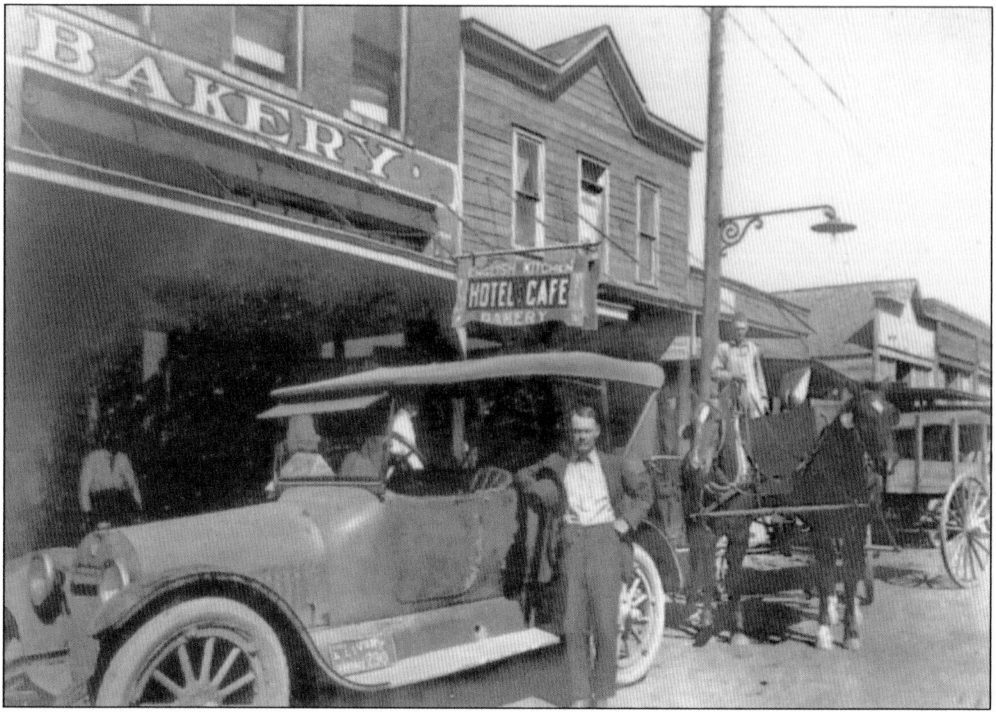

Pictured are a vintage car and a horse and wagon parked in front of the local bakery and the English Kitchen in Sayre in the 1900s.

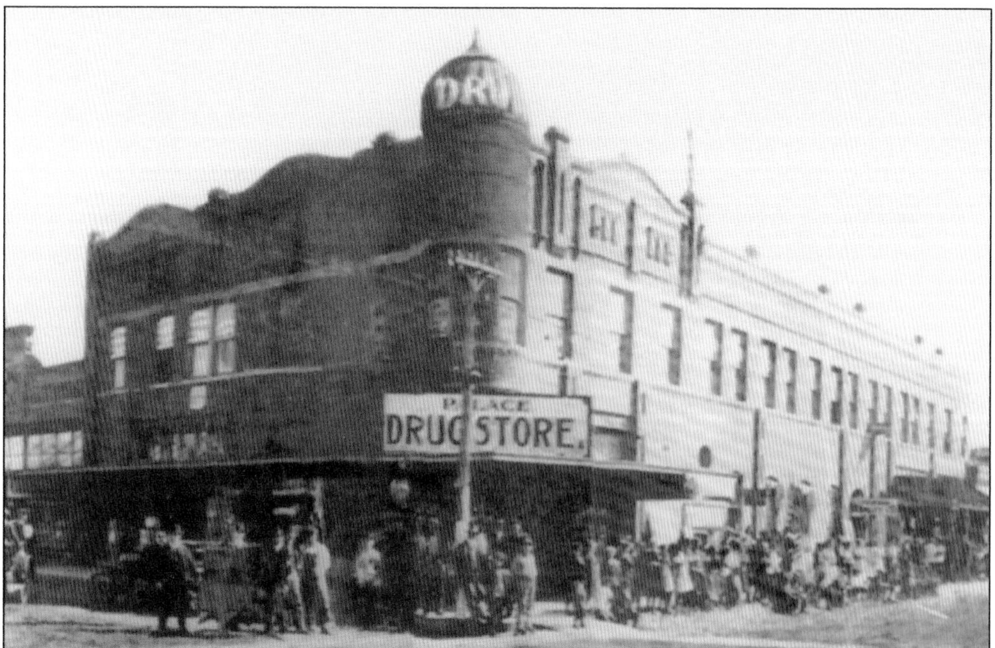

The Old Palace Drug Store on the corner in Sayre is pictured here in the early 1900s; it later became the Hood Drug Store. The upstairs housed various physicians.

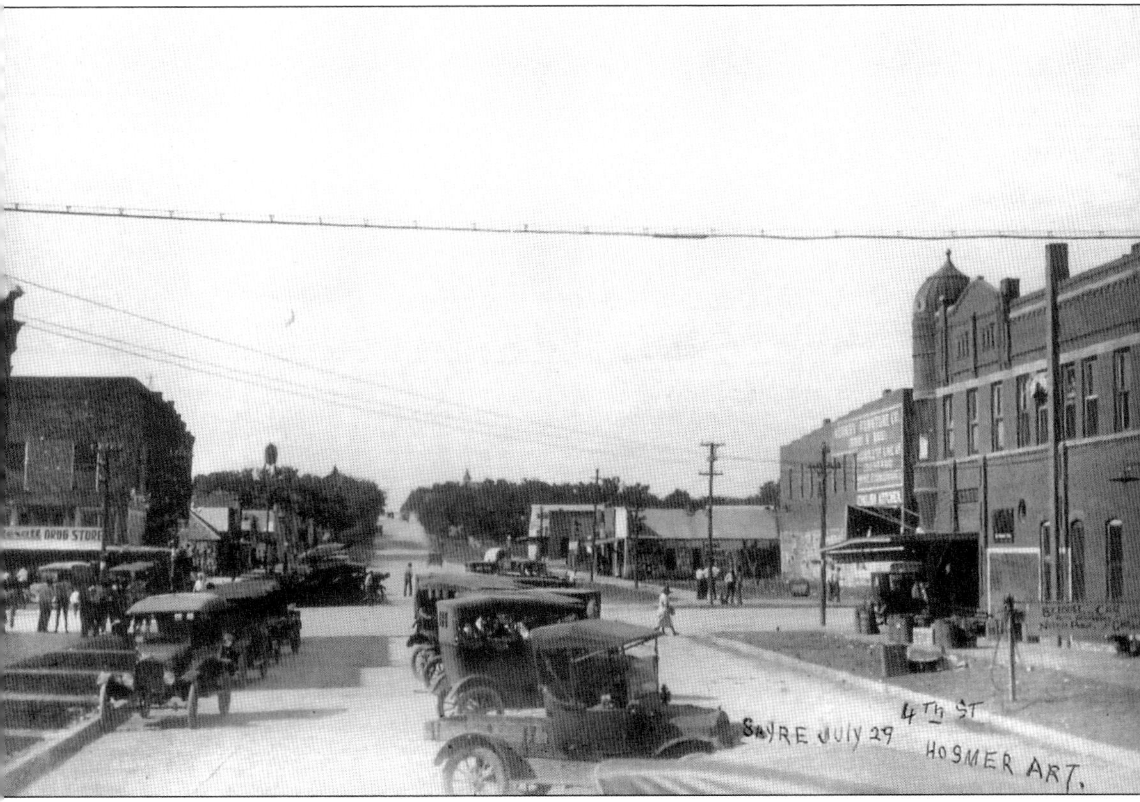

This photograph was taken by Hosmer on July 29, 1900. The First National Bank building can be seen on the right across the street from the Rexall Drug Store. The Hood Drug Store is the building on the right corner.

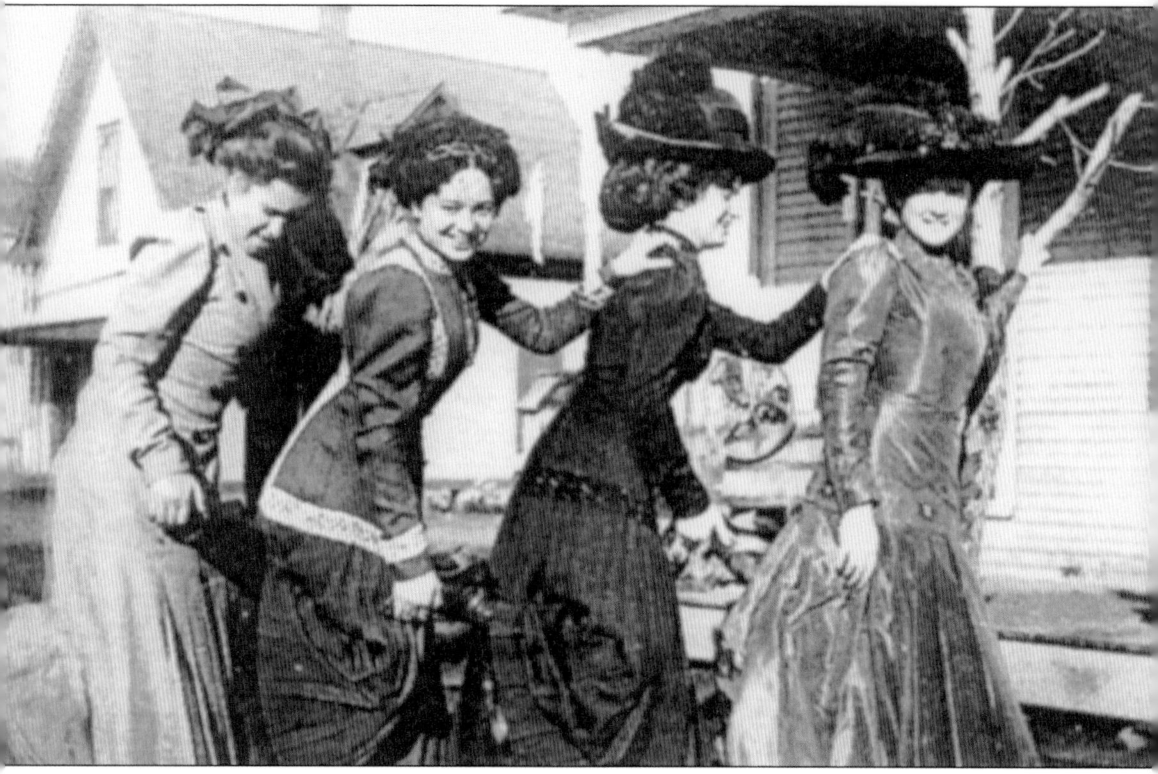

Four friends are acting up while posing in front of one of their wood frame homes in Sayre. Note the dresses of the period and how each lady is holding a foot of the one ahead. (Courtesy of David Brooks.)

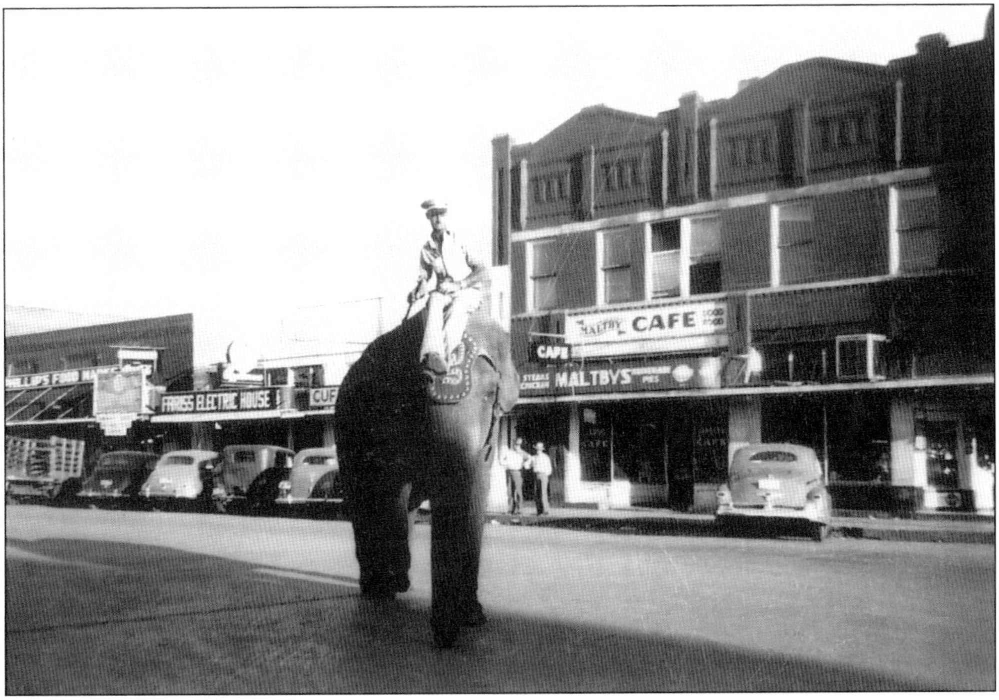

An elephant walks down Main Street in Sayre. It was always an exciting time when the circus or a carnival came to town. Note the vintage cars parked along the side of the street.

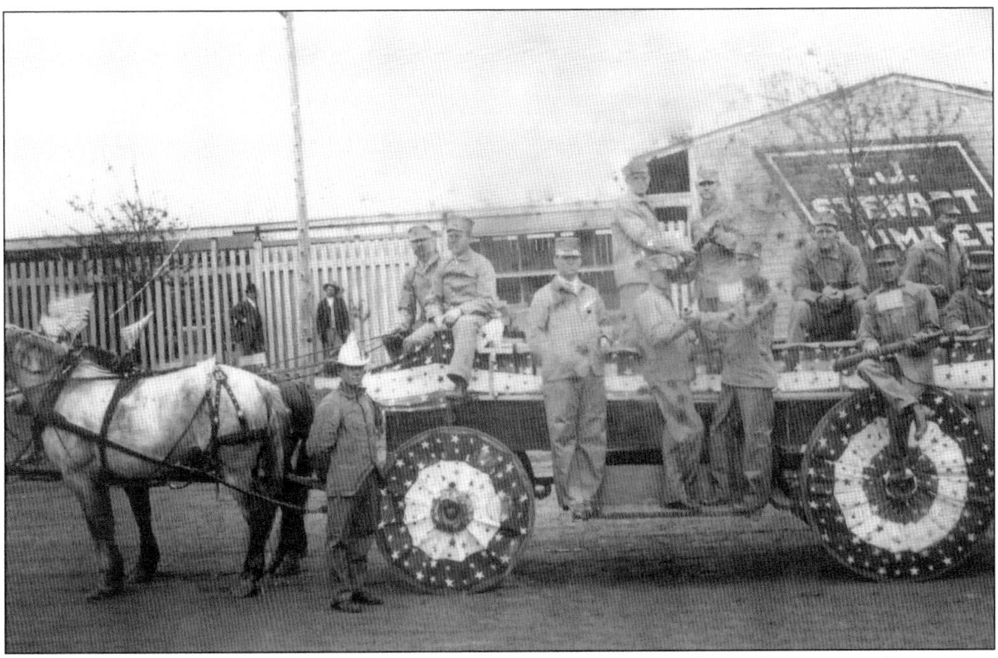

Workers deliver supplies to the T.J. Stewart Lumber Company in Sayre by horse and wagon in the early 1900s. (Courtesy of the *Sayre Record*.)

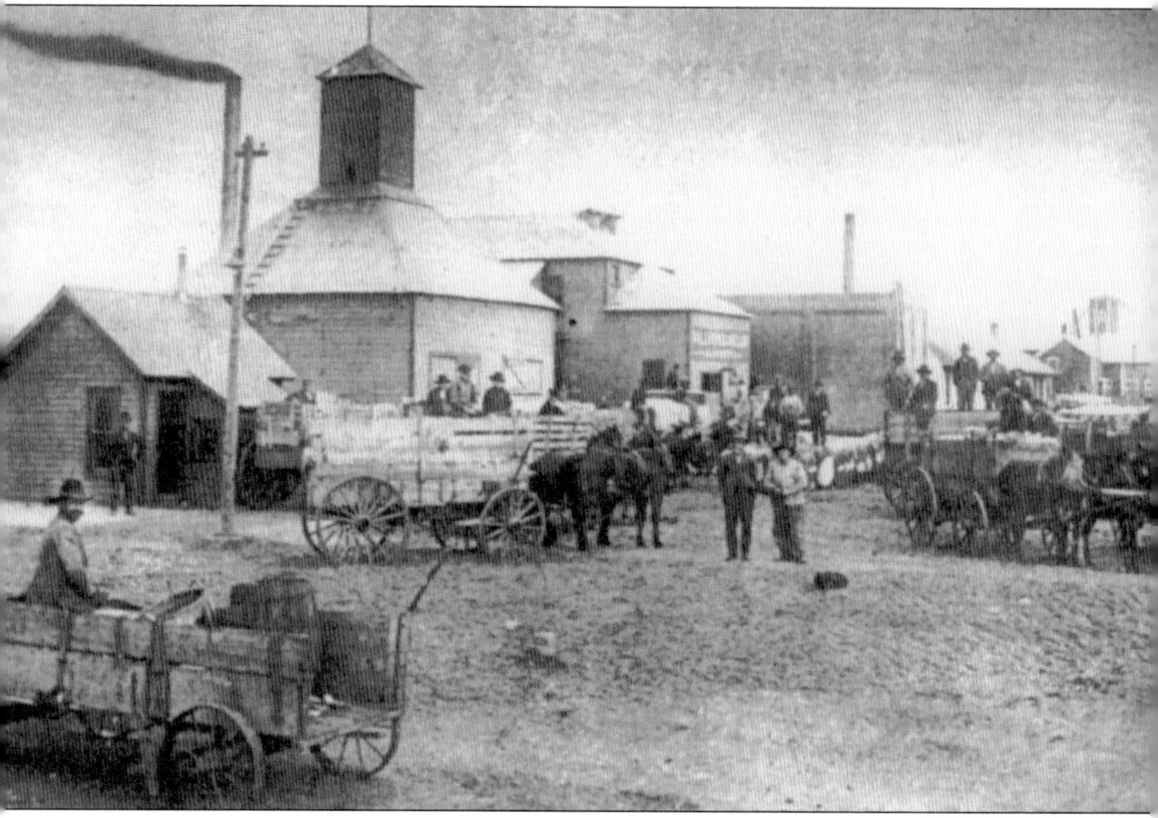

This photograph, taken between 1911 and 1918 from the 200 block between Fourth and Fifth Streets, shows an early gin mill. The business shown is Williams and Miller Ginnery. Note the many farmers from Sayre and surrounding areas who have gathered with their cotton crops. (Courtesy of the Shortgrass County Museum.)

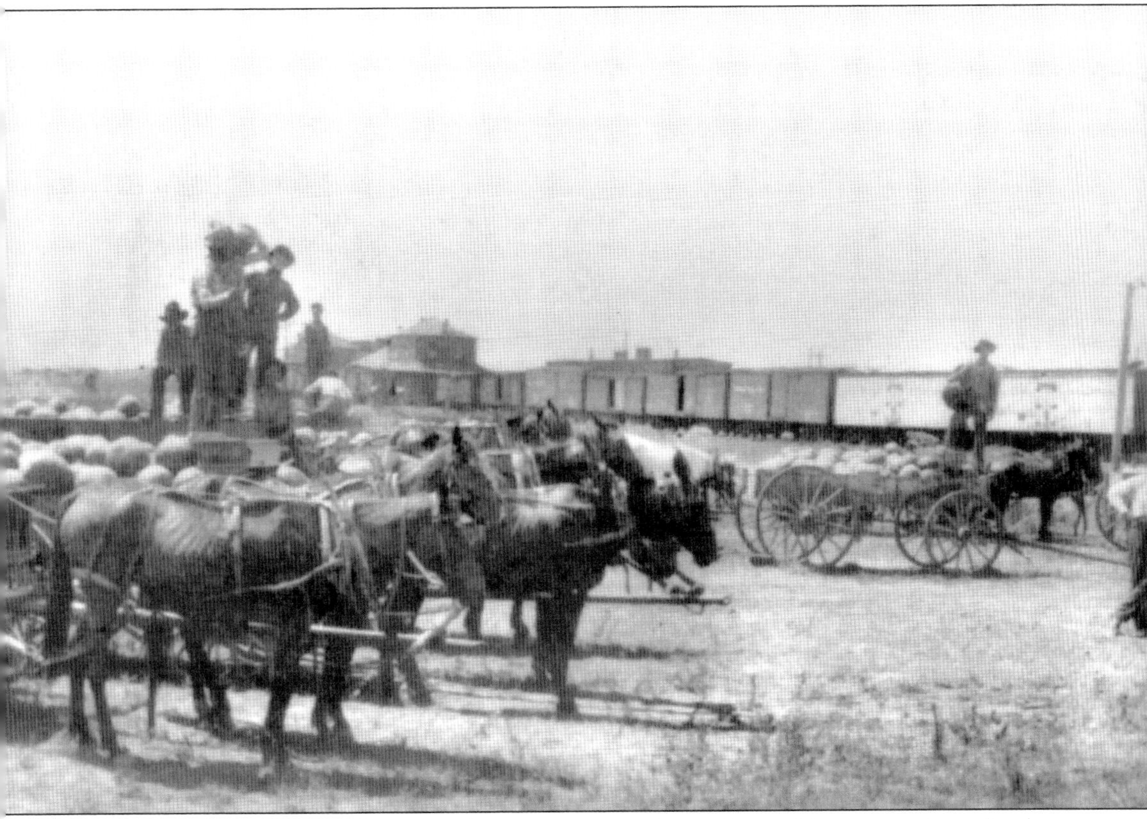

Pictured are several farmers bringing their goods to market at Sayre. They are waiting for the harvest to be put aboard the Rock Island train pictured in the background. The depot and the top of the Harvey House can also be seen as well. (Courtesy of Blevins and Henderson.)

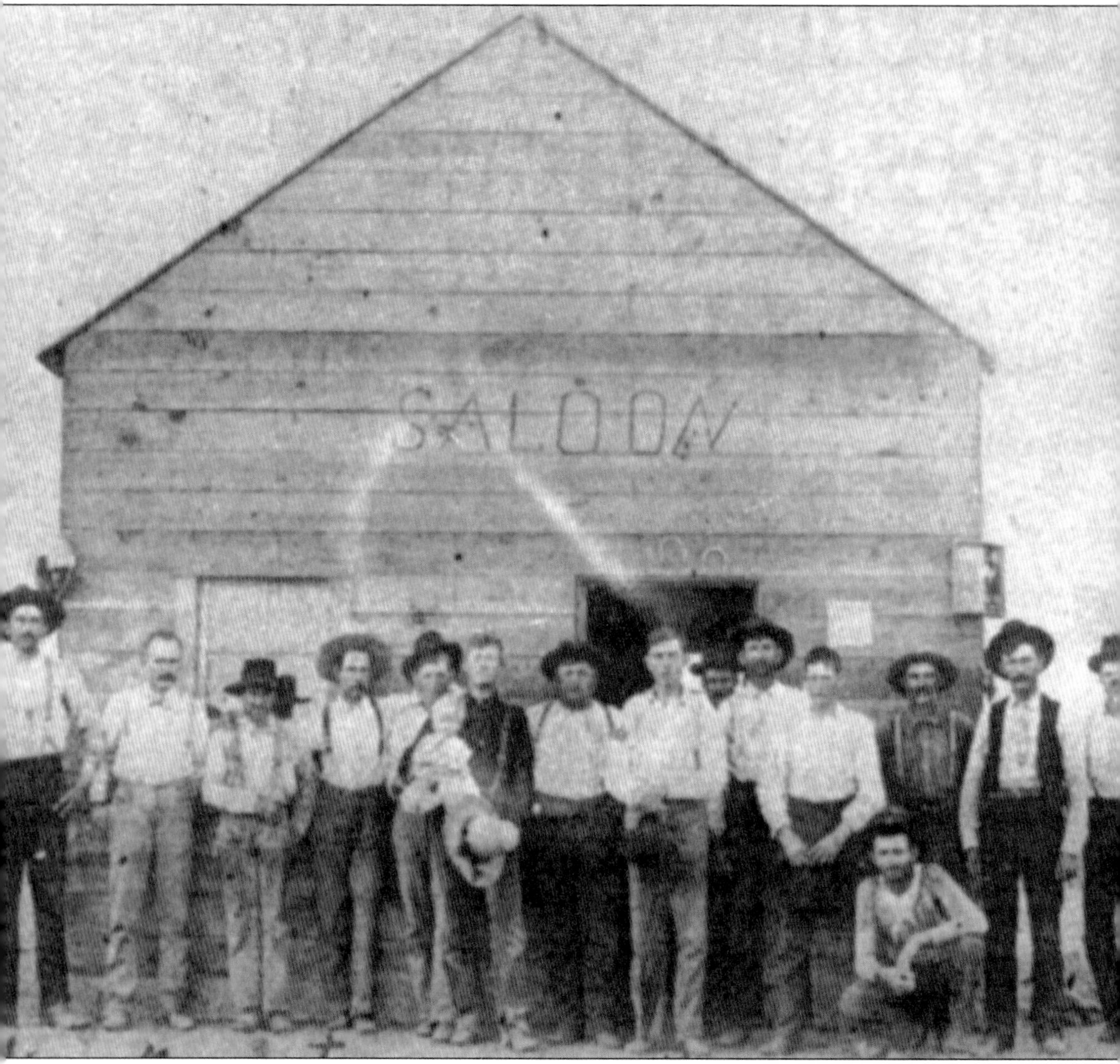

This is the Sullivan Brothers Saloon in 1901. The saloon was supposedly the first building constructed in the early days of Sayre. The town was full of booming businesses, and various saloons were soon aplenty, not only here but in every small upstart Western town. (Courtesy of the *Sayre Record*.)

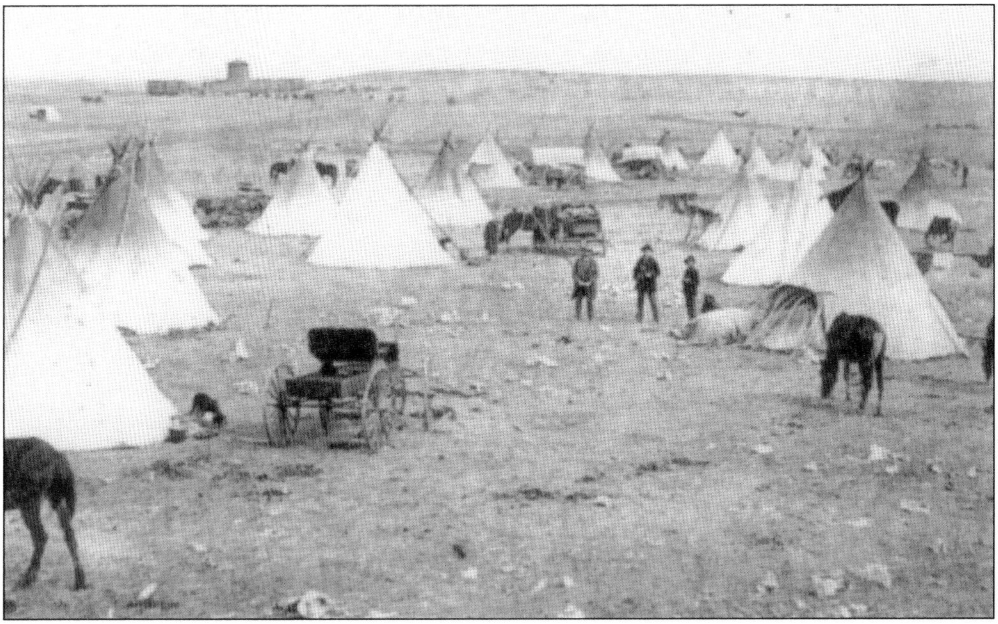

Many cowboys and Native Americans alike lived in tents along the riverbank in Sayre when it was just getting started. In those days, the town was called Riverton because the North Fork of the Red River was nearby. Looking closely, one can see a water tower and some boxcars in the background. (Courtesy of David Brooks.)

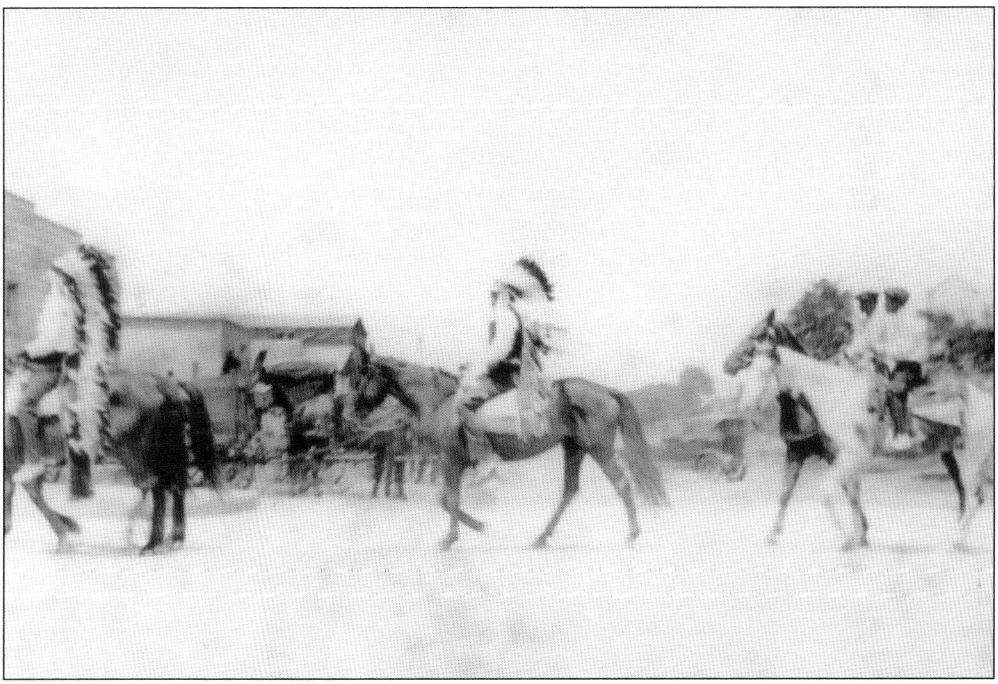

Native Americans are coming into town in the early days of Sayre. Note the horses and wagon, as well as the automobile, in the background; there is also a soldier on a horse. (Courtesy of David Brooks.)

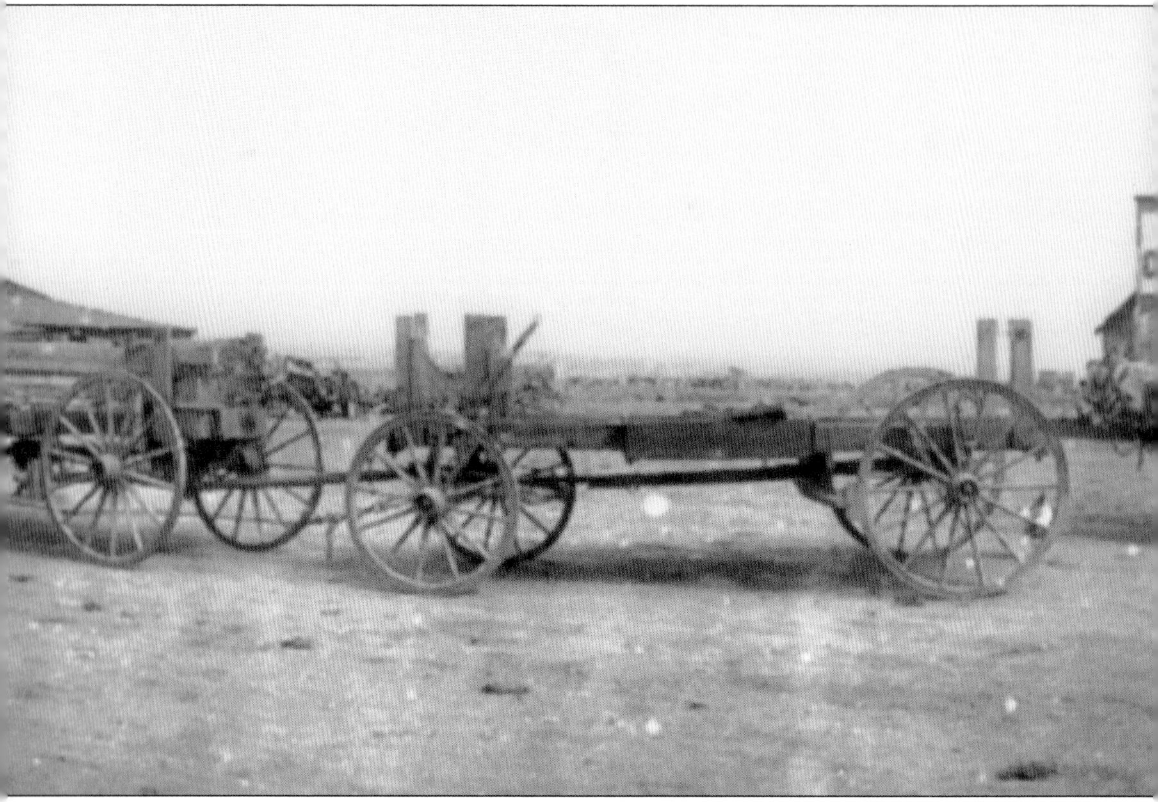

These are some of the wagons used in the early days to transport the farmers' cotton and grain to the Sayre market. The wagons were sometimes chained together so they were able to haul more; these wagons were pulled by horses. Note the photo gallery sign in the background. (Courtesy of David Brooks.)

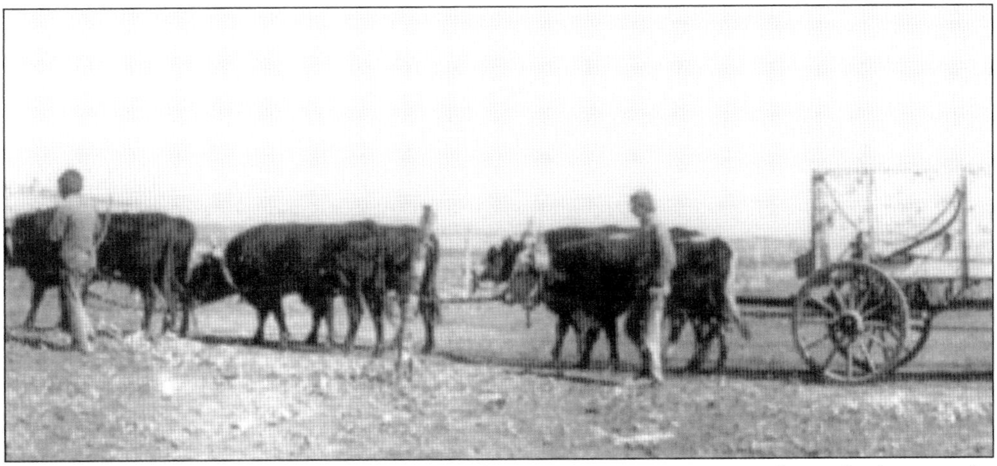

Sometimes wagons were pulled by oxen in early Sayre. Men are running alongside the oxen for encouragement. (Courtesy of David Brooks.)

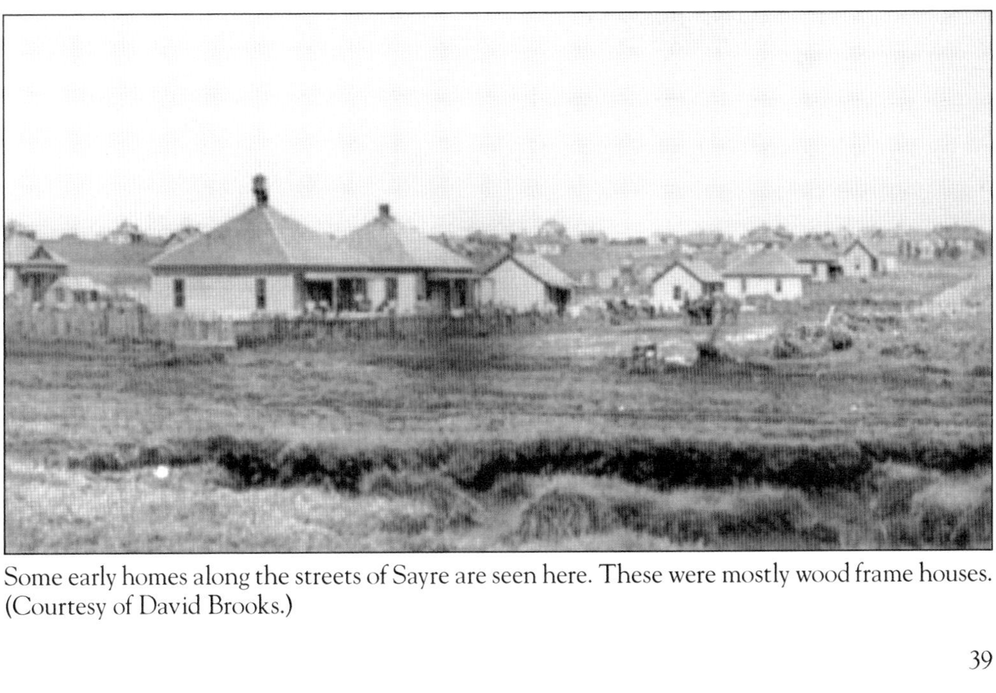

Some early homes along the streets of Sayre are seen here. These were mostly wood frame houses. (Courtesy of David Brooks.)

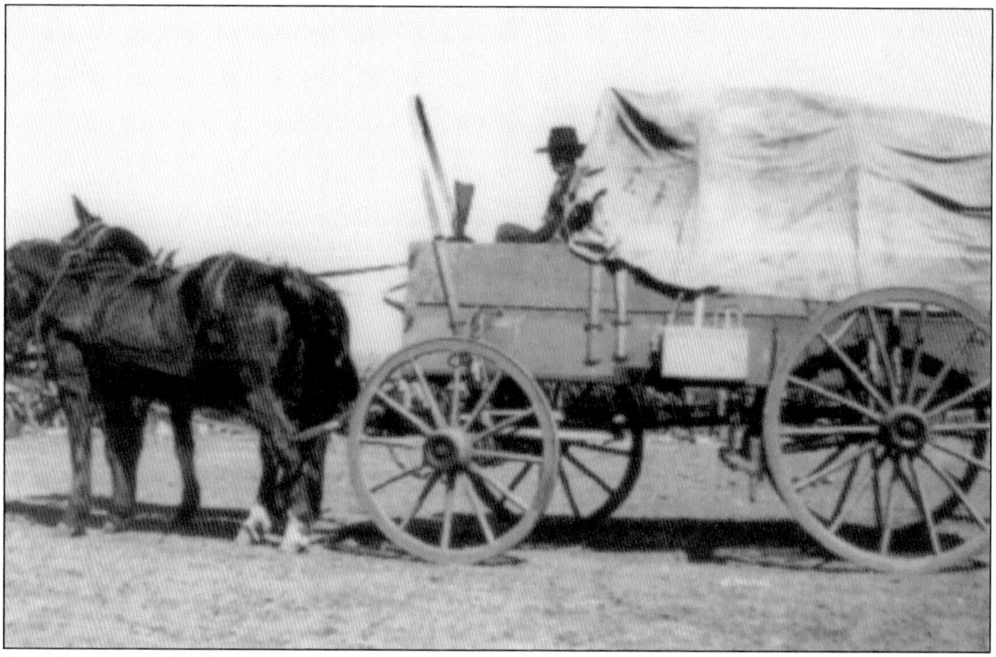

Seen here is a chuckwagon that is being pulled by several horses in early Sayre. Cowboys used them quite a bit when out on a long cattle drive. (Courtesy of David Brooks.)

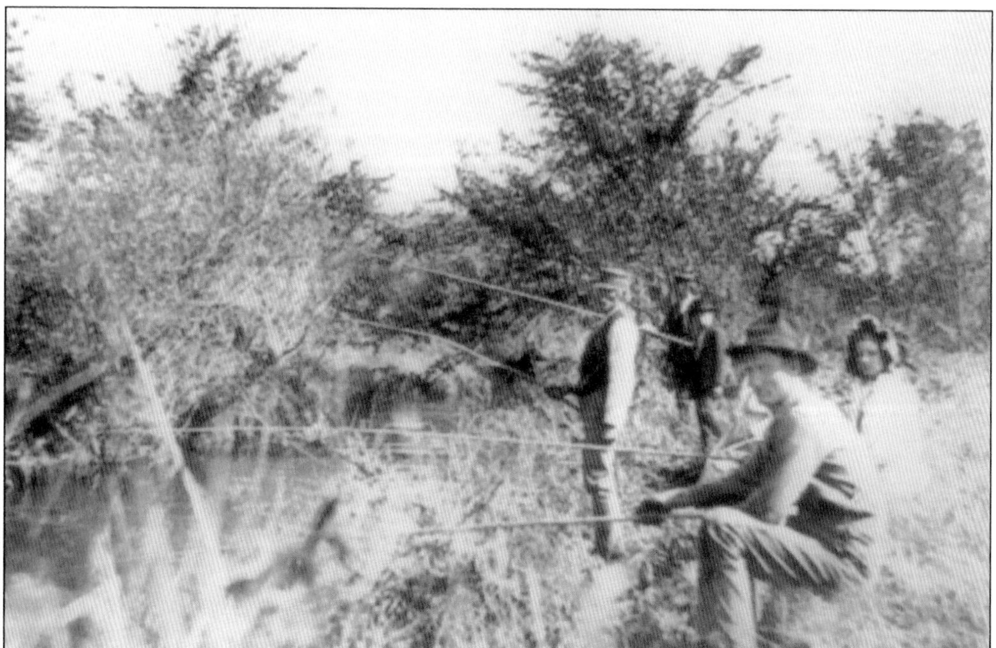

People are gathered to fish along a riverbank near Sayre. Fishing was, and still is, a favorite pastime in Sayre. At the time, it was also a significant source of food. (Courtesy of David Brooks.)

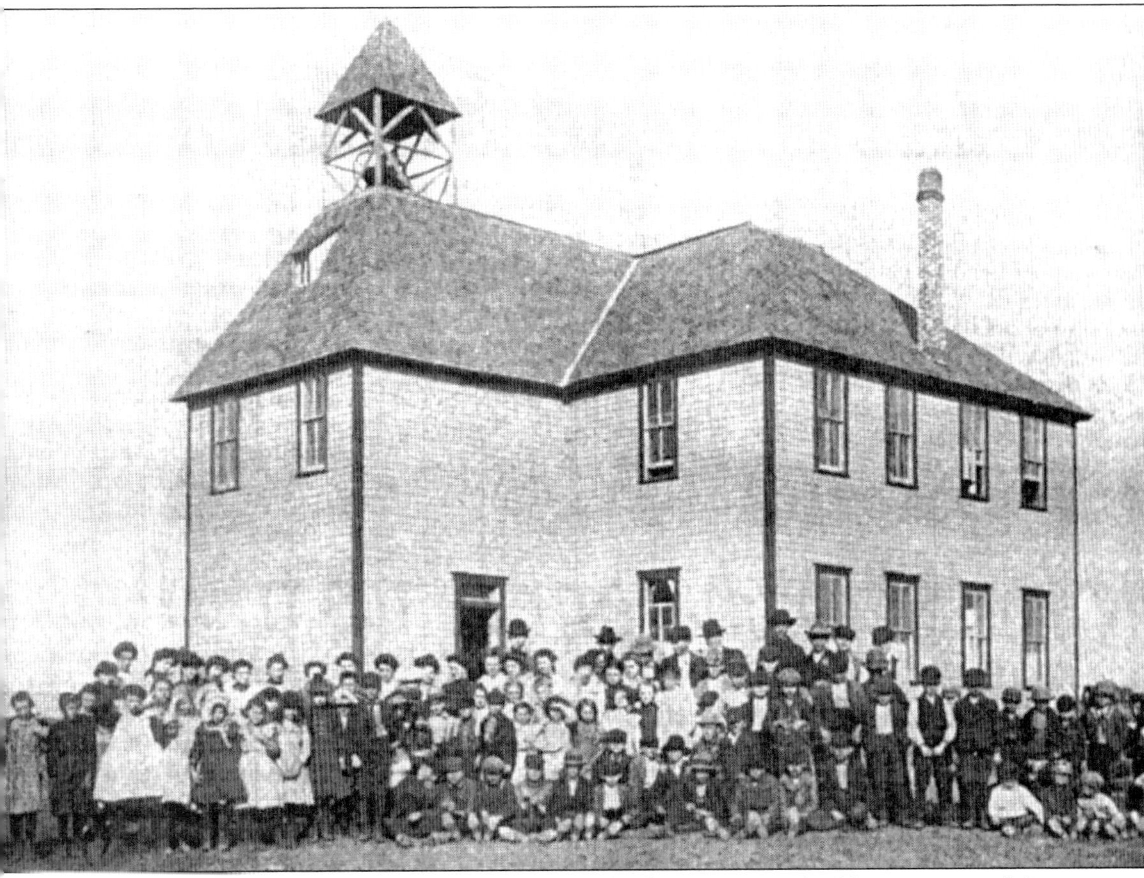

According to Sayre's first superintendent, H.V. Joseph, this nice frame building was one of the first permanent structures built in Sayre. It was constructed in 1902 and was used as the first school building. (Courtesy of the *Sayre Record*.)

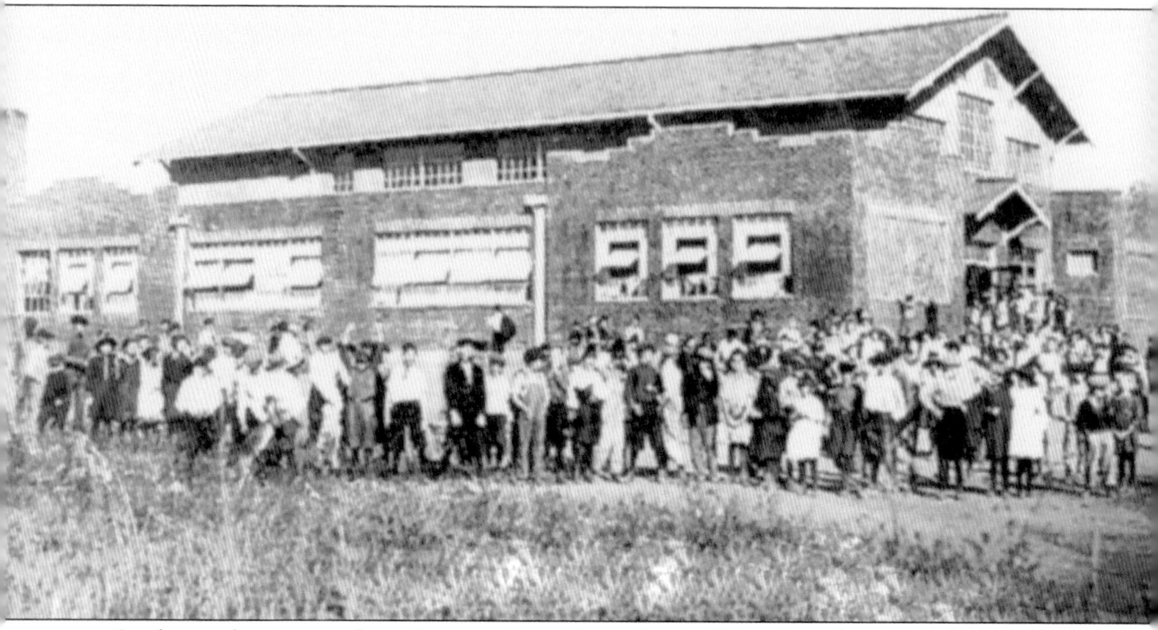

Students take time out for a photograph on November 1, 1922, when classes were held in the old Wilson Building. This structure stood where the old Whitehurst School was in previous years. (Courtesy of Sidney and L.D. Danner.)

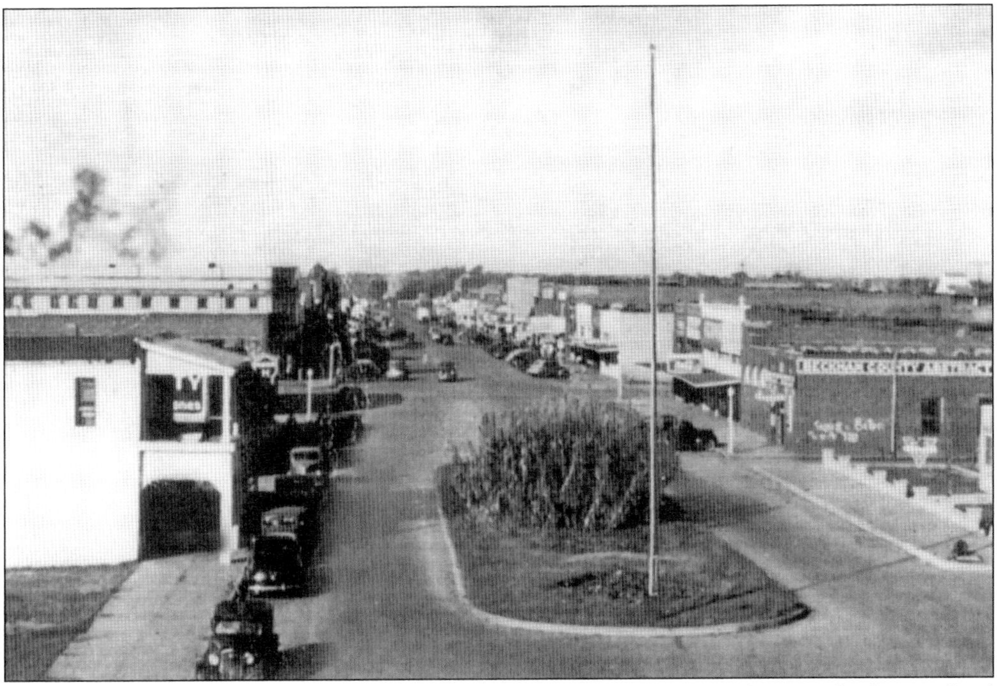

This photograph was taken from the courthouse looking west in Sayre. There used to be an island in the center of the street with a flagpole. There is a hotel to the left, and the Beckham County Abstract is on the right. There are many vintage cars up and down the street.

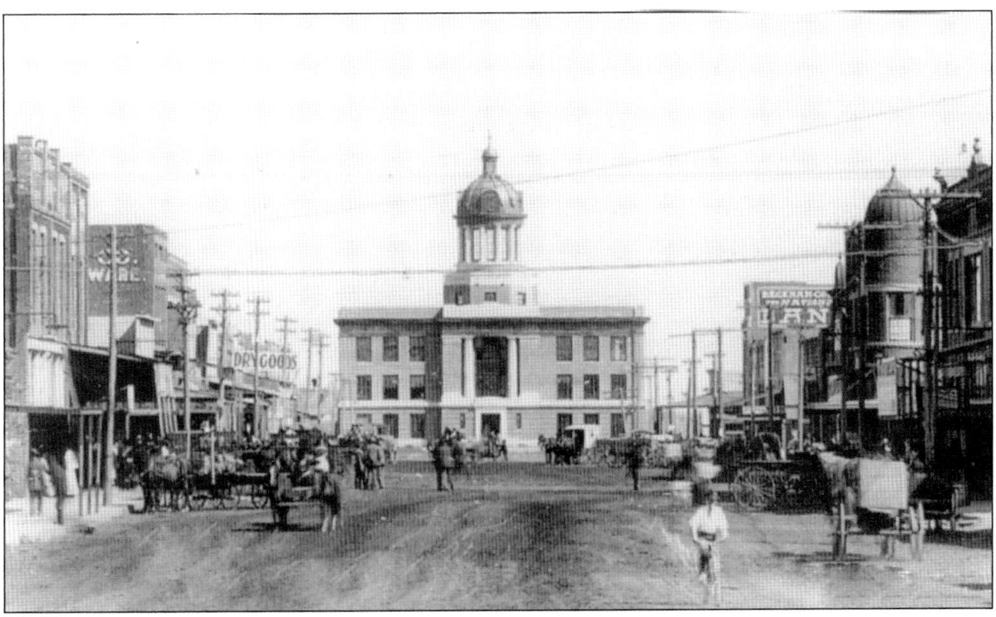

Main Street is seen here in October 1911. Several of the buildings in this photograph are still standing today. The Beckham County Courthouse is in the background.

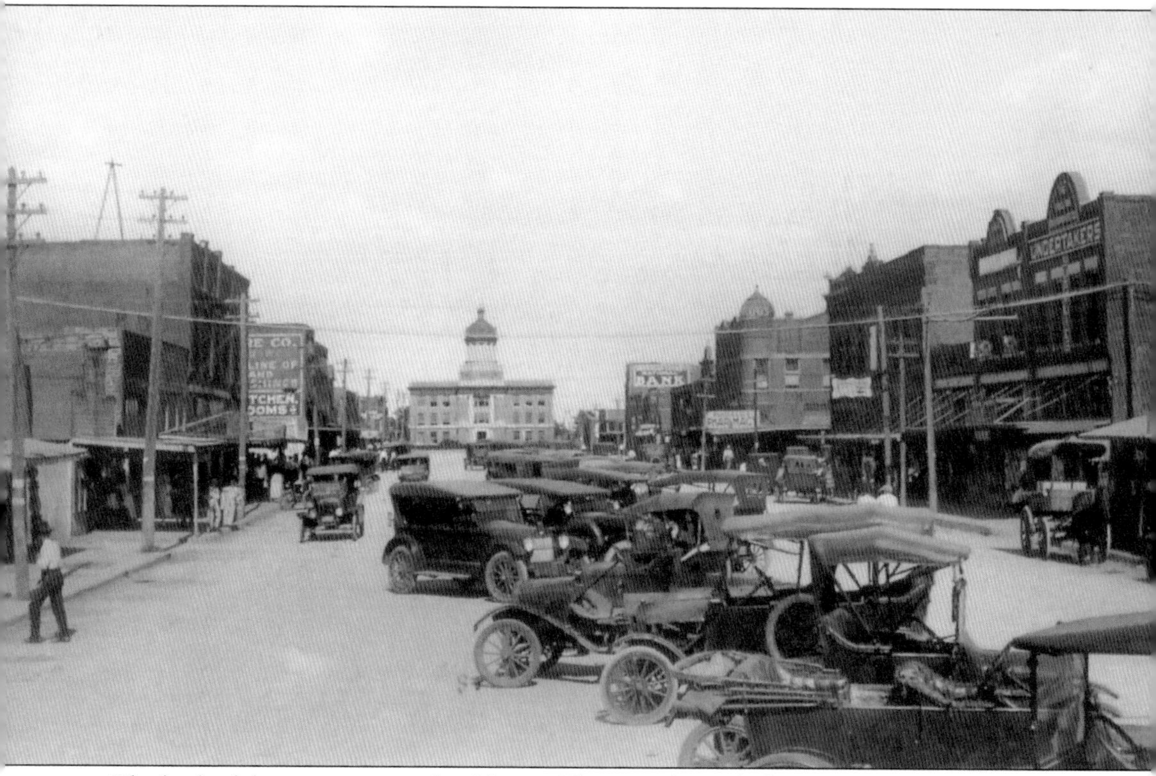

The back of the picture states that Hosmer Photography took this image of Main Street on July 29. It looks like it was taken during the 1920s, and these were busy times in the town. Cars were allowed to park in the middle of the street. There are both Model-Ts and Model-As pictured.

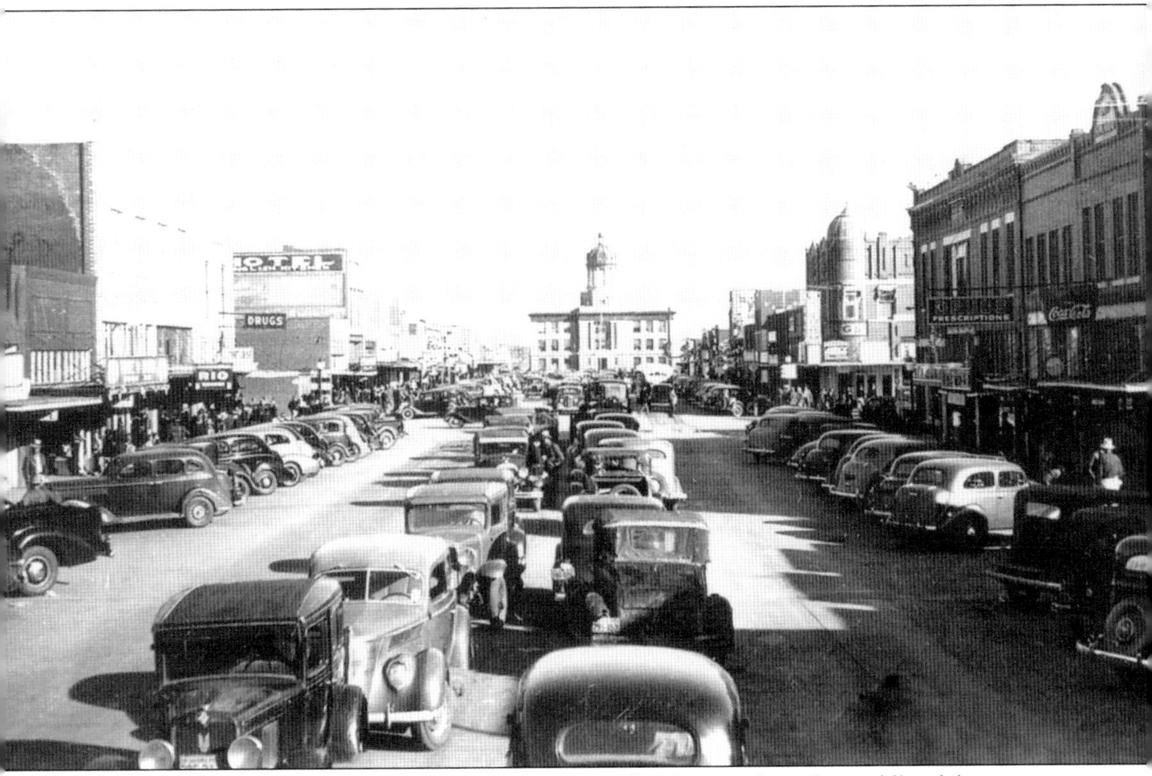

This is Main Street in Sayre in the 1940s. Cars were still able to park in the middle of the street. Note the old Rio movie sign on the left, which showed many cowboy and Indian films. A few hotels can also be seen in this picture.

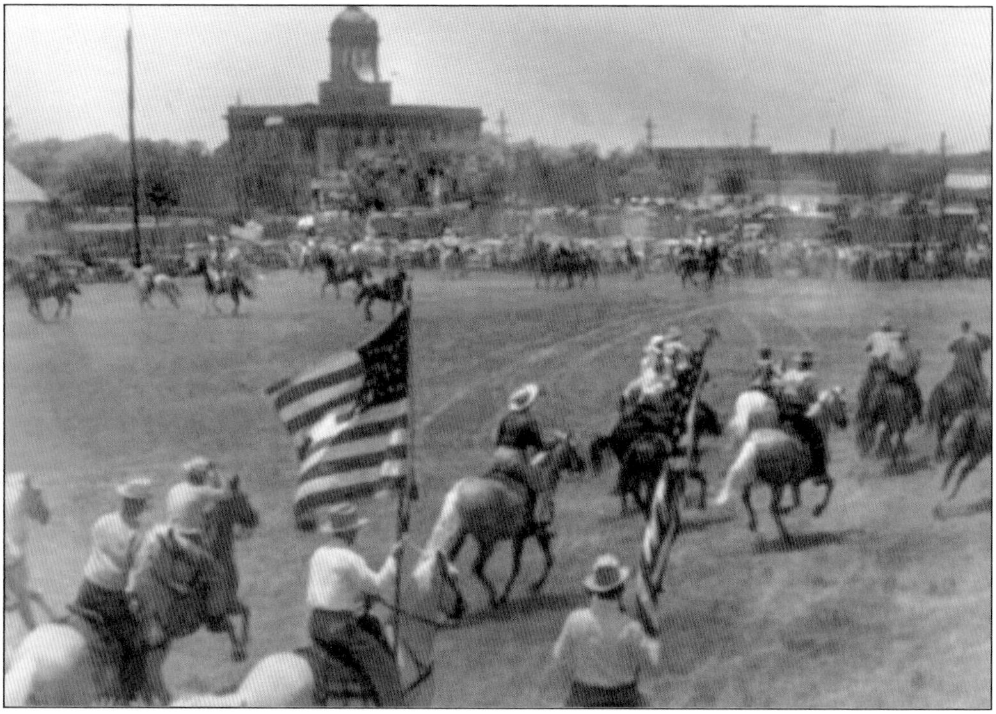

The town of Sayre is preparing for a rodeo in the early 1900s. The rodeo always brought a lot of people and excitement to the town.

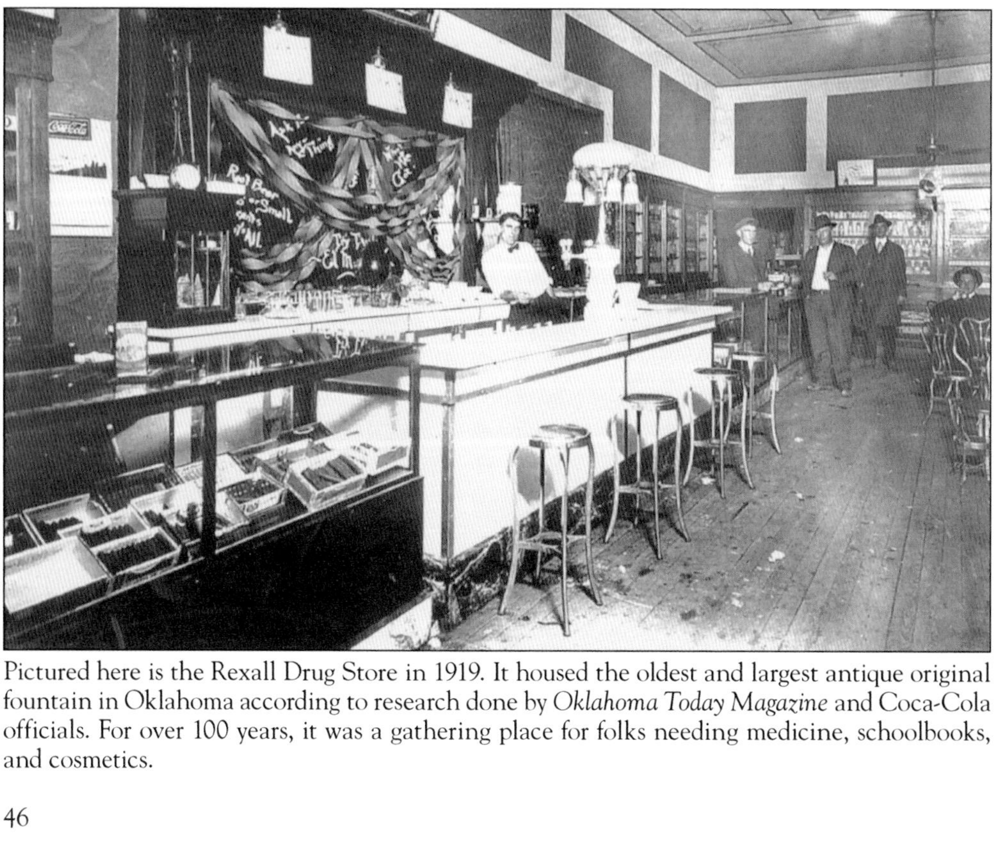

Pictured here is the Rexall Drug Store in 1919. It housed the oldest and largest antique original fountain in Oklahoma according to research done by *Oklahoma Today Magazine* and Coca-Cola officials. For over 100 years, it was a gathering place for folks needing medicine, schoolbooks, and cosmetics.

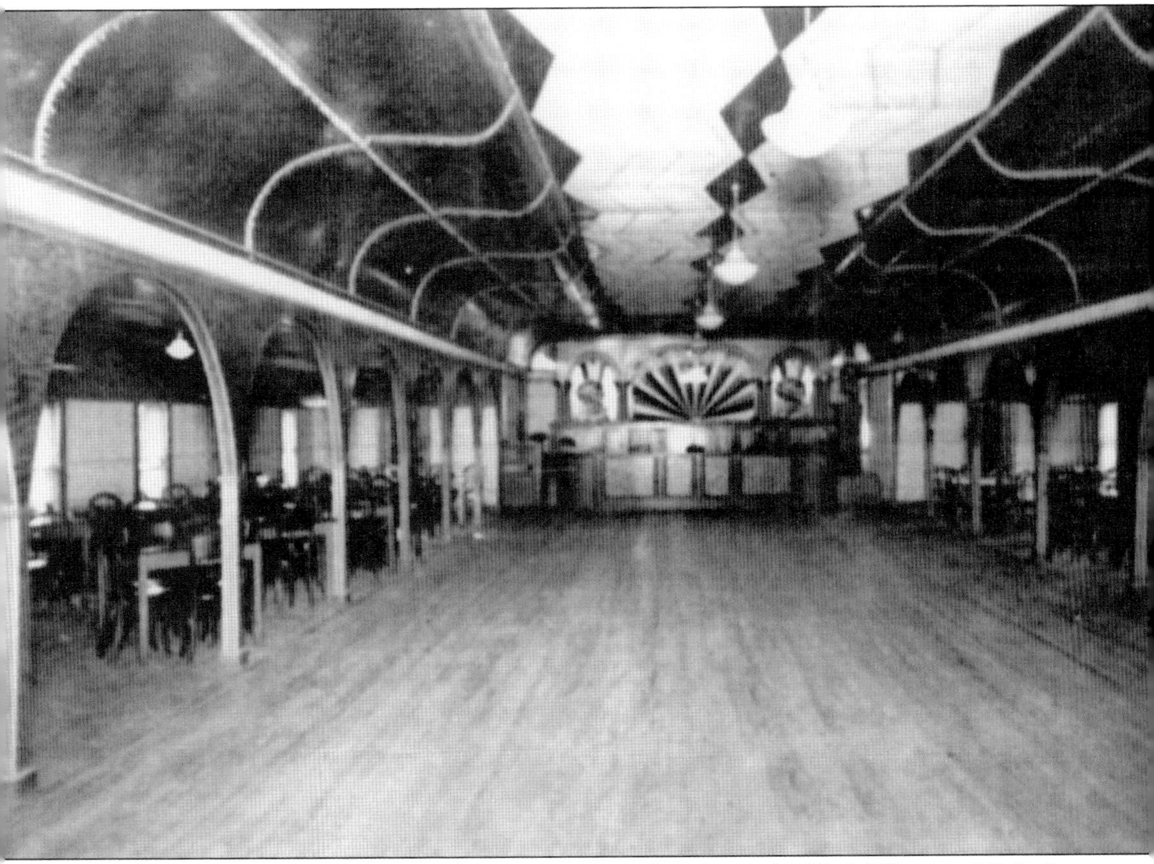

This building was the Red, White, and Blue, sometimes referred to as the "Red, White, and Fight," on the west end of Sayre. It was one of the many dance halls and beer joints during that time. It was located close to Route 66 and Highways 283 and 152.

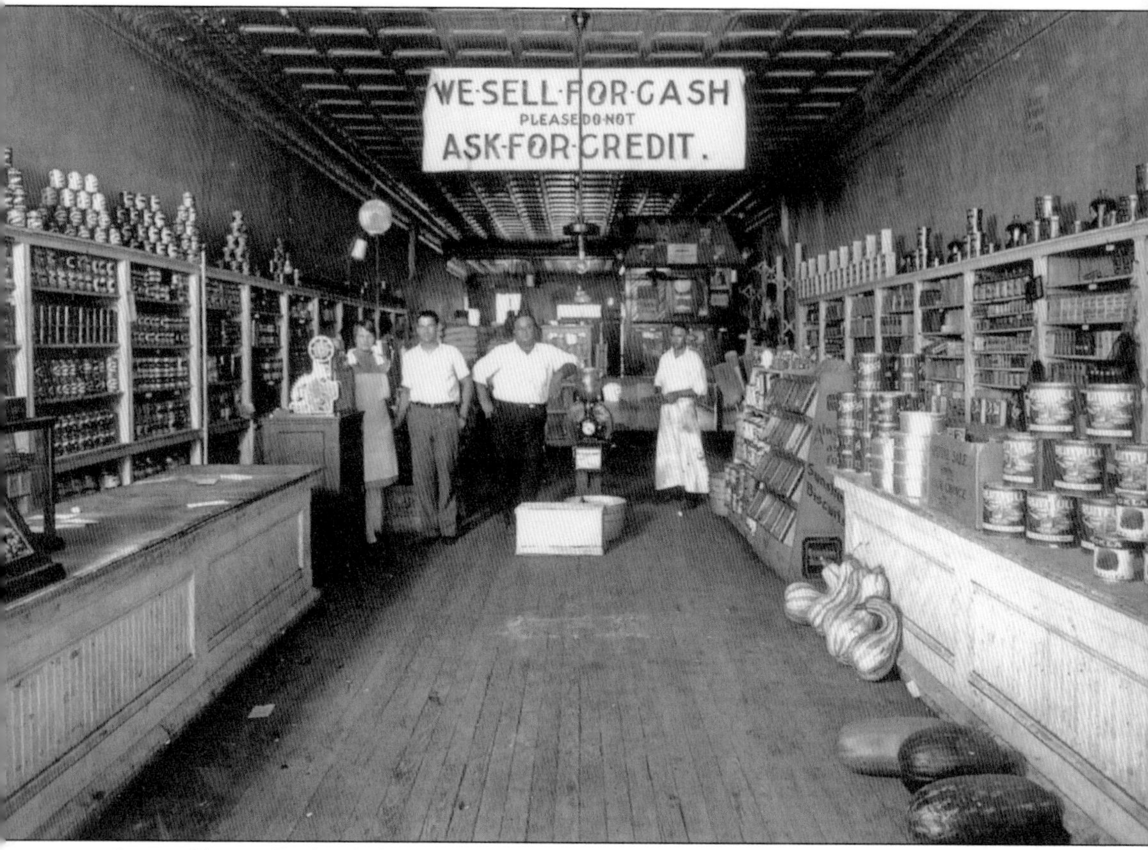

Pictured here is Puckett's Grocery Store in the early decades of the 20th century. The sign in the middle of the building requests patrons not to ask for credit. There are gourds and watermelons in the foreground, and cans that are stacked high on the shelves.

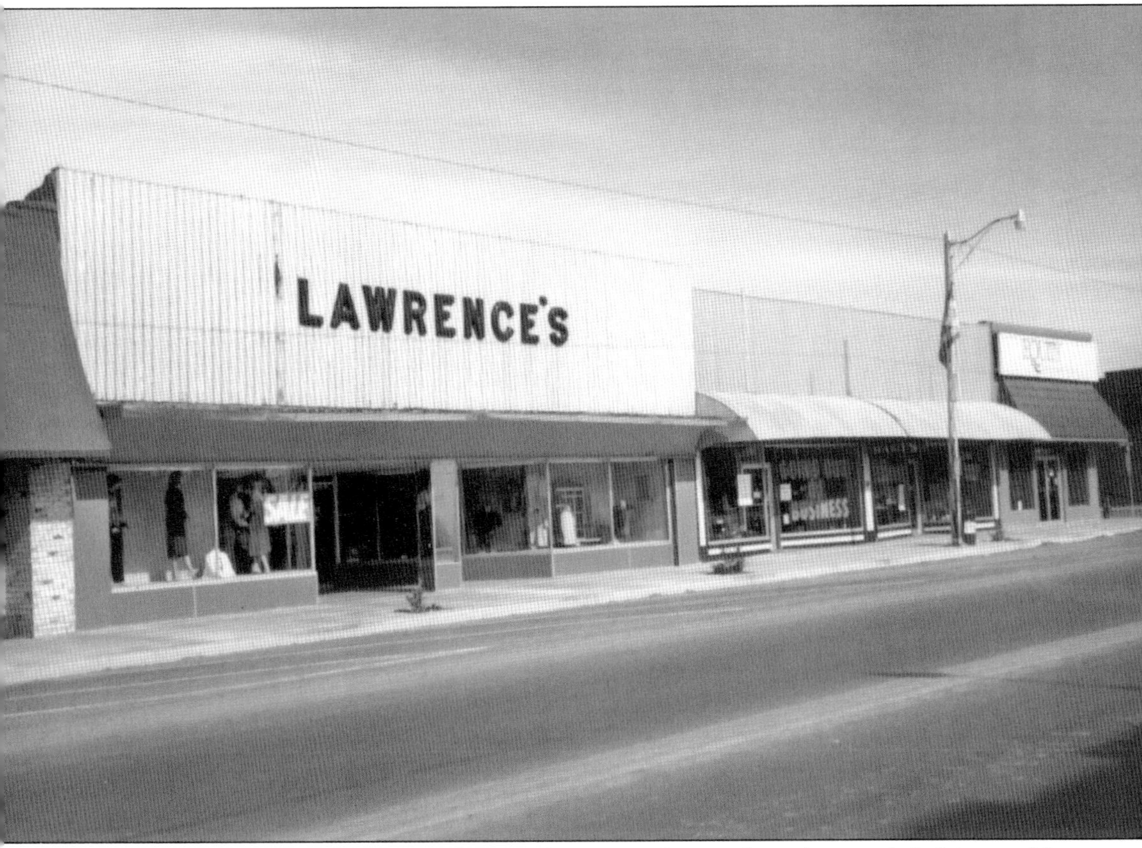

This is the old Lawrence Department Store in downtown Sayre, where shoes and clothing could be bought for the whole family. Children used to enjoy the Santa Claus that jumped up and down out of a chimney put in the window at Christmastime.

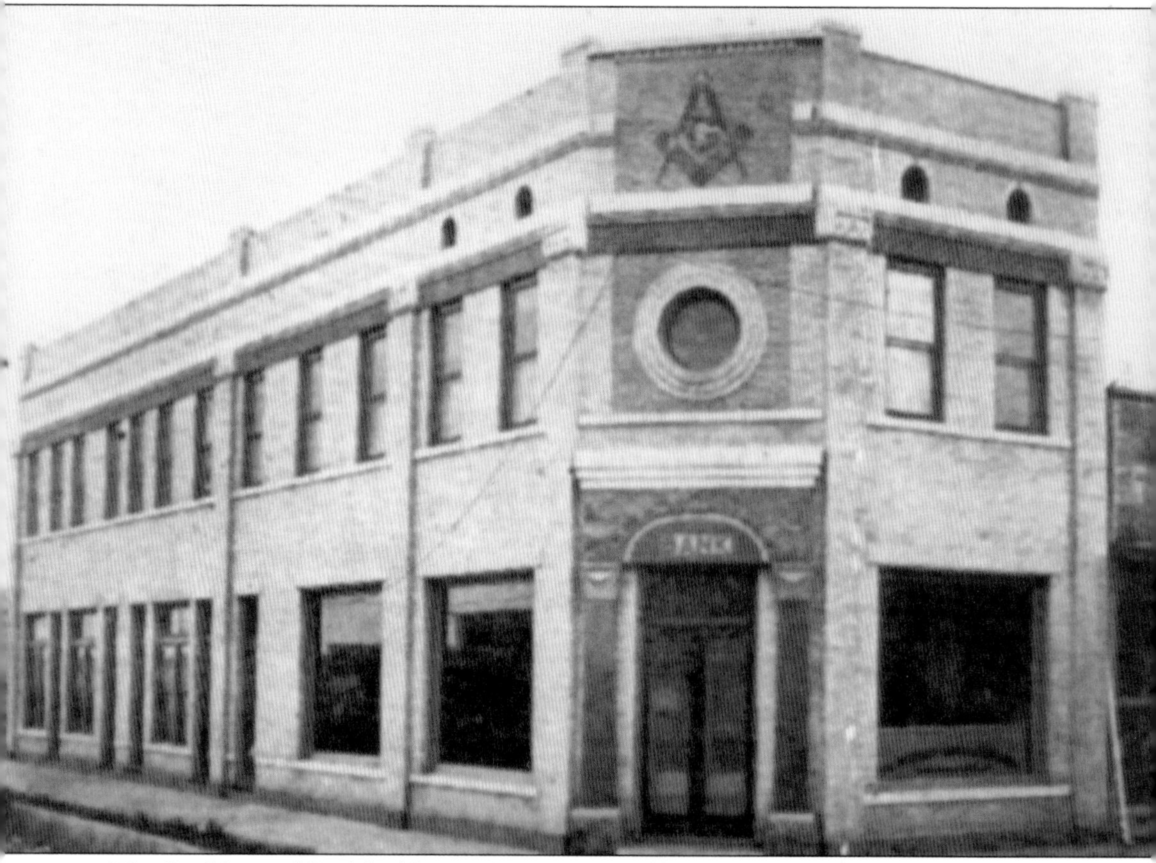

The City National Bank building in Sayre is pictured here, where the bank did business for many years until it was replaced by the Great Plains National Bank. Above the bank was where the Sayre Masonic Lodge no. 195 met. This lodge was issued its charter from the Grand Lodge of Oklahoma in Guthrie on February 11, 1903.

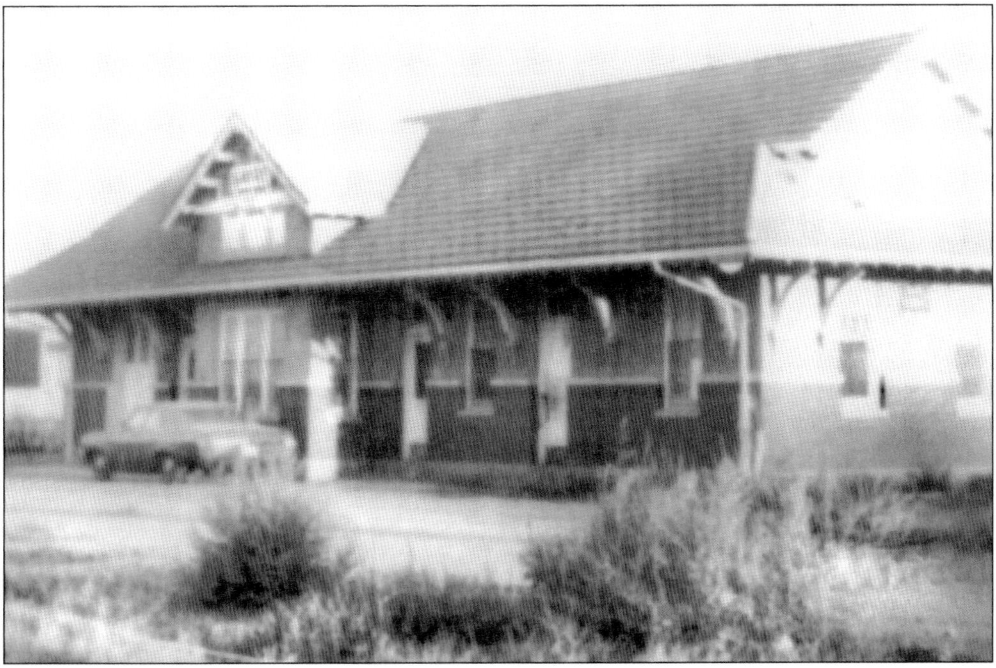

The Rock Island Depot is pictured before it was made into a museum. It was constructed in Sayre in 1927 and served the railroads for many years until the Rock Island Railroad was no longer in use.

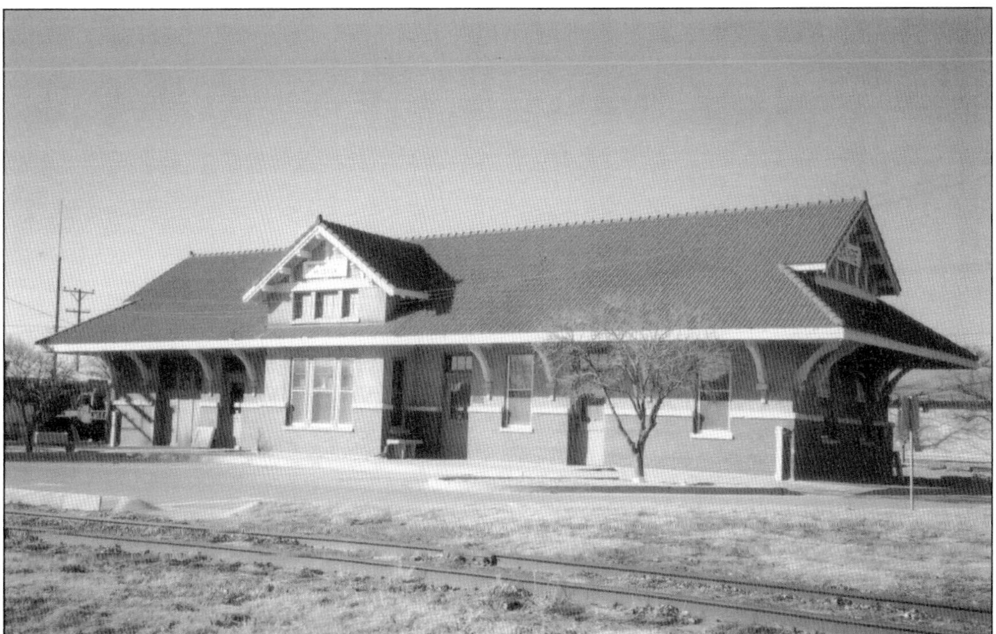

Rock Island Depot was built near the center of Sayre in 1927, and it is now the home of the Shortgrass County Museum. It was placed in the National Register of Historic Places in 2000.

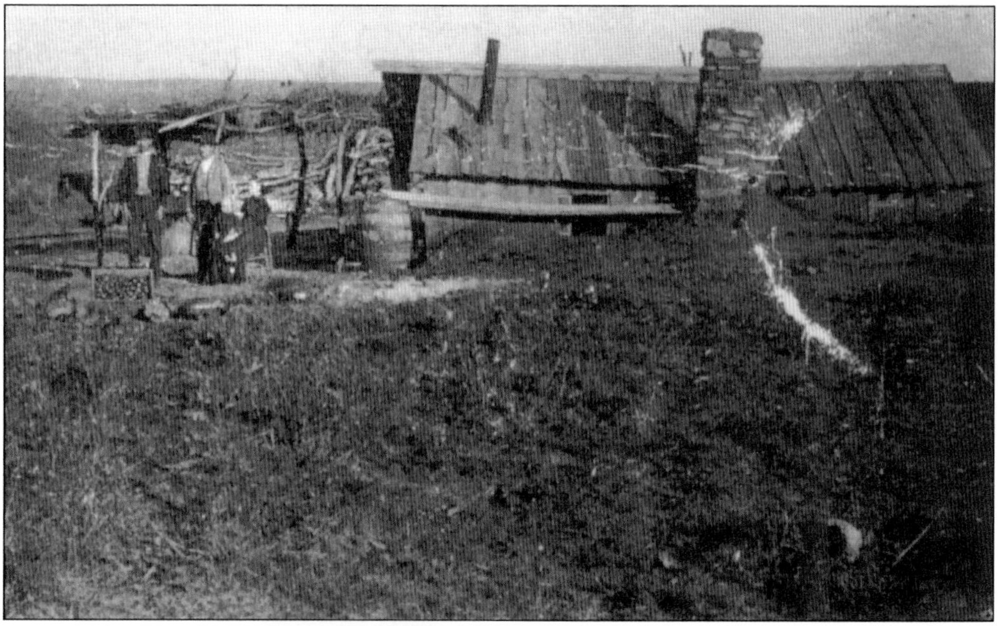

This is the first home of some early-day settlers, Mr. and Mrs. D. A. Vineyard. This dugout is typical of many dwellings in the area in 1897. A lot of early settlers used these as their first homes and then built final homes on the same property. (Courtesy of the *Sayre Record*.)

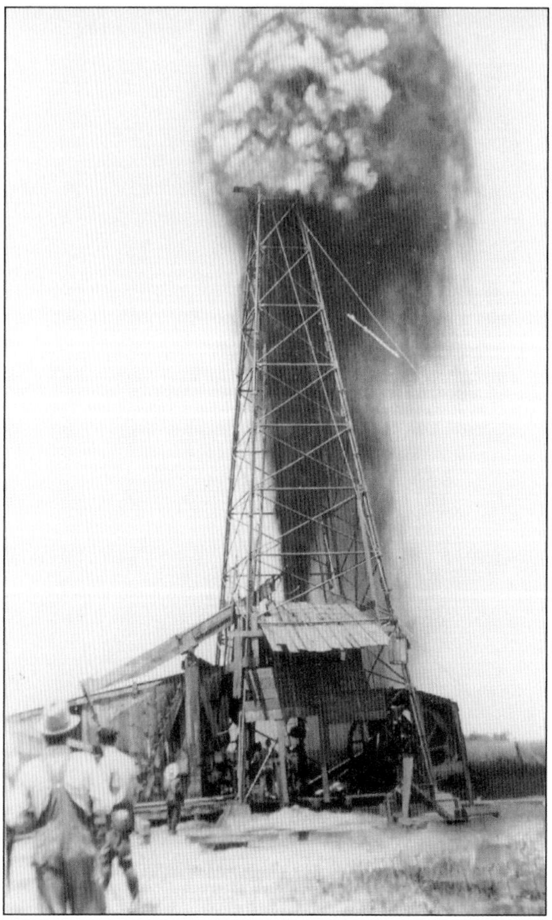

This early-1900s photograph shows an oil well blowing. The oil boom helped Sayre to double in size.

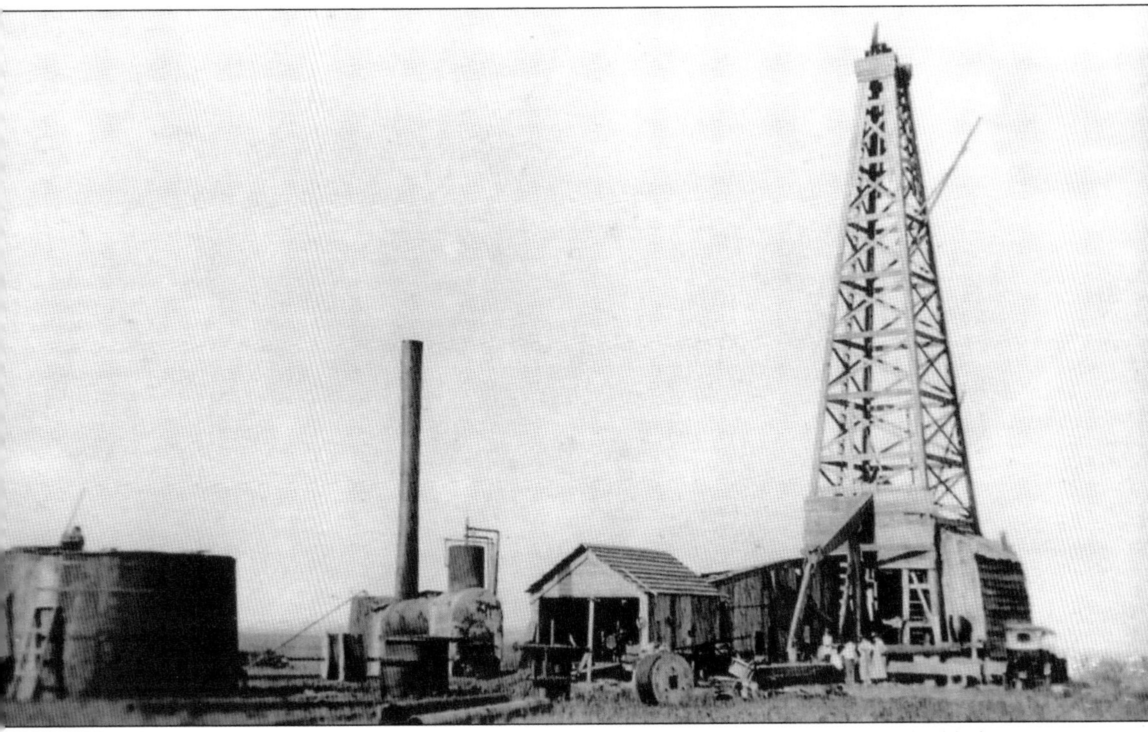

This oil rig near Sayre dates from the early 1900s. It is said that the town almost doubled in size during this oil boom. Hosmer Photography took the image.

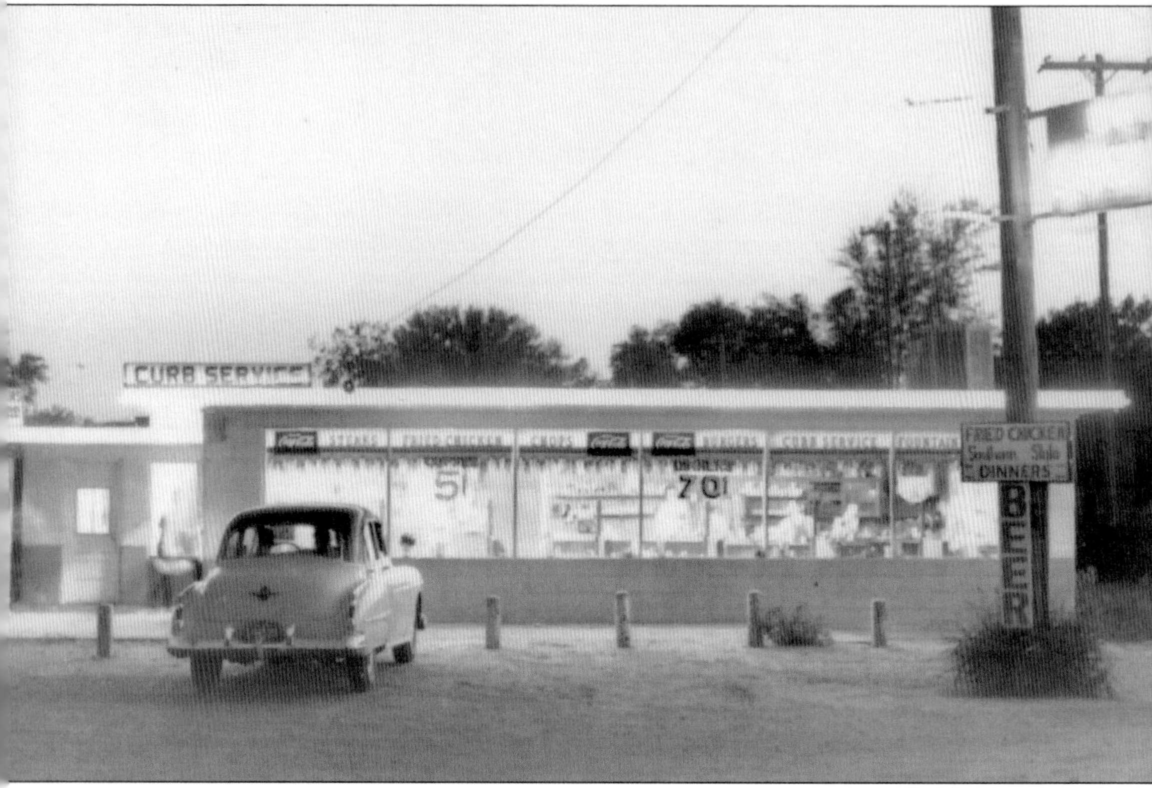

Rays Drive-In was on the west end of Sayre and was popular in the 1950s and served fountain drinks, steaks, chicken, chops, and burgers. The author and her husband had a fountain drink there on their first date.

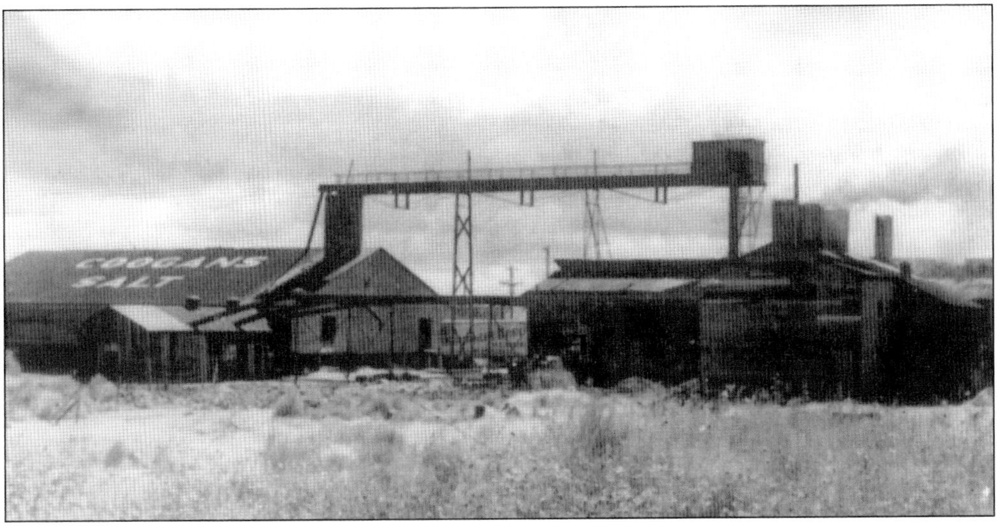

Pictured above is the Western Oklahoma Salt Manufacturing Plant, southwest of Sayre, in the early 1900s. Fred Coogan Sr.'s family owned this plant. It is still in operation today under new ownership. The image below shows what used to be the home of Fred Coogan Sr. Most recently, Joan Ellison, a teacher and museum director, has owned the home. (Courtesy of the Shortgrass County Museum.)

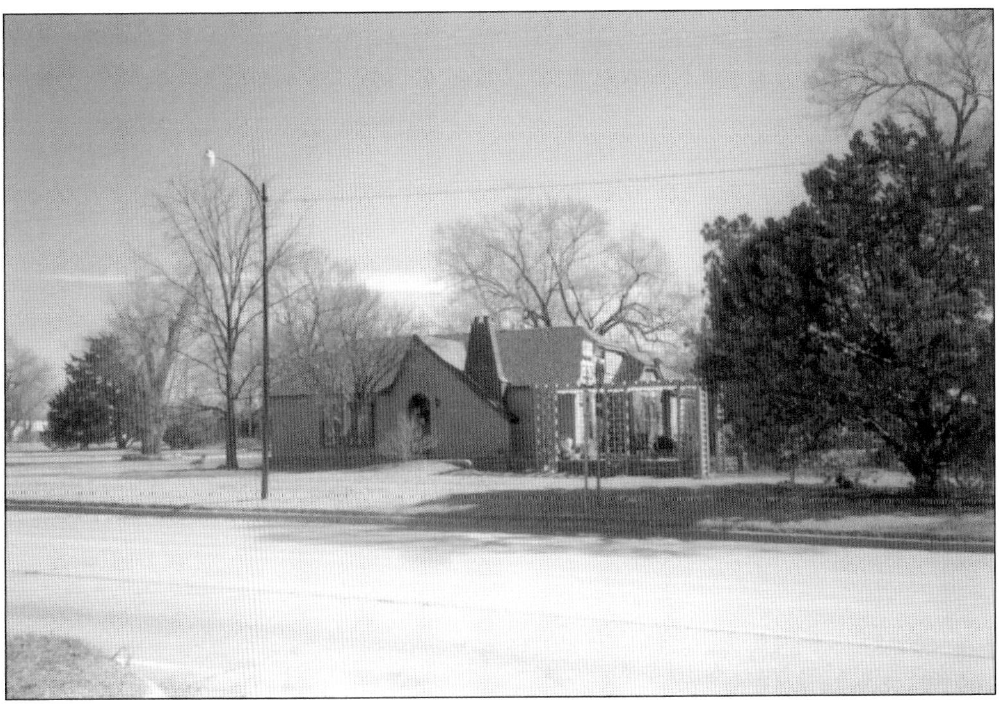

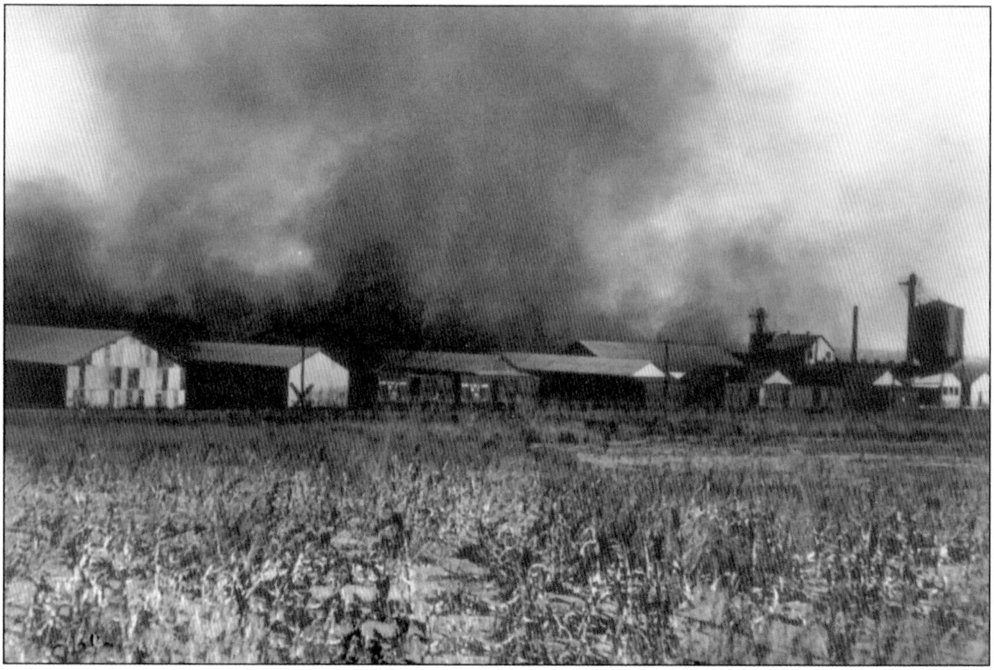

Pictured above is the Carbon Black Channel Plant, southwest of Sayre. It made black ink, shoe soles, and tires. In the early 1990s, C.K. Springfield owned it, but today it is no longer in operation. The house in the image below was the home of C.K. Springfield. He had offices in a two-story building to the southeast of his home. (Courtesy of the Shortgrass County Museum.)

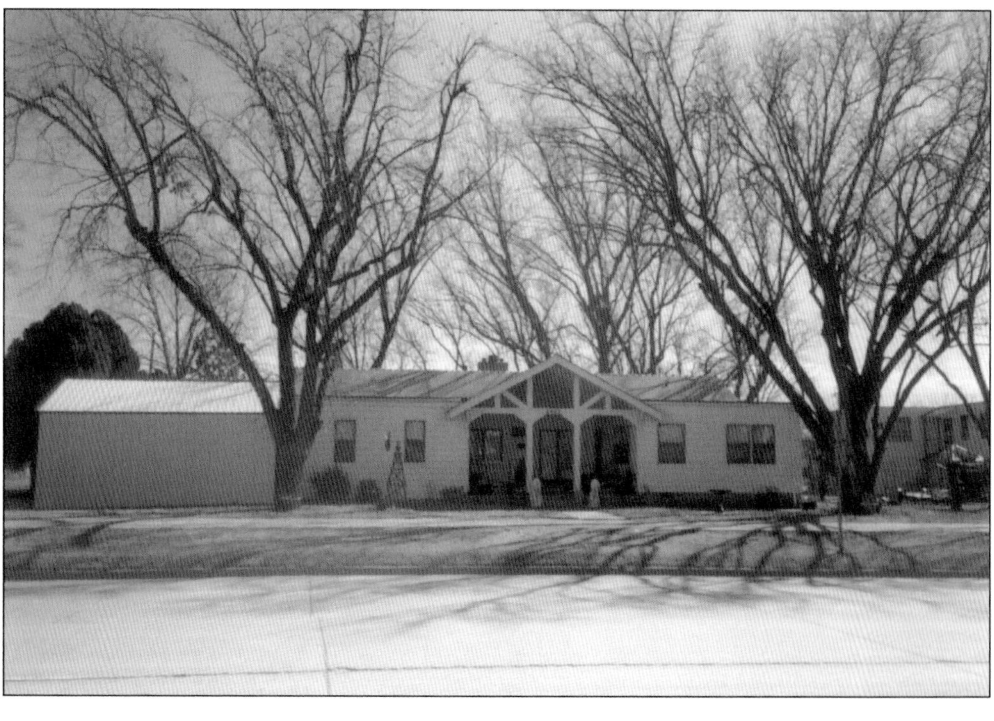

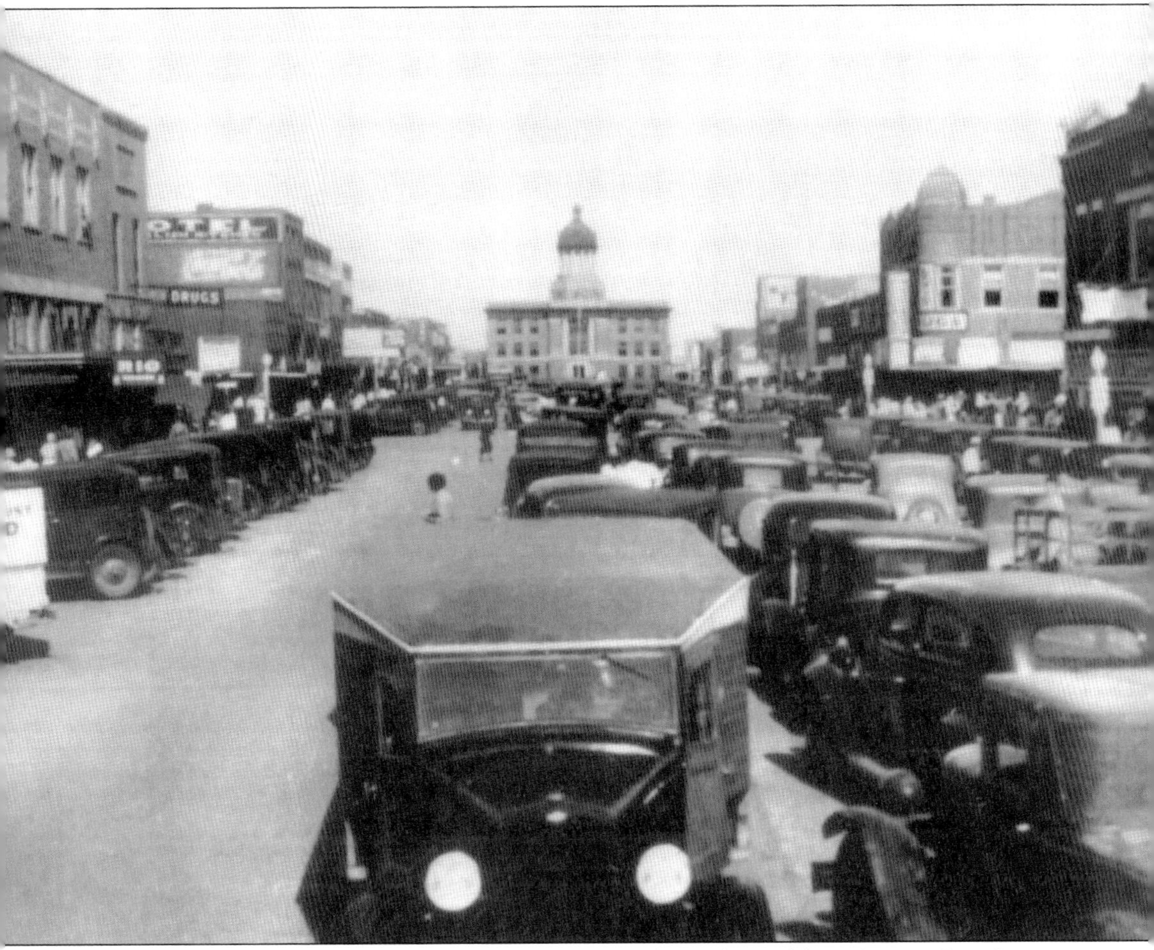

This 1930s photograph of Main Street in downtown Sayre shows the Beckham County Courthouse in the background. The courthouse was built in 1911 and was featured in the movie based on John Steinbeck's novel, *The Grapes of Wrath*.

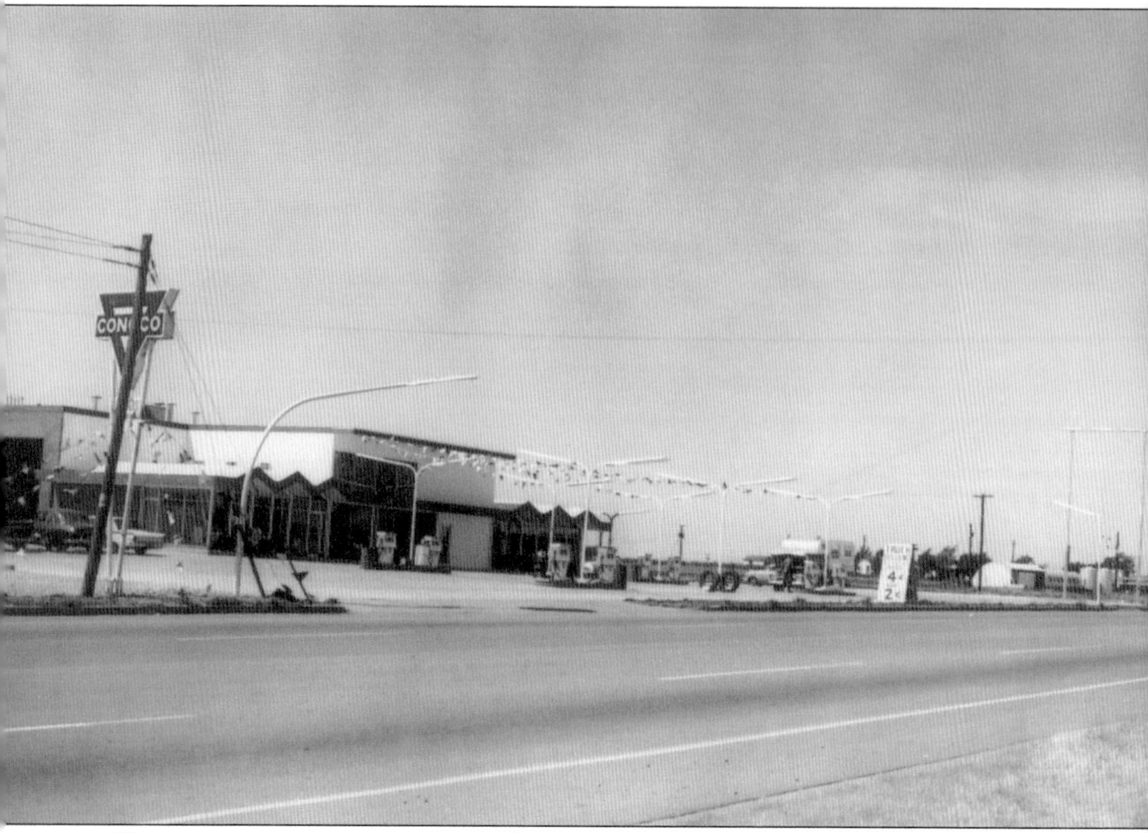

The Conoco station that was owned and operated by Kings Truck Oasis, along Route 66, is pictured here in the 1960s. It is now the administration building for Sayre Public Schools. (Courtesy of the Shortgrass County Museum.)

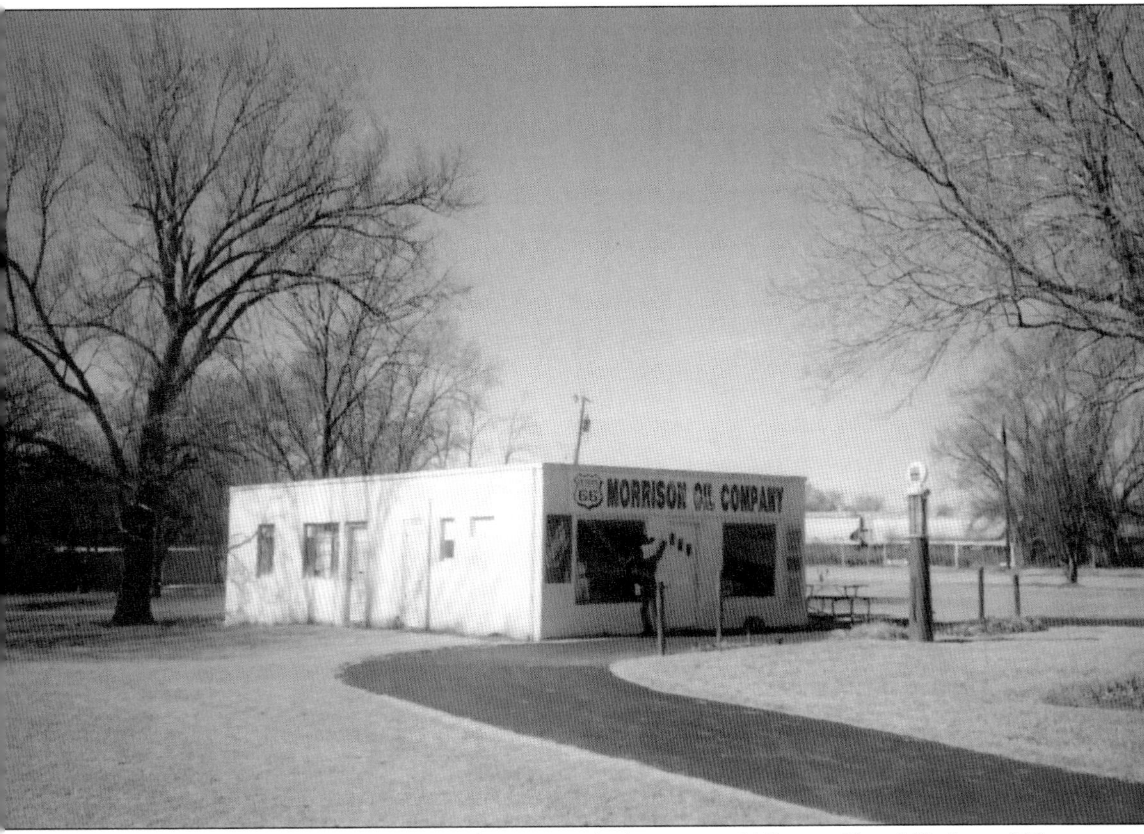

Here is the Old Deep Rock Station on the west end of town on old Route 66 and Highway 283. Back in the 1950s, it was a busy little station with two to four gas pumps out front and a grease rack on the north side. Bill Craig and his wife lived in the back of the station.

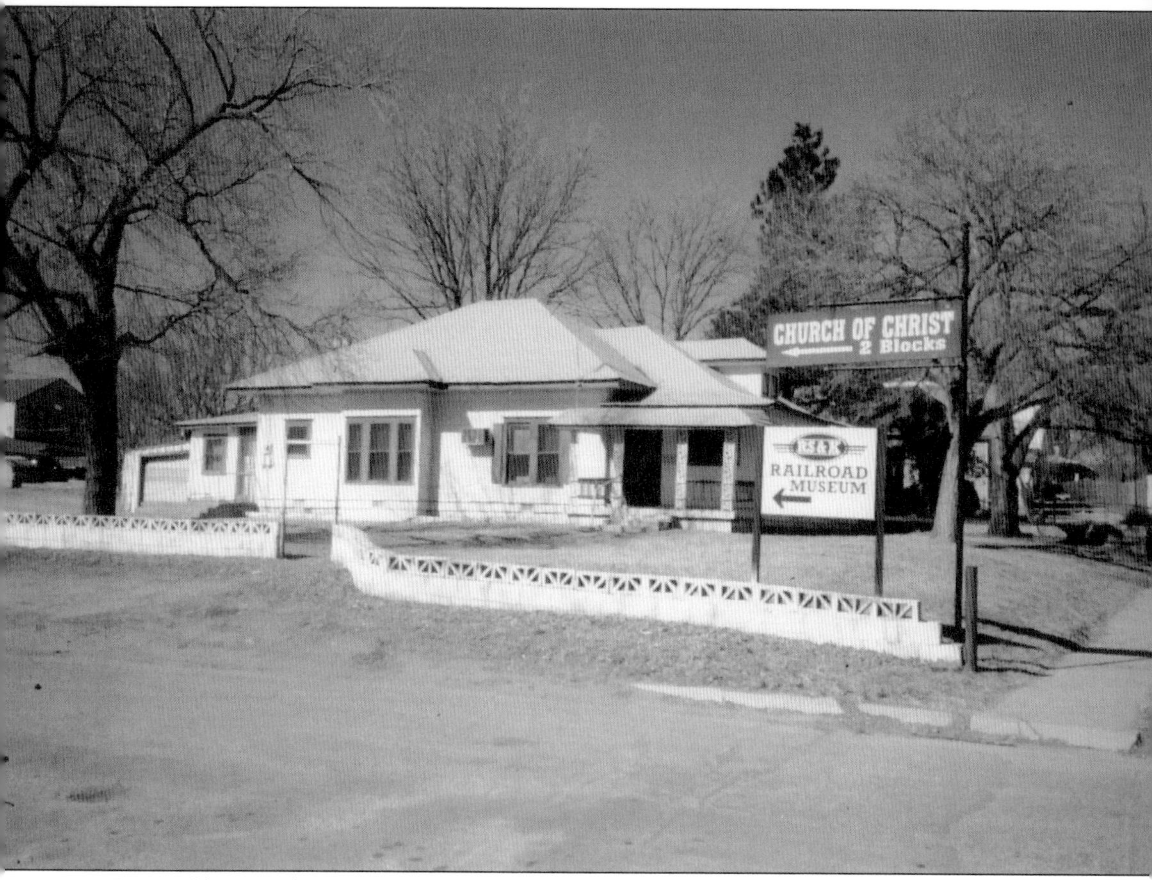

Pictured here is the R.S. and K. Railroad Museum sign on the corner of Fourth Street (Route 66) and Locust Avenue in Sayre. The home in the background belongs to the Bain family. They settled in Sayre around 1907.

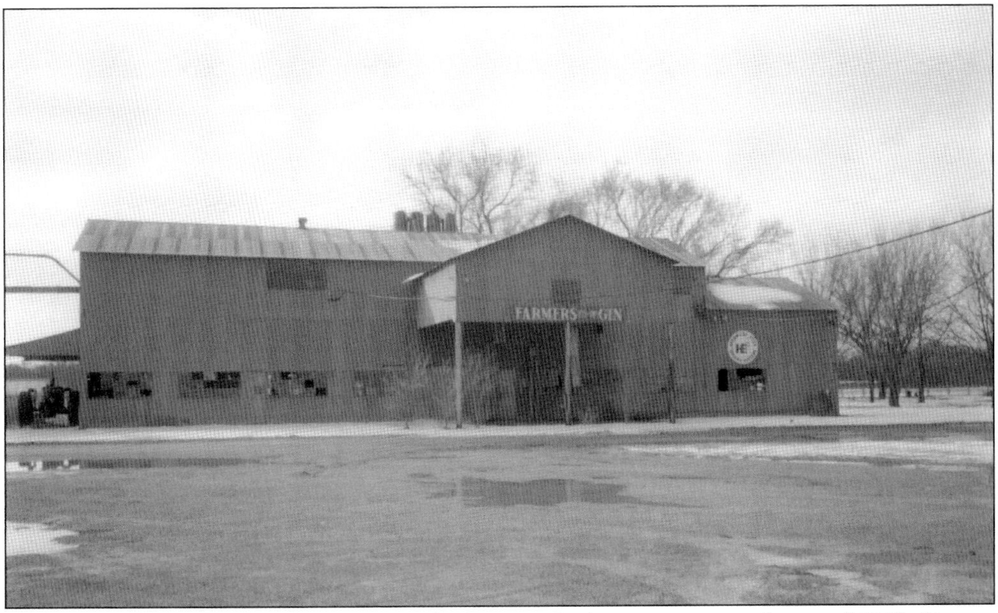

This is the old cotton gin on the west end of town, which was in use until around 2009. Cotton was once big business in Sayre, but now it is manufactured elsewhere.

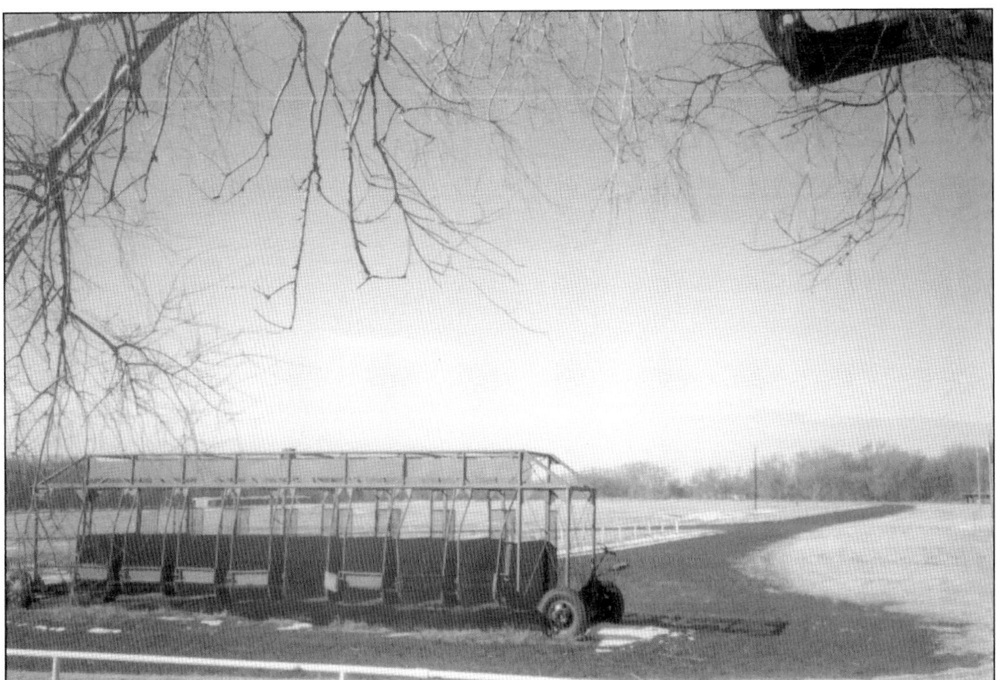

This racetrack was referred to as the Cradle of the Quarter Horse up until around 10 years ago. Now it is called the J. and J. Training Center and is still in use today.

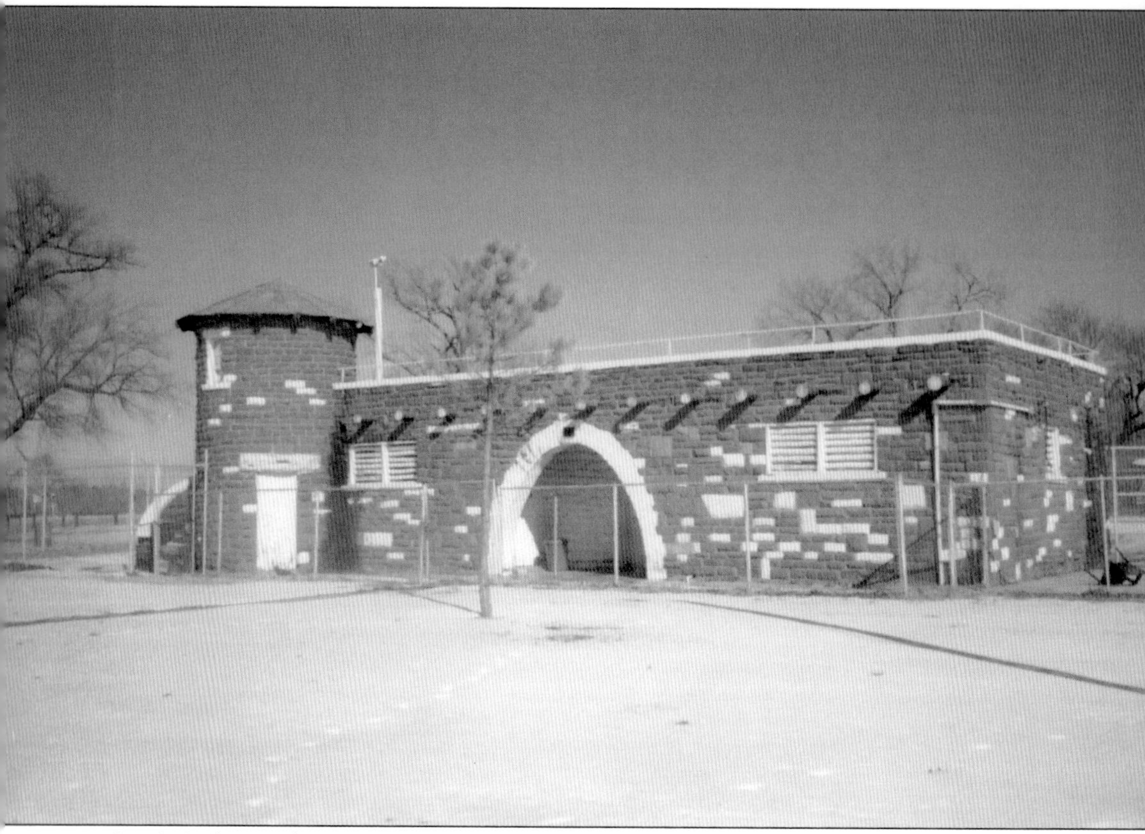

In 1940, the Works Projects Administration constructed the Sayre swimming pool. It was part of the project to put men to work during the Great Depression, and it was welcomed by the men of Sayre. The program also constructed bridges and schools in the area.

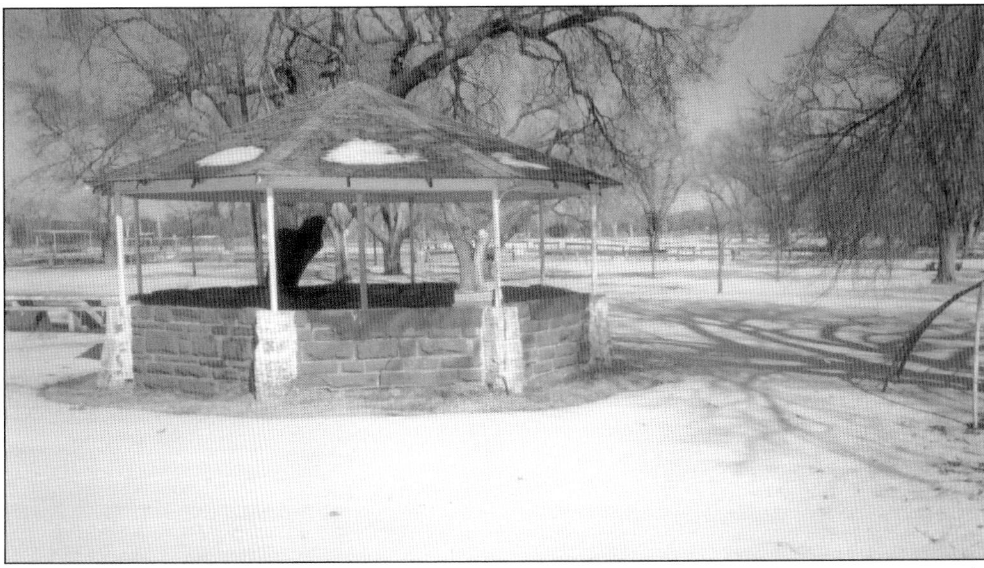

In 1940, the WPA constructed this gazebo in Sayre Park. It constructed bridges, swimming pools, bathhouses, schools, and cellars to help put people to work during hard times.

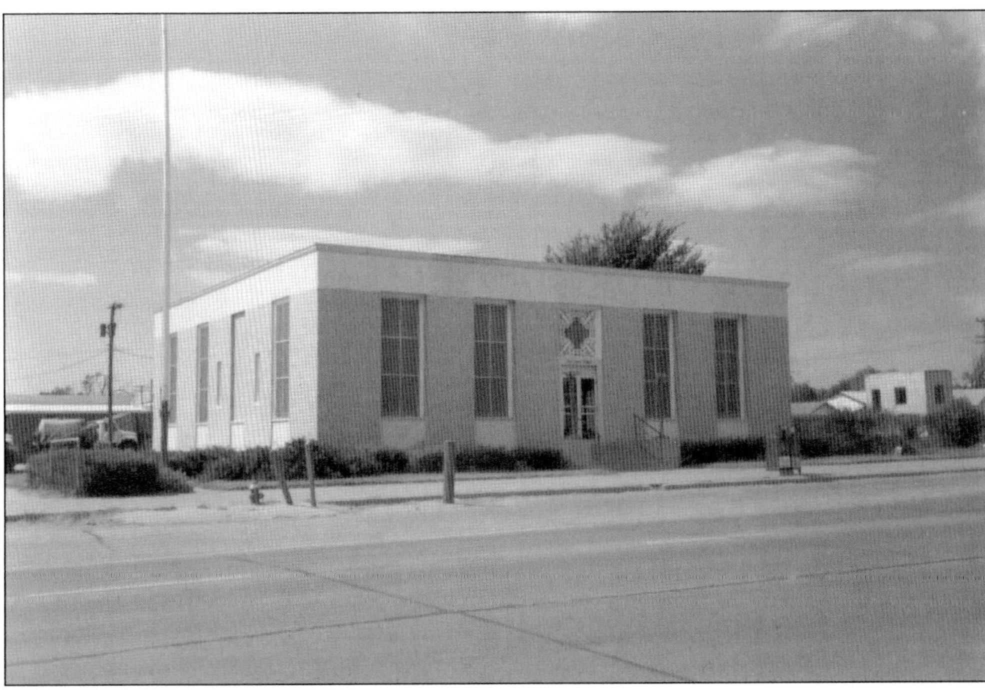

This is the US post office in Sayre, which was constructed in 1938. The author's husband, Ray, worked in the building as a distribution clerk. He took care of the mail that came in on the train and tied the bag out on the hook for the outgoing mail on the train.

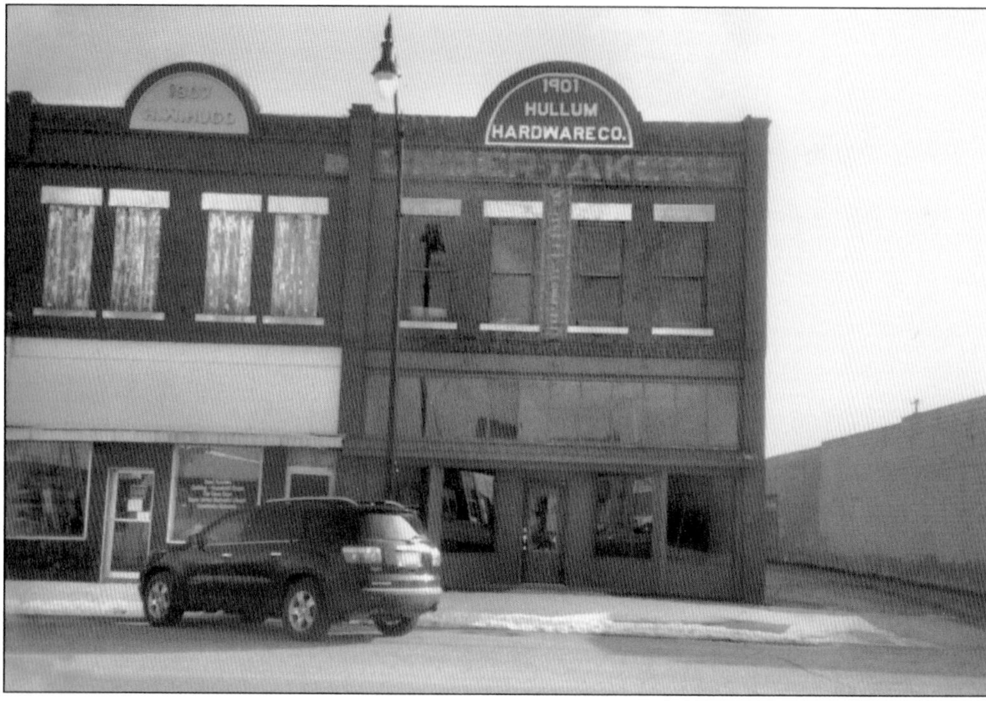

The building on the right in the above image houses the Hullum Hardware Company; it was constructed in 1901. The building on the left is H.W. Hugo, also constructed in the early 1900s. Pictured below is the Hullum home.

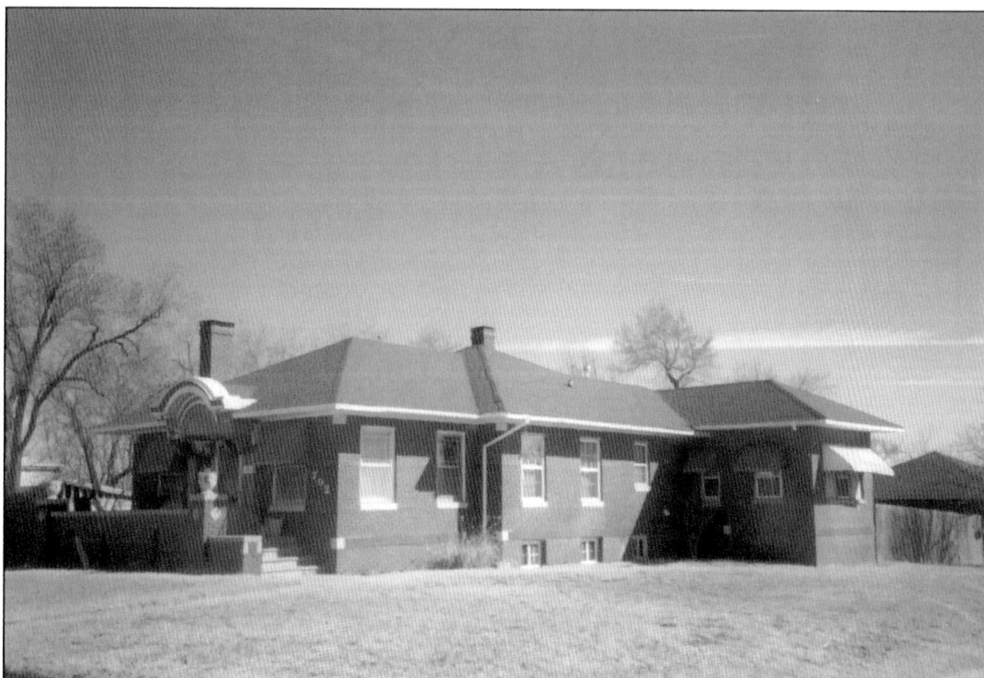

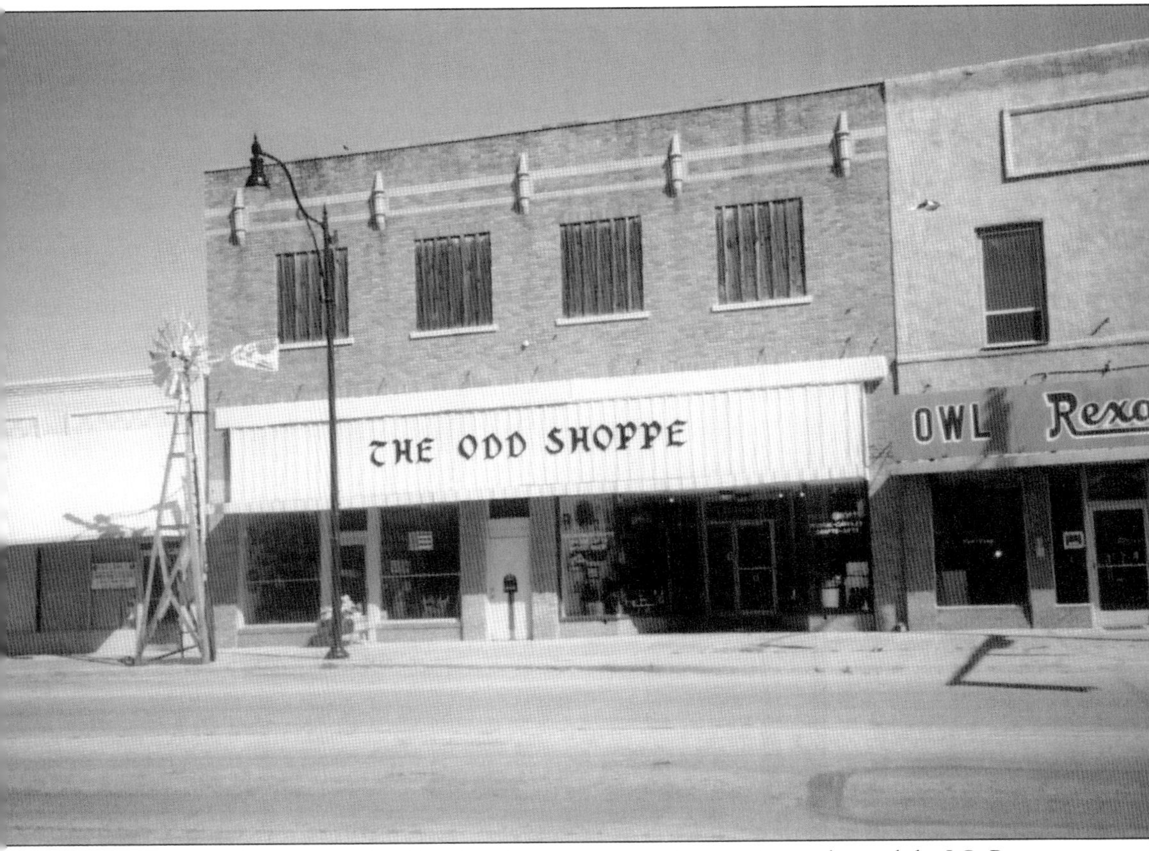

This is the Odd Shoppe, which sells a lot of antique items. At one time, it housed the J.C. Penny Dry Goods Store. The old Rio movie theater was to the left of this building.

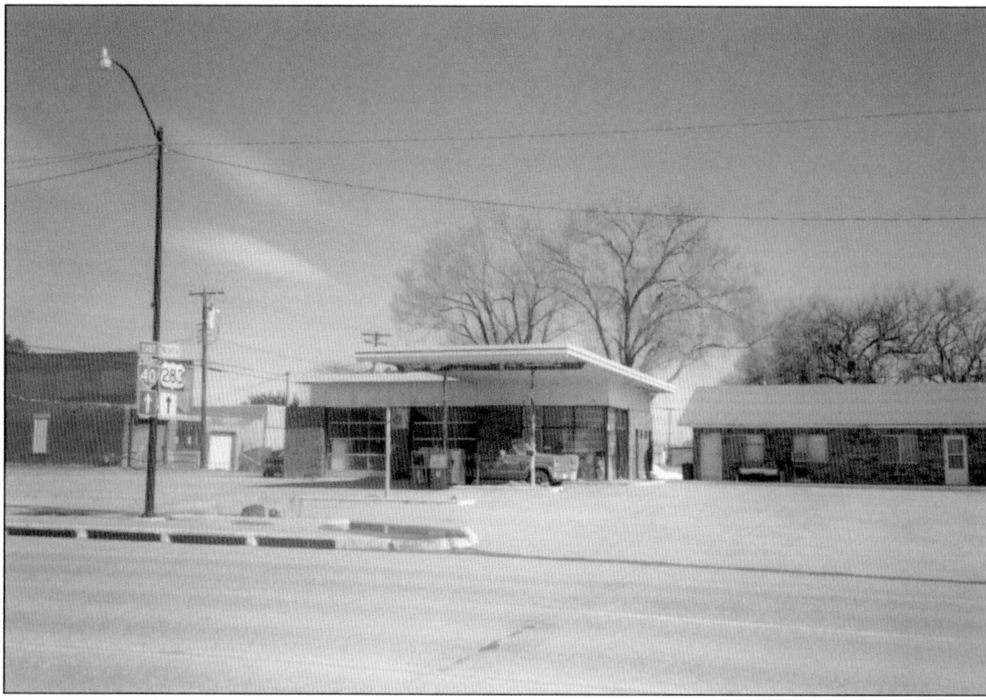

Above is the Mobile Oil Company that used to be owned and operated by Jimmy Winget's family. More recently, the Easter family ran it along with a small motel in the background. The gas pumps have been removed from the station. Pictured below is the Winget home on North Fourth Street. They lived here for many years, and the family still gathers at this house from time to time.

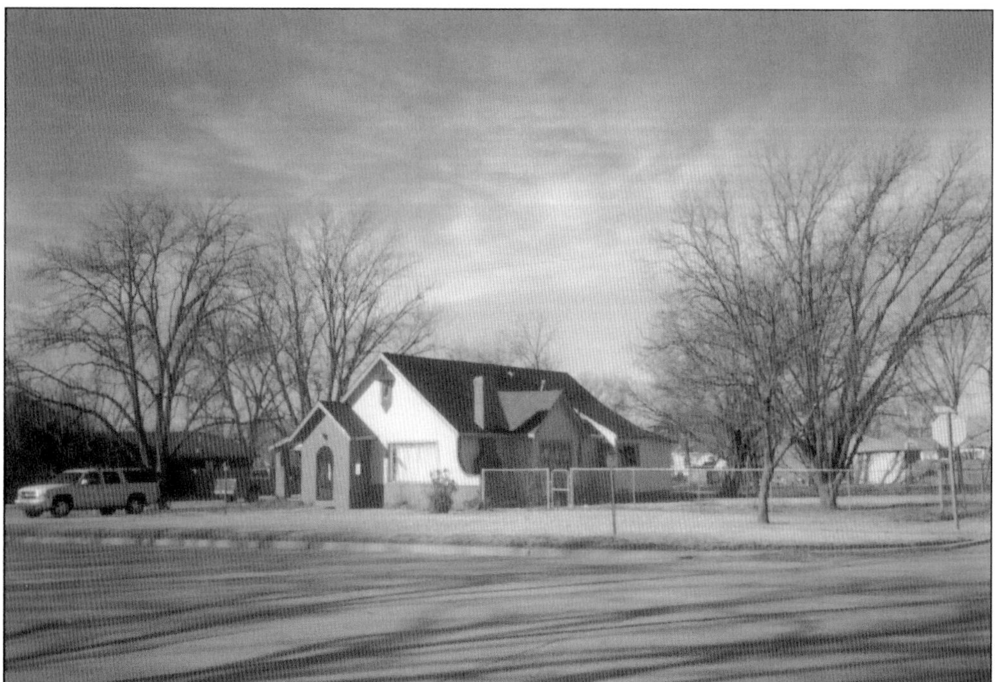

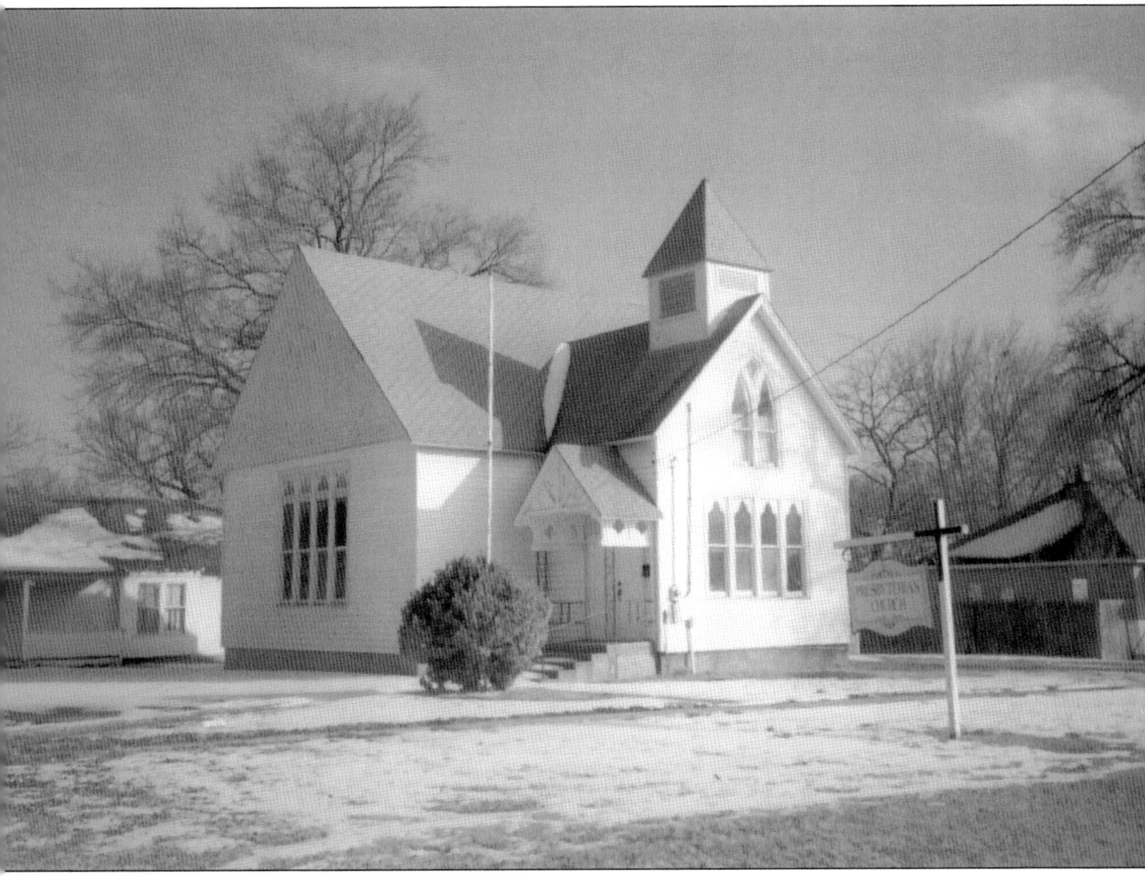

The Presbyterian Church, pictured here, was organized as a congregation in 1908 and constructed this building in 1913. In 1968, this church disbanded due to the lack of membership. The church was donated to the Shortgrass County Museum and Historical Society for use by the community.

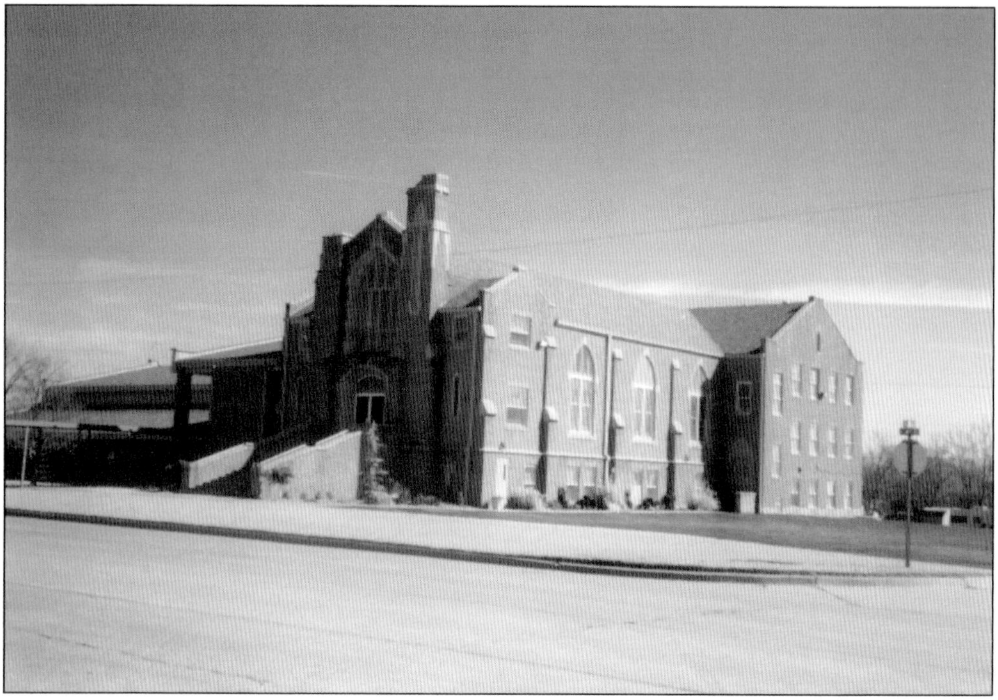

This is the Methodist Church building on Fourth Street in Sayre. It was constructed in the 1900s.

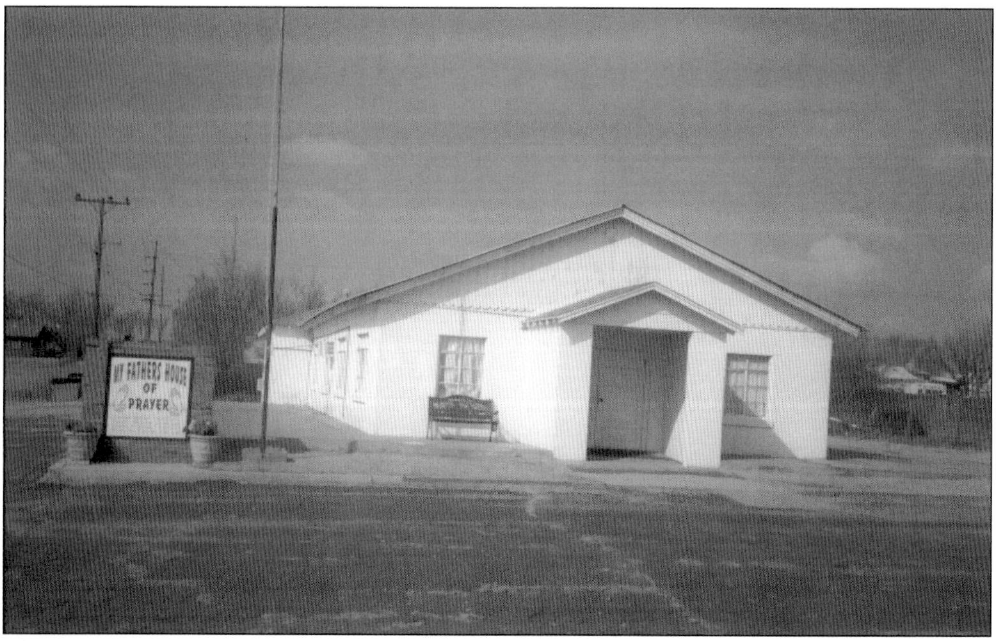

This is My Fathers House of Prayer on the west side of Sayre. It used to be a Baptist mission that was attended by railroad workers and their families who lived on what was affectionately called "Railroad Hill."

This furniture store was once Sharpes Dry Goods store. It is now Dean Properties, a real estate office. The Deans also own a hair salon and a copper cross ranch.

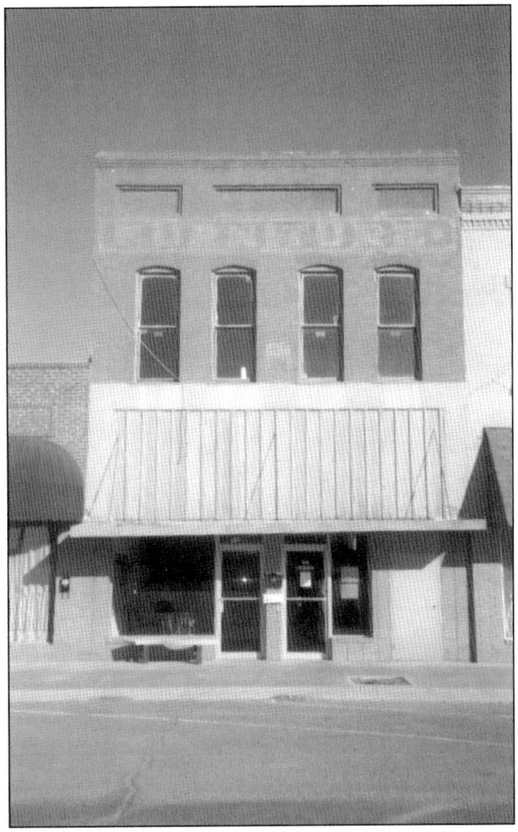

This is the Hood Drug Store building. Doctors had practices upstairs, and Dr. Wendel, Dr. Gum, and Dr. Spence were located in the rear of the building.

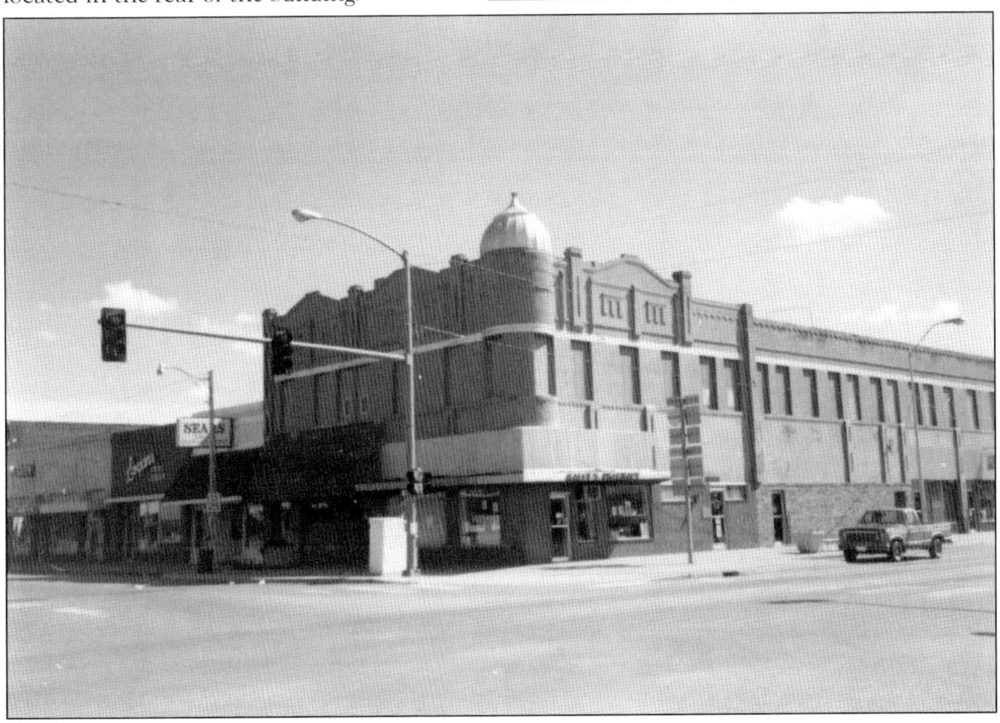

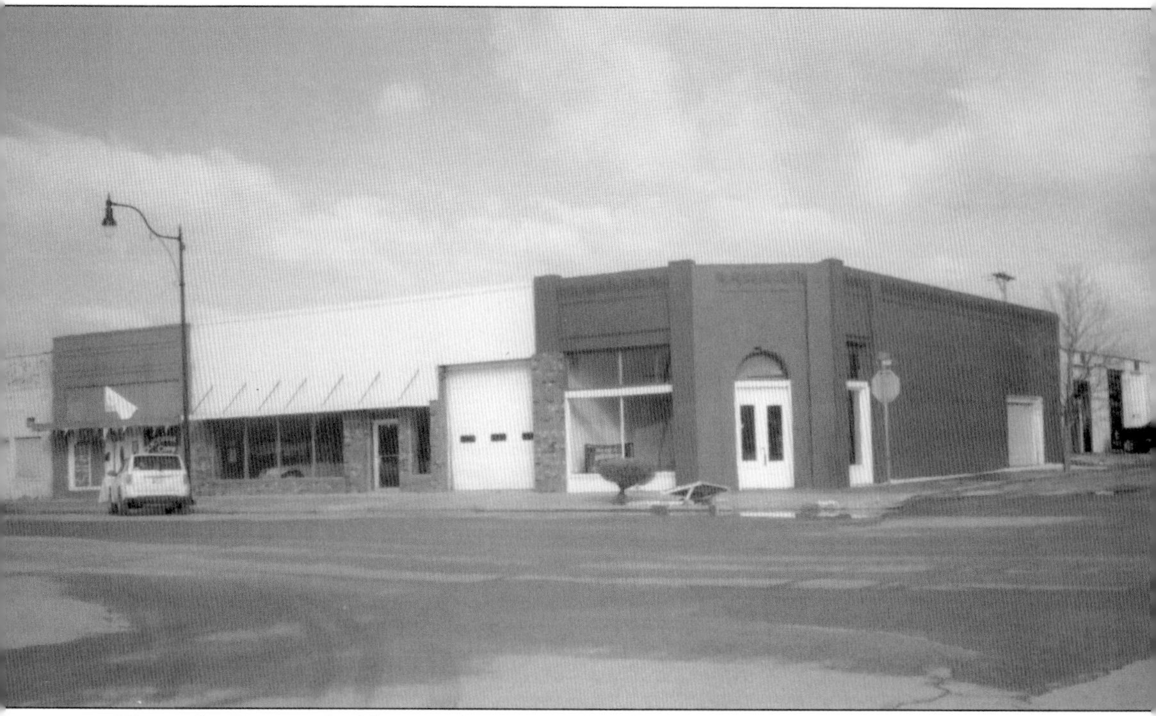

This is the Drapper Building on the corner of Fifth and Main Streets. Drapper was a car dealer in Sayre for many years, and once upon a time it was a Coca-Cola Bottling Company. Today, it stores remodeled cars and a fire engine in the building.

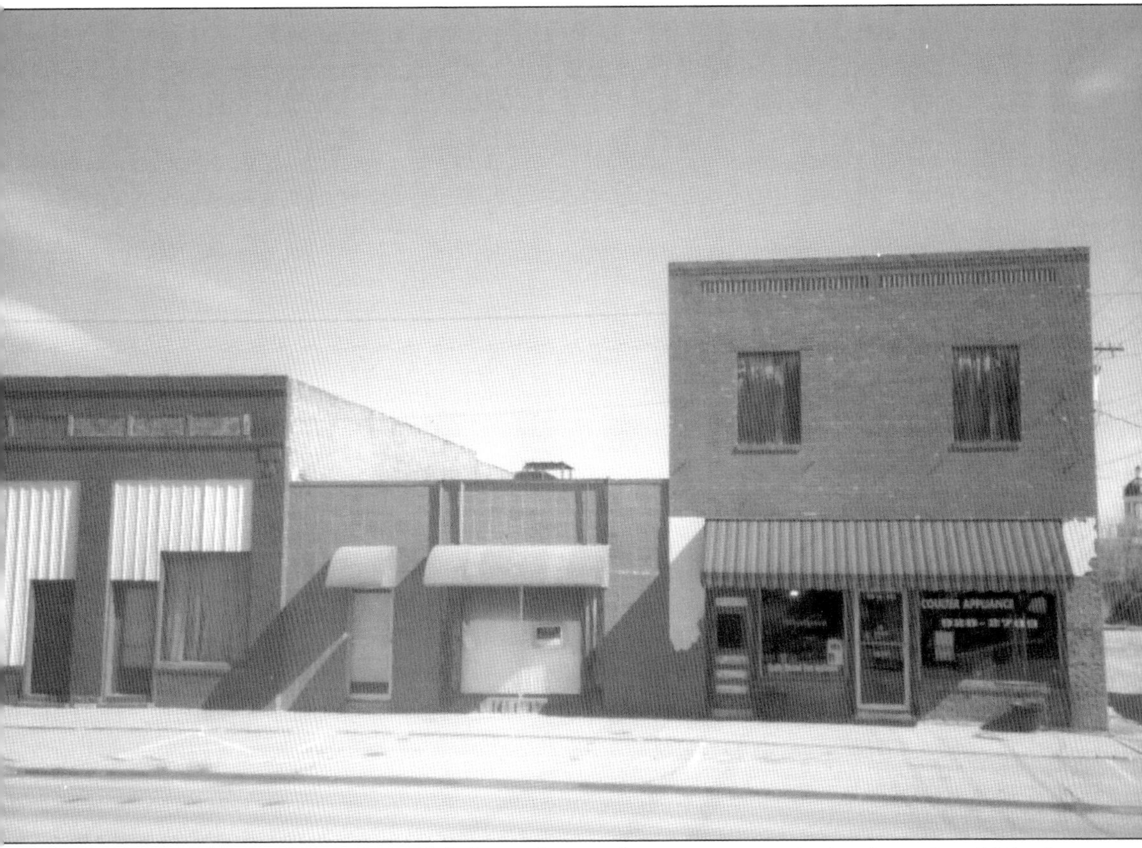

This was the home of the *Sayre Headlight Journal,* a popular newspaper in the local area. It published daily newspapers and was owned and operated by Bill Bacon for many years. Previously, Tom Higley was the publisher and editor. Under his leadership, the newspaper changed over to being a weekly publication. It is now the Coulter Appliance Center. The Odd Fellows Lodge used to meet in the upstairs of the building. Note the courthouse in the background on the right.

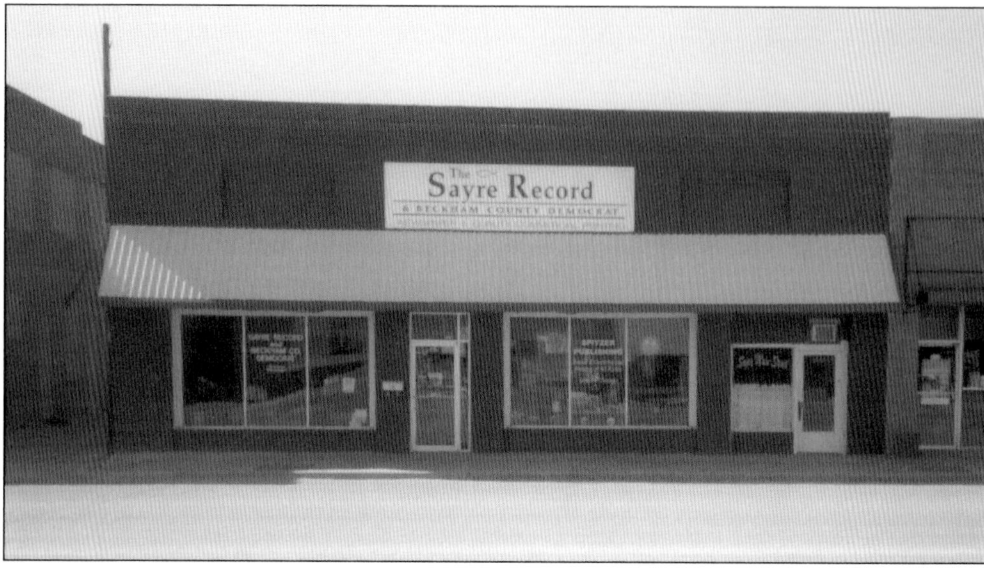

Pictured here is the local newspaper, the *Sayre Record and Beckham County Democrat*. The building used to house the Fox Drug Store and later Whites Auto Store.

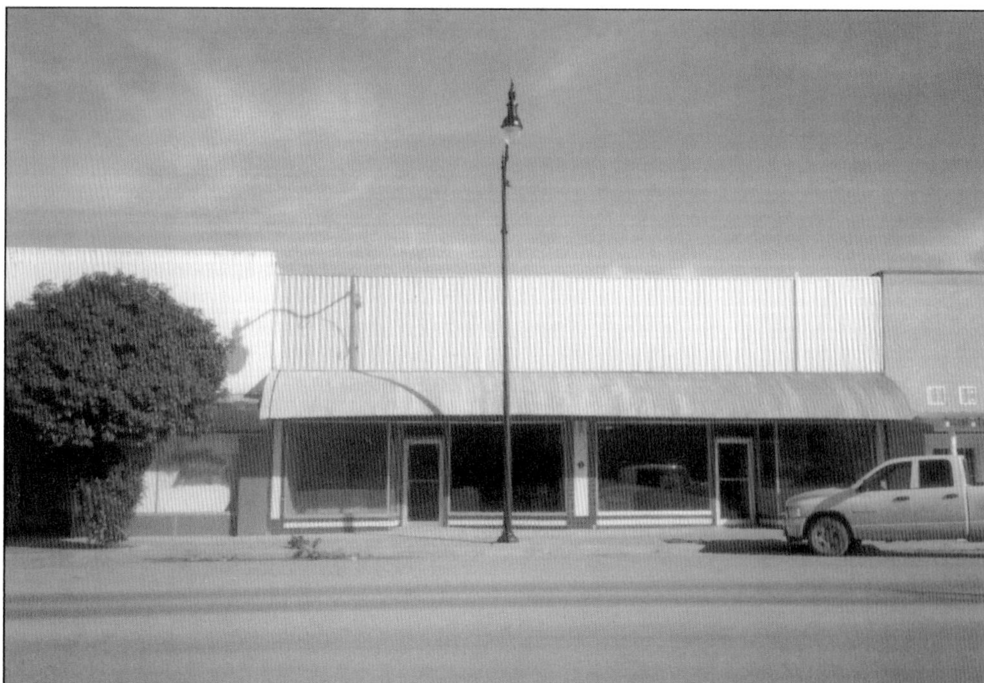

In the center of this image is the old Hart Building, which was a variety store. It was owned and operated for many years by the Hart family and was located on Main Street.

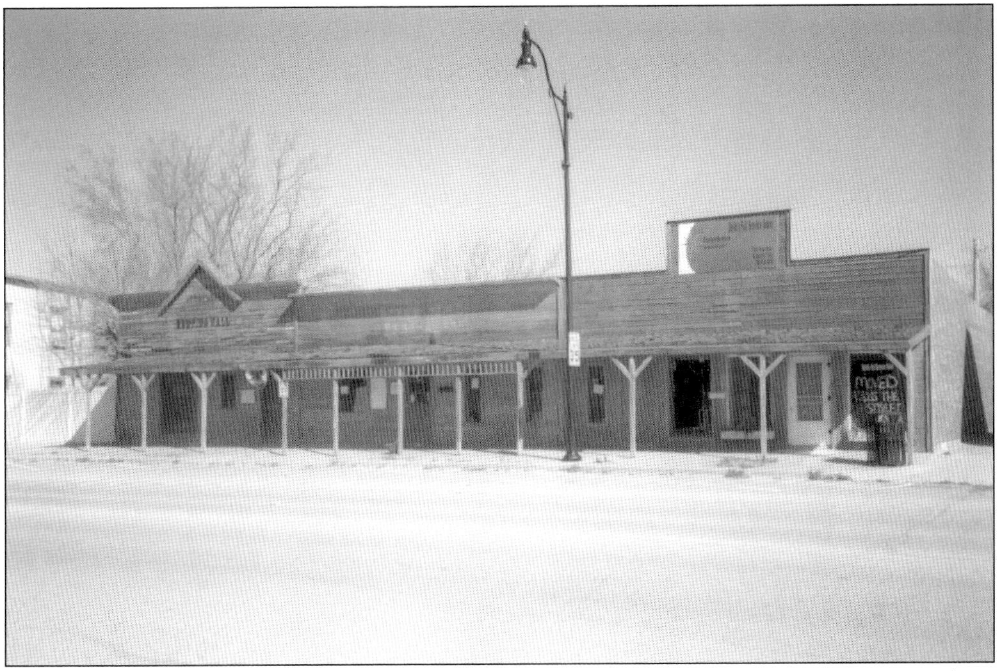

Pictured here is the Riverbend Steakhouse on the west end of Main Street in Sayre. It was later used for a meeting place for various organizations.

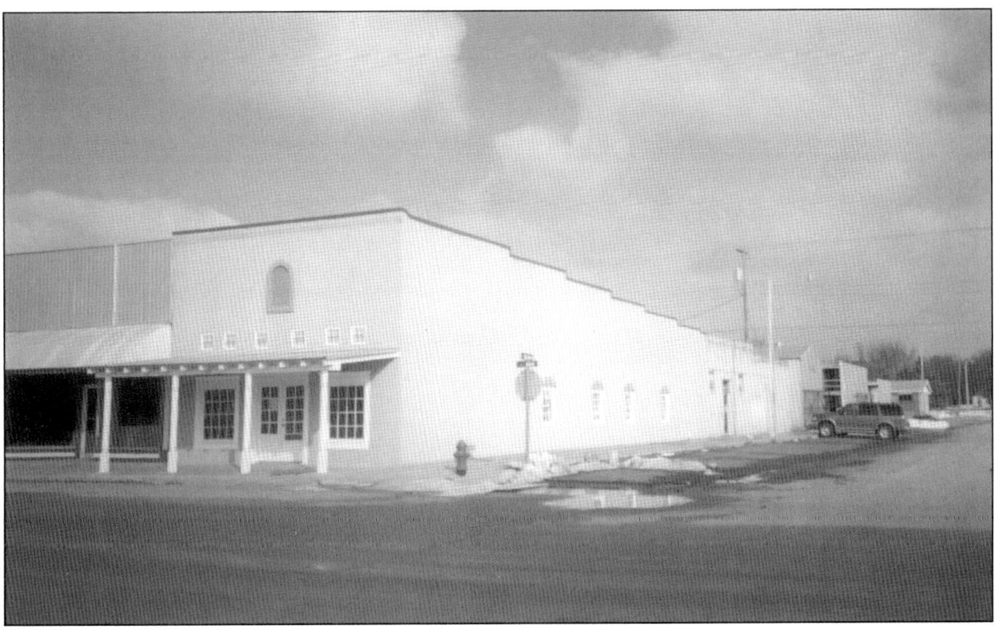

This is Blevins Law Office, located on the corner of Broadway and Main Street in Sayre. It was constructed in 1910 and used to be Puckett's Grocery Store. Later, it became Gurley Matag, Ben Lewis Hardware, and finally a bank.

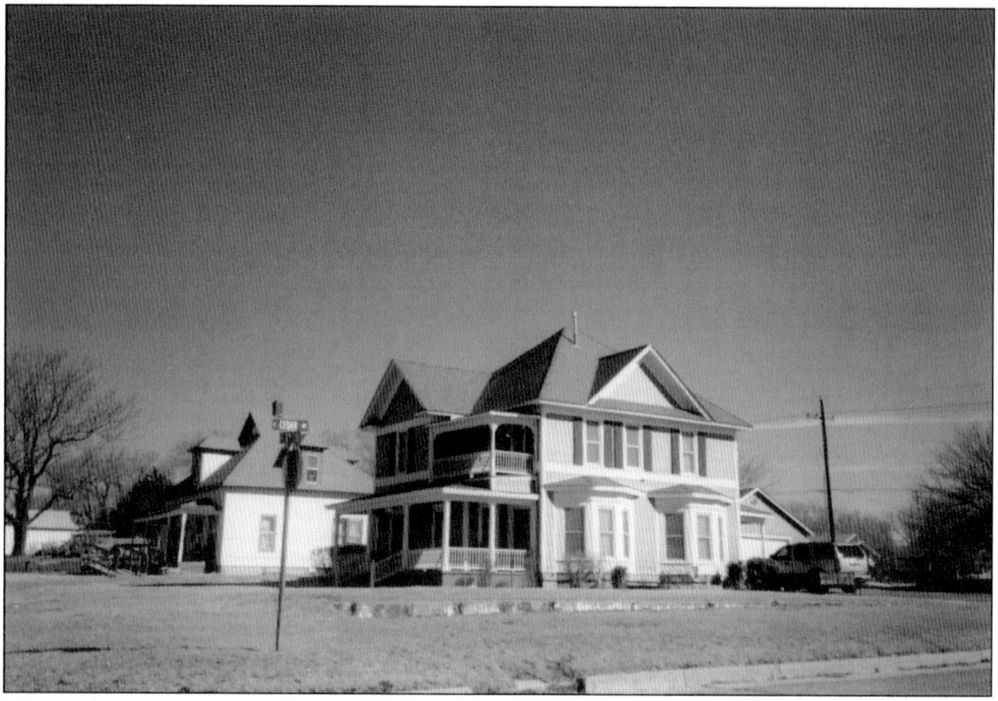

This is a historic home, newly remodeled, on Second Street in Sayre. The Gipson and Bell families once owned this home, and it is now under the ownership of the Copeland family.

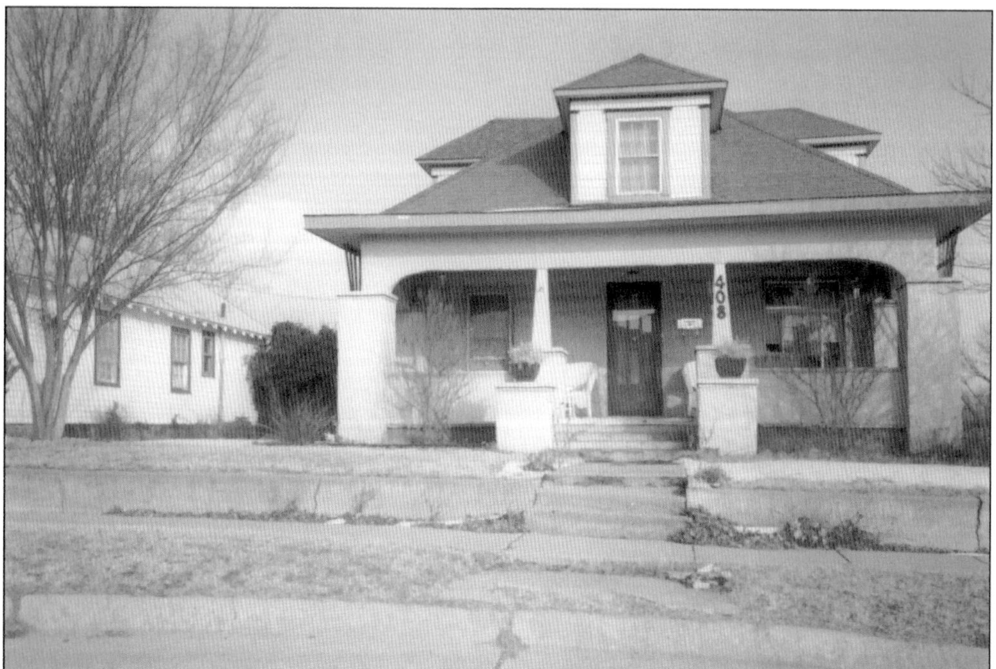

Here is the Dean home, which is located on Fourth Street. It is a rock house with interesting lines and has been placed in the National Register of Historic Places.

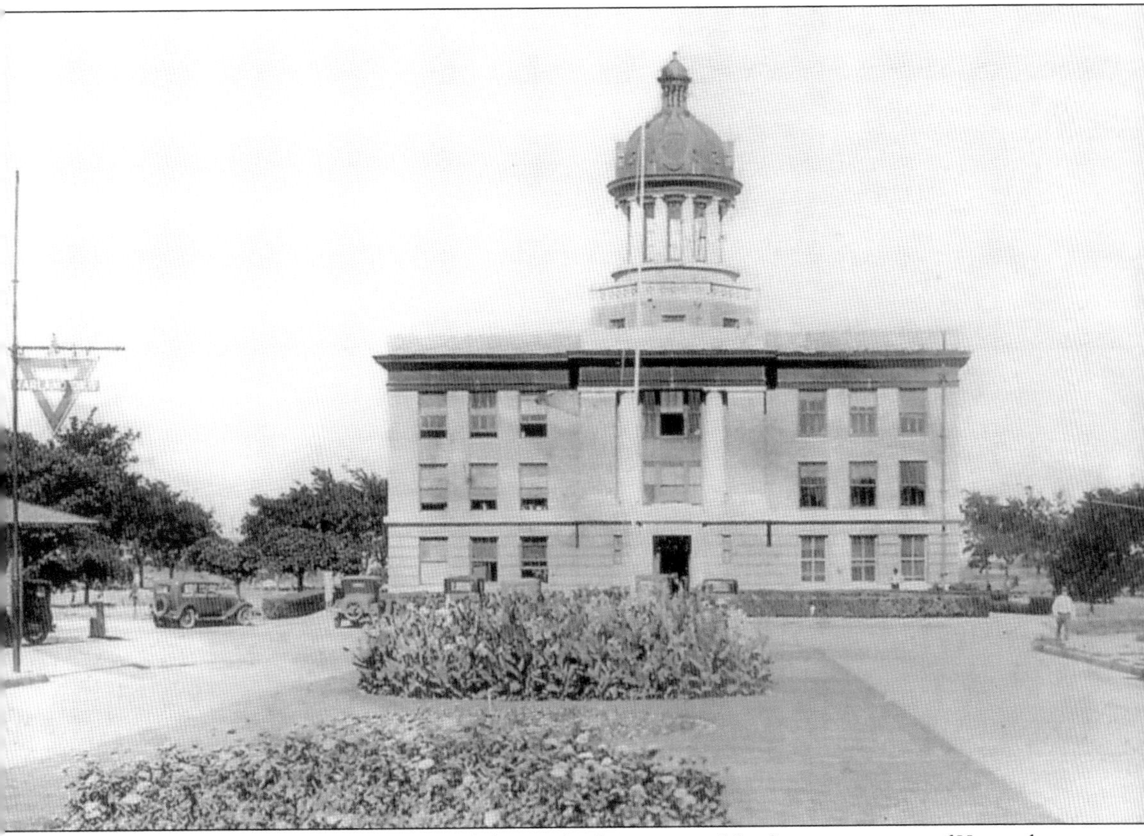

The Beckham County Courthouse stands here, which was named for former governor of Kentucky J.C. Beckham. Built in 1910–1911, the courthouse was listed in the National Register of Historic Places in 1984. (Courtesy of the *Sayre Record*.)

BECKHAM COUNTY COURTHOUSE
SAYRE, OKLAHOMA

Beckham County was created at statehood from portions of territorial Greer and Roger Mills counties. It was named for J.C. Beckham, former governor of Kentucky.

Sayre, a town founded in 1891 and named for a railroad promoter, won the title of county seat in an election held June 16, 1908, edging Erick by only eleven votes. The county courthouse was completed in 1911 at a cost of $69,000.00. Designed bySolomon A. Layton, an associate of the turn-of-the century firm Layton, Wemyss Smith and Hawk. Historians have dubbed Layton "Father of Oklahoma courthouses." The cornerstone for the present courthouse was laid in 1911, built by Oklahoma Quarries and Construction Company. The building was a symmetrical blend of Neo-Classical and Second Renaissance Revival styles. Outstanding features include colossal Doric columns above the main entryway, classical pilasters, a grooved surface on the ground floor, and distinctive belt courses. The most unique part of the design was the dome, with a colonnade supporting a vaulted and babbled roof. On top of that was a smaller dome reproduced to scale. And for just a few seconds, the courthouse has a cameo role in the 1940's movie, "The Grapes of Wrath." As the Okies round a corner on their way out of Oklahoma, they drive past the picturesque, domed building.

The Beckham County Courthouse is described on the plaque that is in front of the courthouse. It explains how it received its name and some of its outstanding features. The county courthouse was constructed in 1911, and it was featured in the movie *The Grapes of Wrath*. Note the clocks accenting the dome. The city ran out of money before it could add all four, but the task was completed for the centennial.

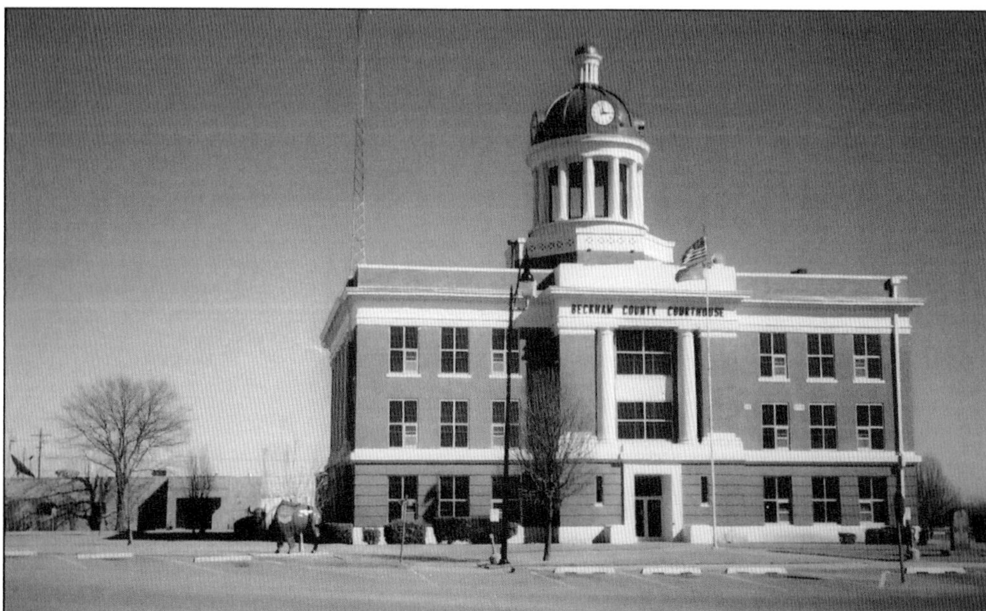

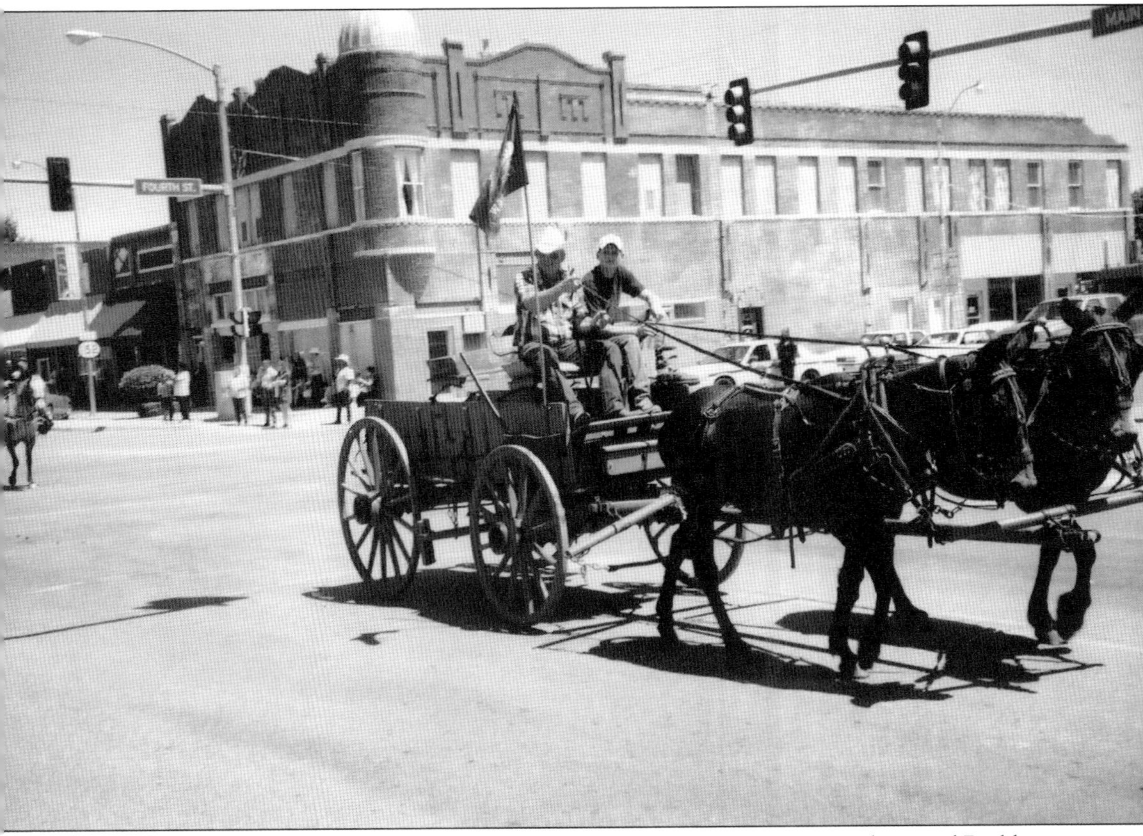

This is part of the Centennial Parade in downtown Sayre in September 2001. The Hood Building sits in the background. (Courtesy of the *Sayre Record*.)

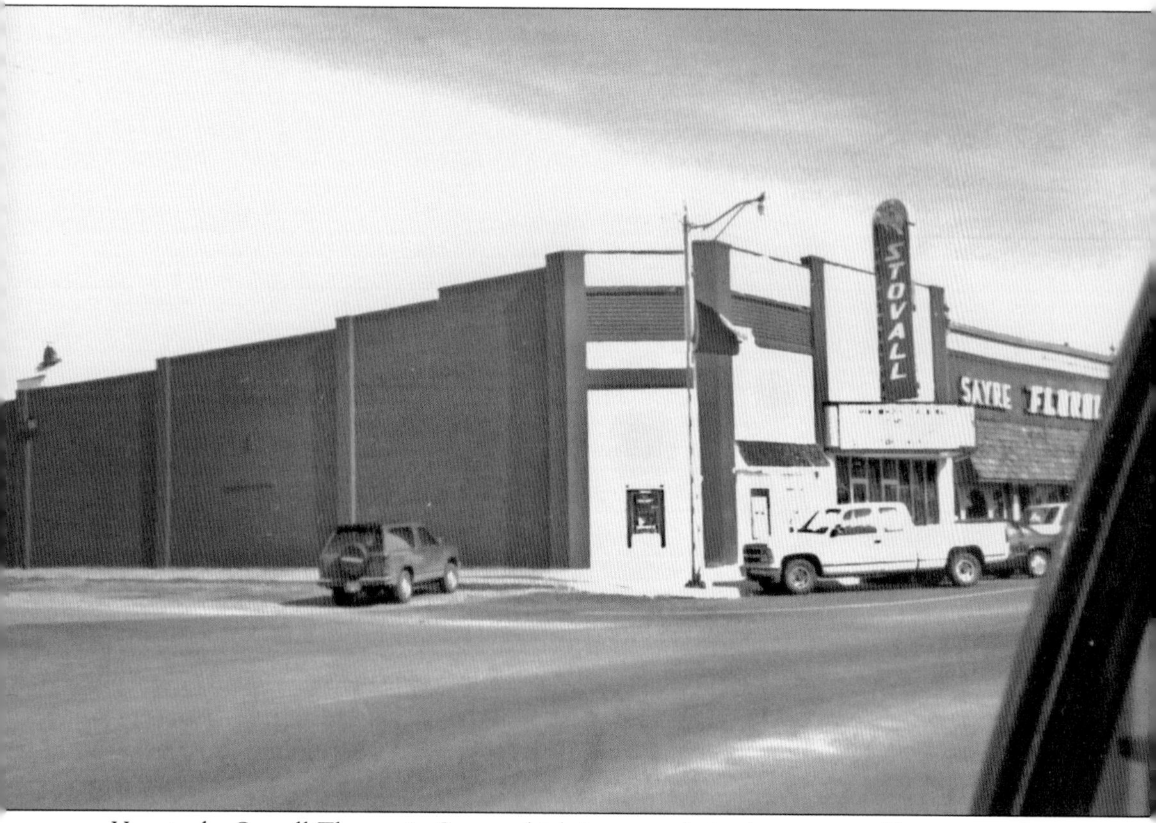

Here is the Stovall Theater in Sayre, which is presently in the process of being turned into a community theater by the city.

Three

Farmrail-Grainbelt

Farmrail has been running a short-line regional railroad through Sayre and the surrounding area since 1981. It has 89 miles of track between Hydro and Erick, Oklahoma. It leased another 89 miles of track in 1992, which was used to belong to the Atchison, Topeka and Santa Fe Railway Company. Farmrail's affiliate, Grainbelt, owns 176 miles, linking Enid and Frederick, Oklahoma. These miles were acquired from the Burlington Northern Railroad Company in 1987. The 354 miles that make up the coordinated regional network serves agricultural, manufacturing, and mineral interests in western Oklahoma.

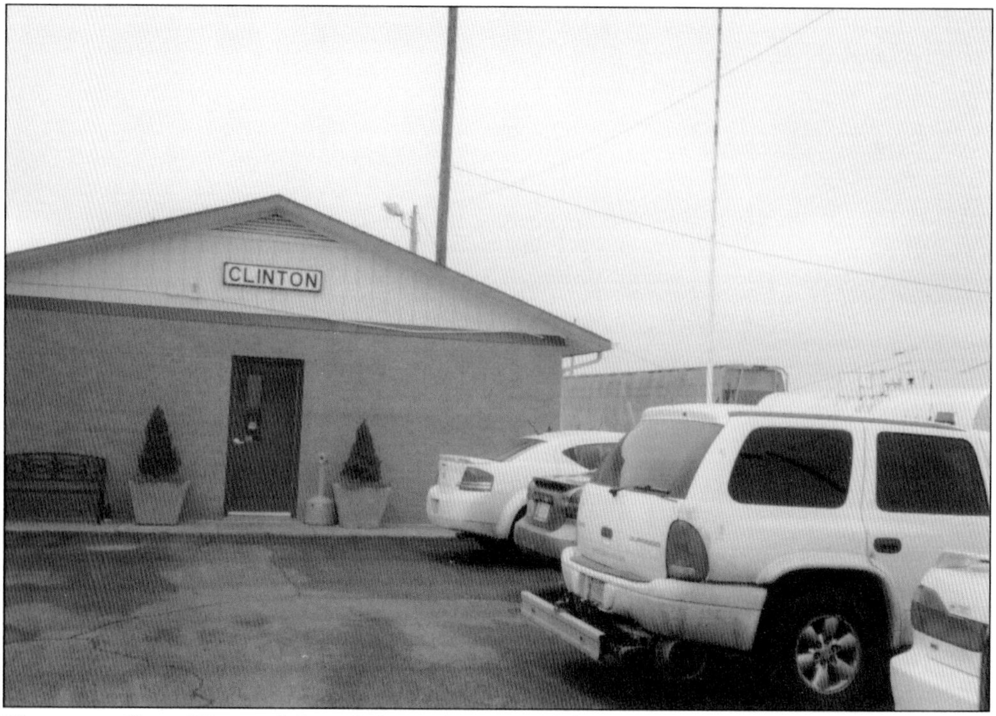

The main office of Farmrail-Grainbelt in Clinton, Oklahoma, is pictured here. Rodney Roof, the marketing manager, has his office in this building. It also employs quite a few ladies.

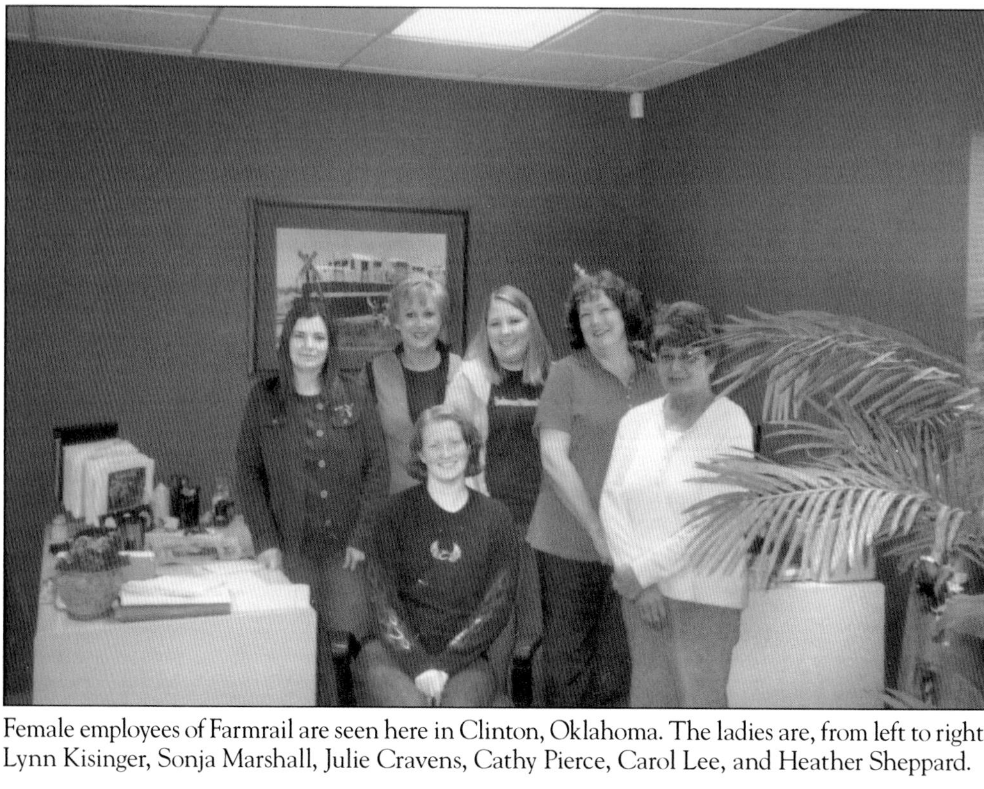

Female employees of Farmrail are seen here in Clinton, Oklahoma. The ladies are, from left to right, Lynn Kisinger, Sonja Marshall, Julie Cravens, Cathy Pierce, Carol Lee, and Heather Sheppard.

Craig Wolf (front) and Eddie Williams board a Farmrail engine in the yard in Clinton. (Courtesy of Eddie Williams.)

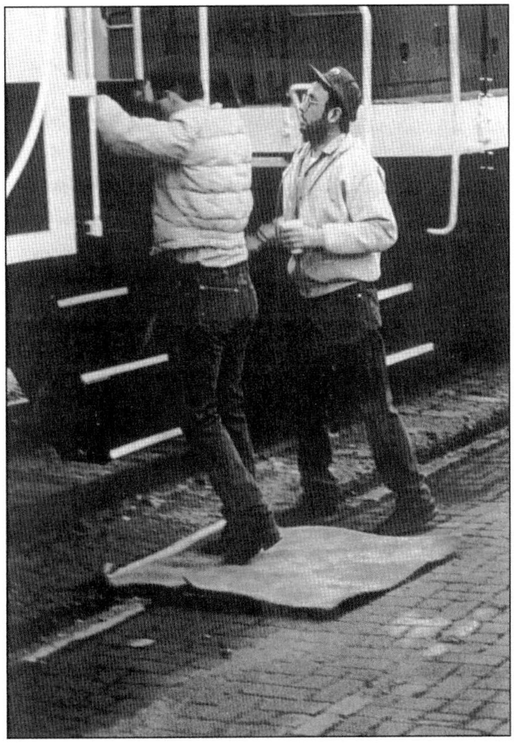

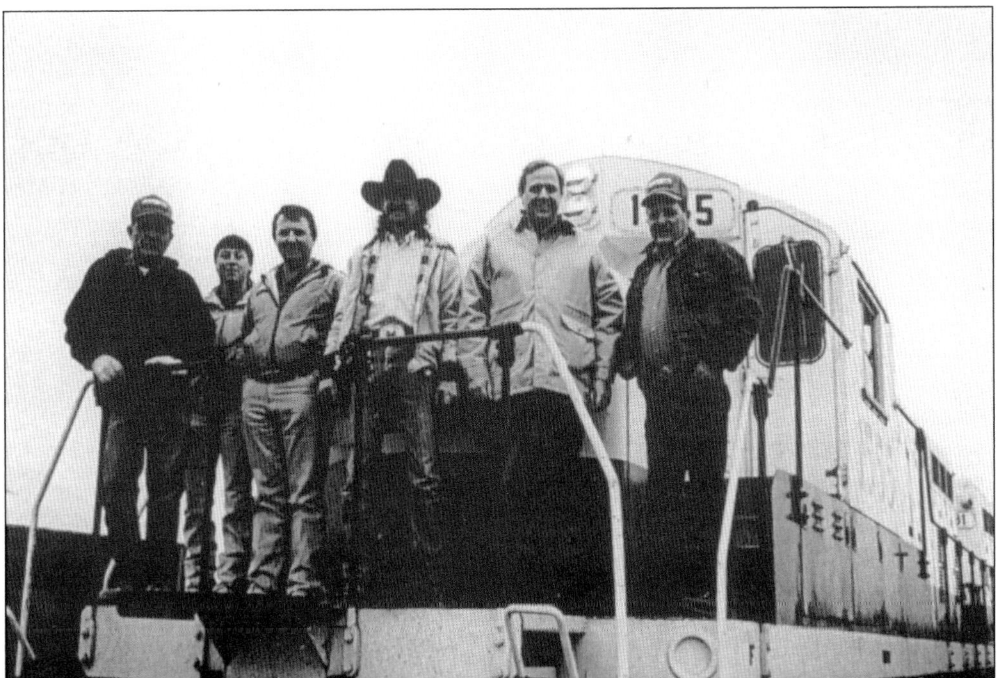

Six Farmrail employees stand on the front of a Farmrail engine. The men are, from left to right, Eugene Dungan, Ronnie White, Dan Knight, J.R. Gelnar, Rodney Roof, and Ray Rogers. (Courtesy of Eddie Williams.)

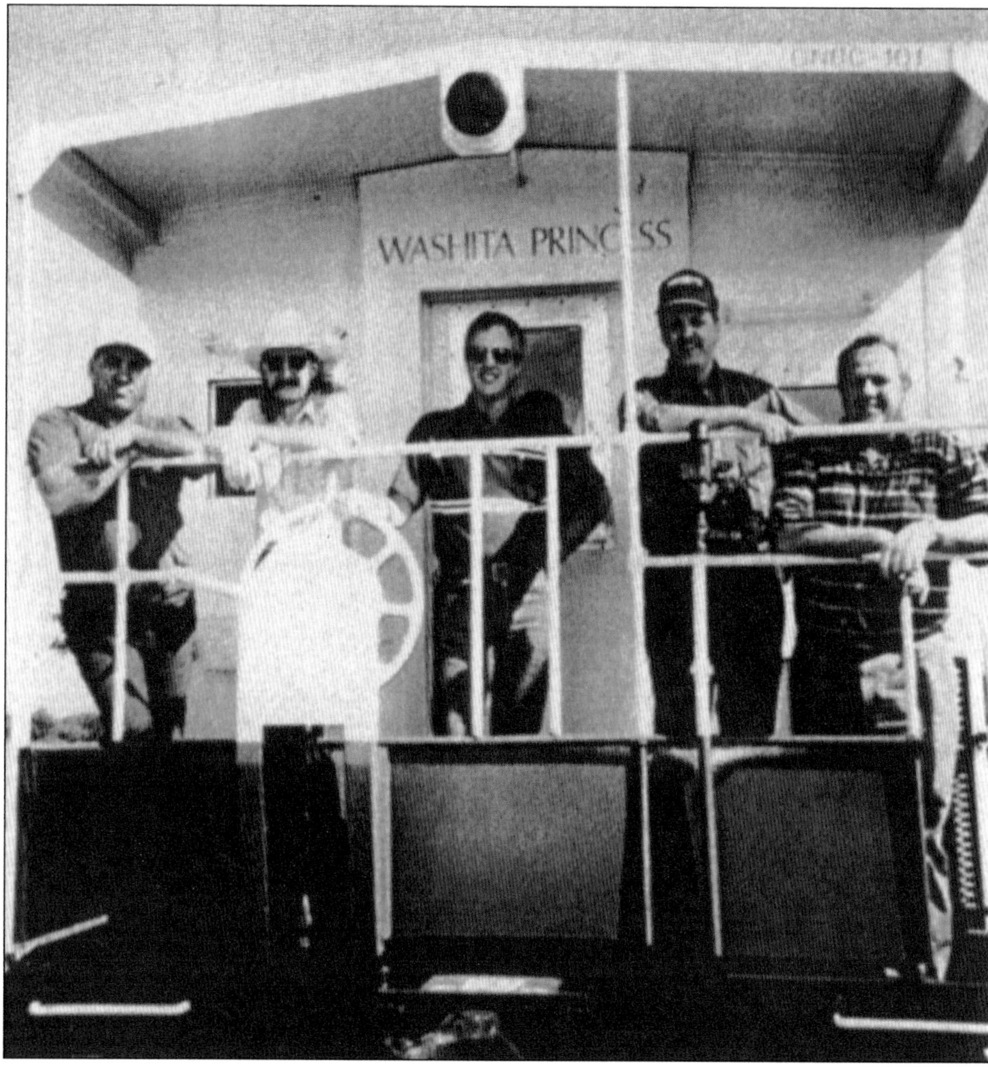

Five Farmrail employees take a trial run on the *Washita Princess* caboose right after it was restored. The men are, from left to right, Larry Rippetoe, J.R. Gelnar, unidentified, George C. Betke Jr., and Rodney Roof. (Courtesy of Eddie Williams.)

This is an image of some Farmrail employees at Clinton, Oklahoma. Pictured from left to right are Devin Martin, Jeff Blanchard, trainmaster Kevin Eckel, Bryan Reed, and equipment superintendant Craig Wolf. These guys do a great job reconstructing engines in old boxcars. They also won the Jake Award for safety, which is a great achievement.

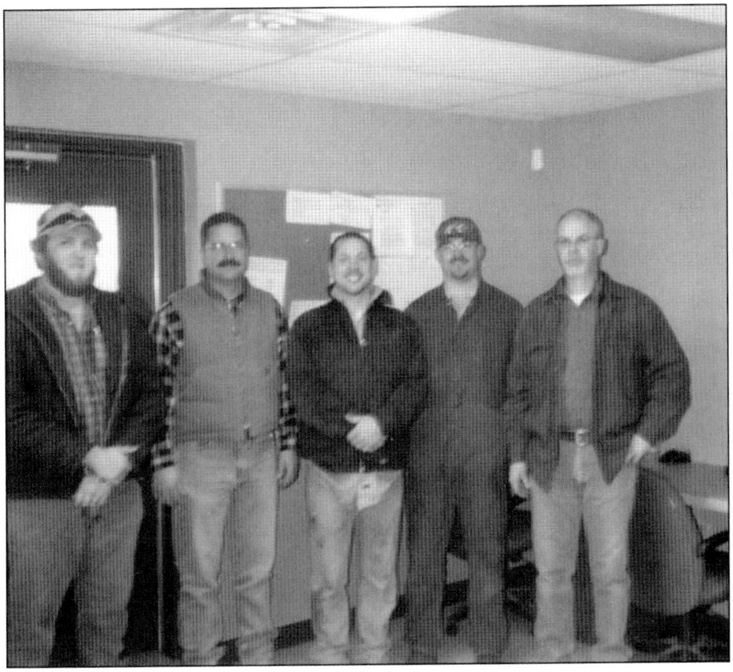

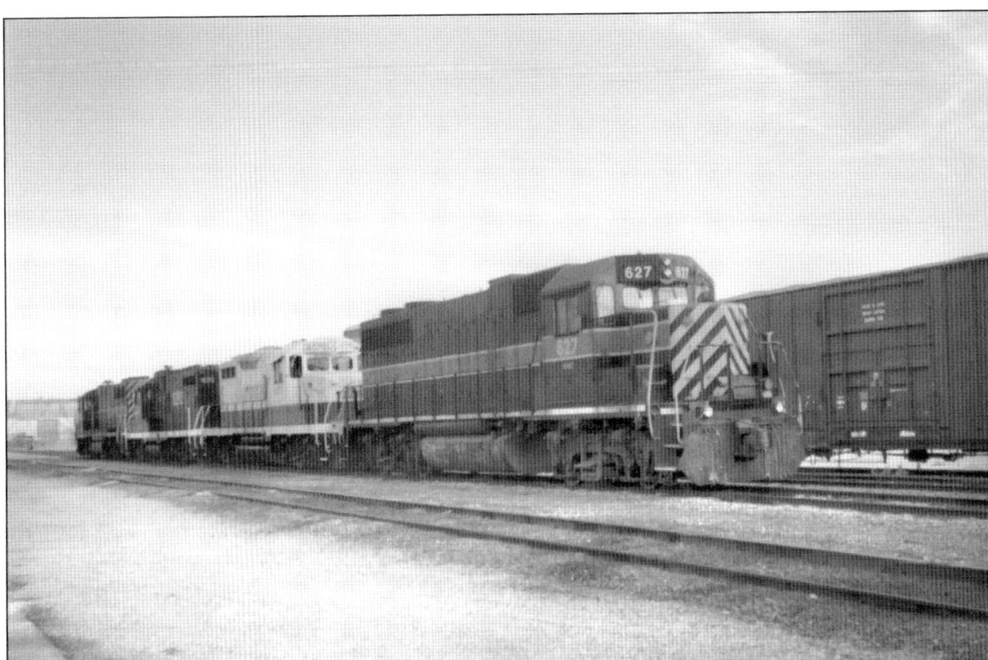

In front in the railroad yard in Clinton, Oklahoma, sits engine no. 627, a Farmrail locomotive, with two other engines behind it. Most of these trains have 16-cylinder engines.

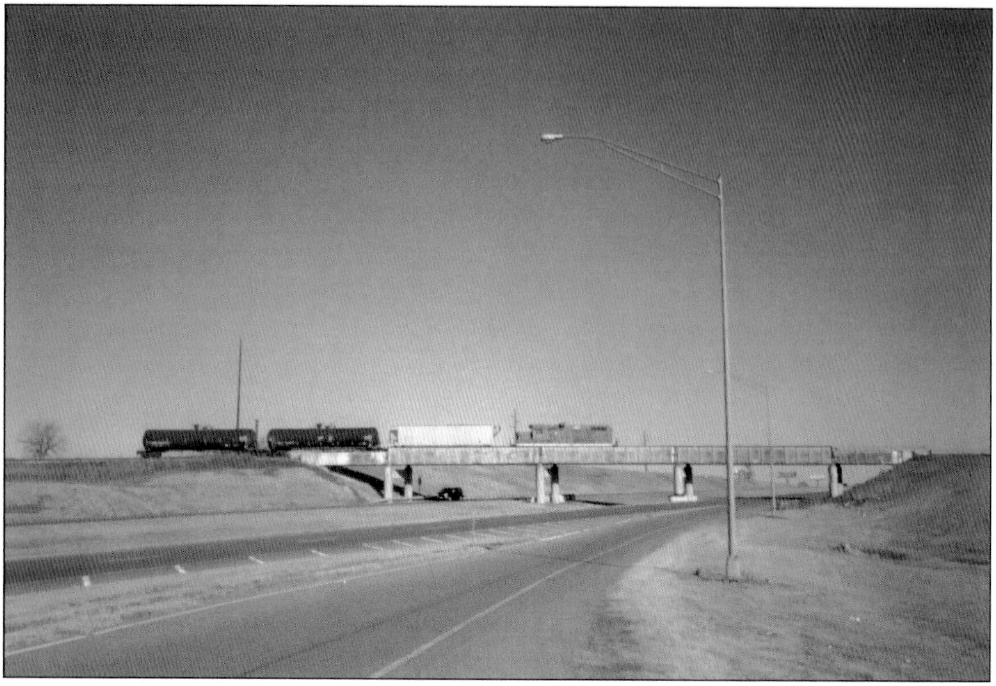

A Farmrail engine and three cars cross the I-40 Bridge one mile east of Sayre on its journey back to Clinton.

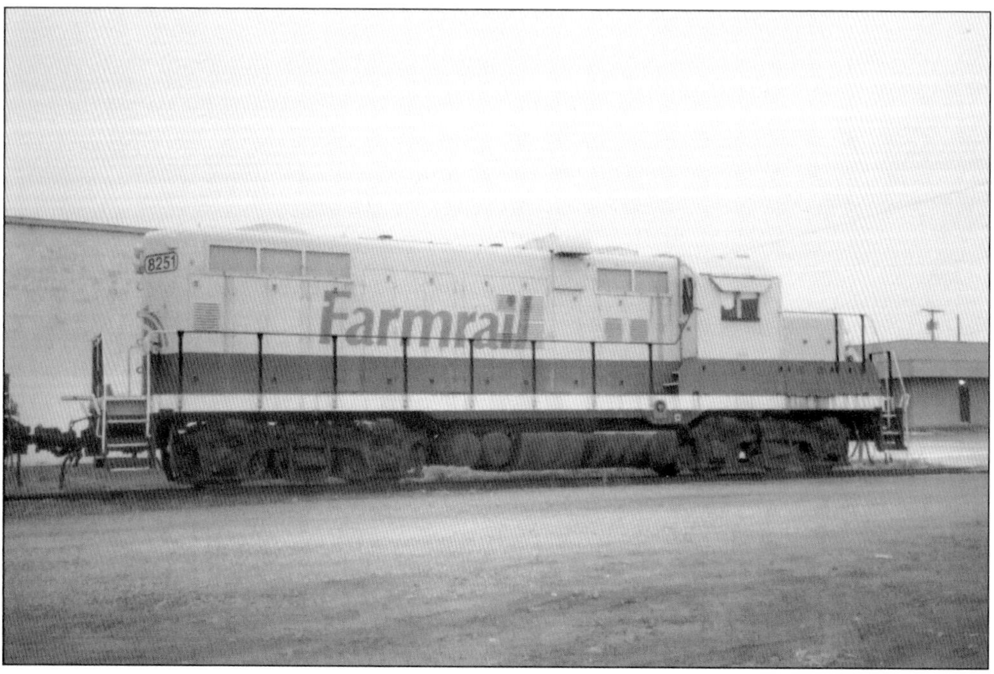

Farmrail engine no. 8251, named *Catawba*, is parked in the rail yard at Clinton, Oklahoma.

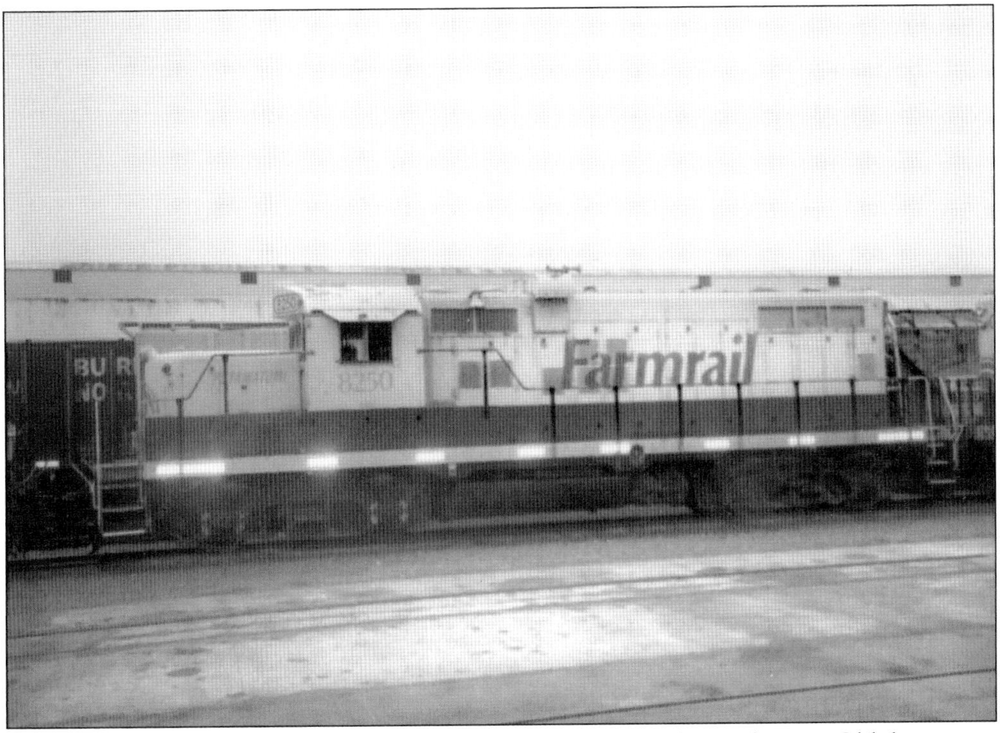

Farmrail engine no. 8250, the Potawatomi, sits on the track at Clinton, Oklahoma, on a Sunday.

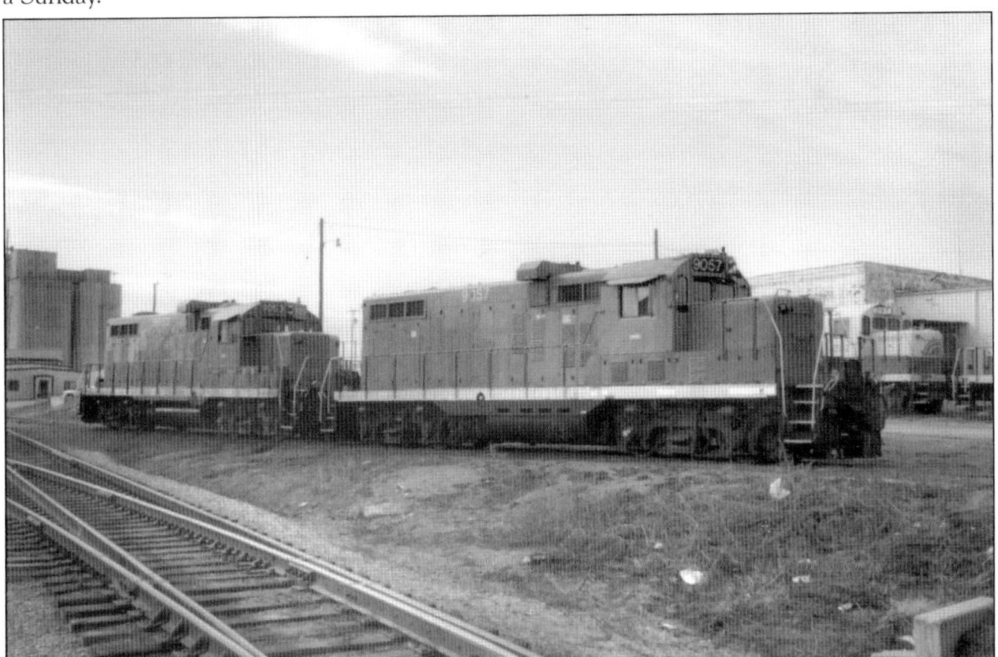

Engine no. 9057 and engine no. 9053 sit in the train yard in Clinton. There are elevators in the background, as well as a Farmrail engine to the right. The GP10 locomotives provide 1,500 horsepower.

These freight cars are sitting on the track on the west end of town waiting to be picked up and used by Farmrail Corporation or another rail service.

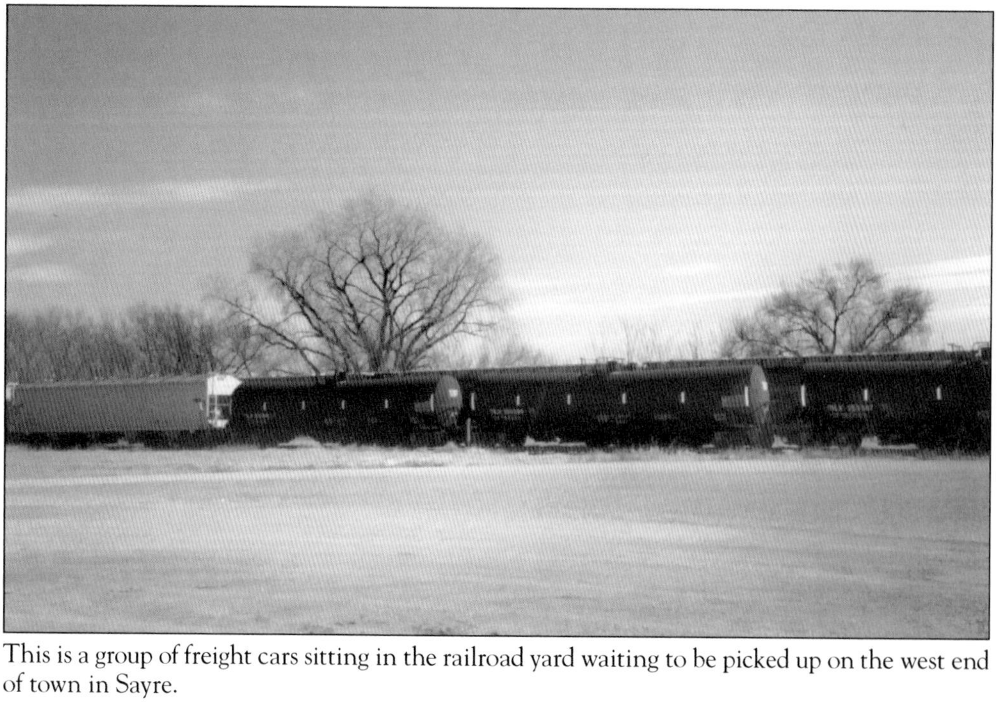

This is a group of freight cars sitting in the railroad yard waiting to be picked up on the west end of town in Sayre.

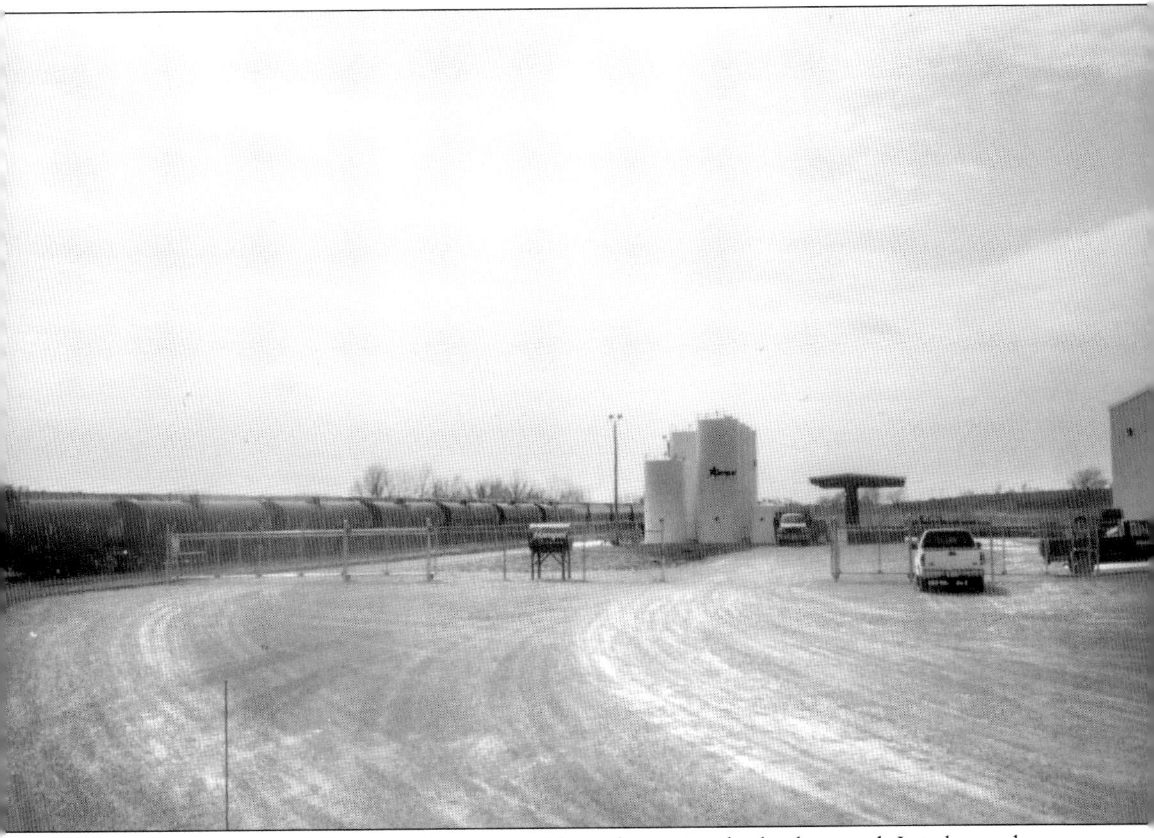

This is the Hampel Oil Company in Sayre with tank cars in the background. It is located on the west end of town next to the railroad track. It ships up to 45,000 gallons of methanol weekly. Hampel Oil is headquartered in Oklahoma City.

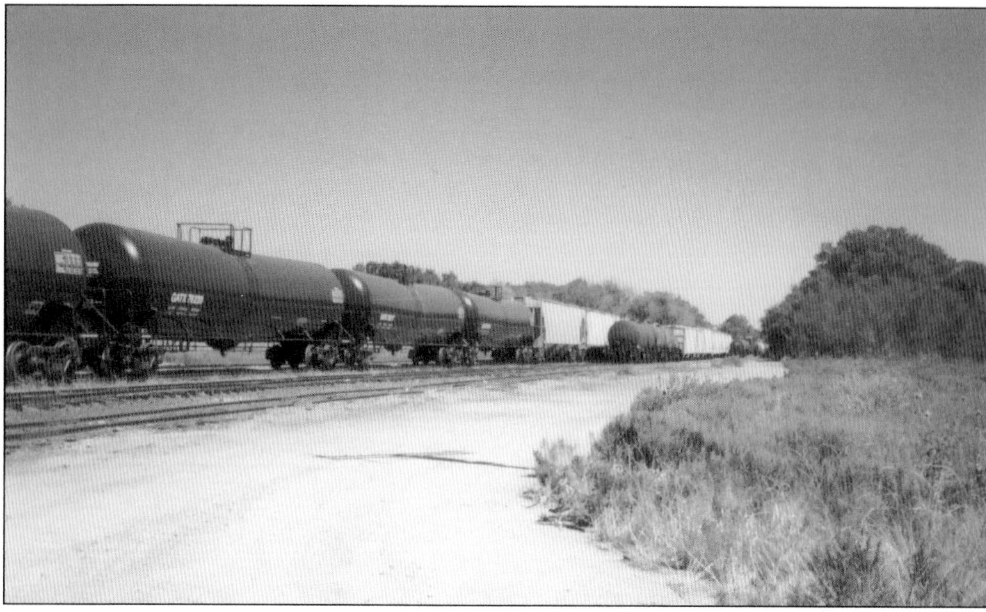

A couple of lines of freight cars are seen in the yard on the west end of town. Farmrail and other lines store some of their cars on this track between Sayre and Erick, Oklahoma.

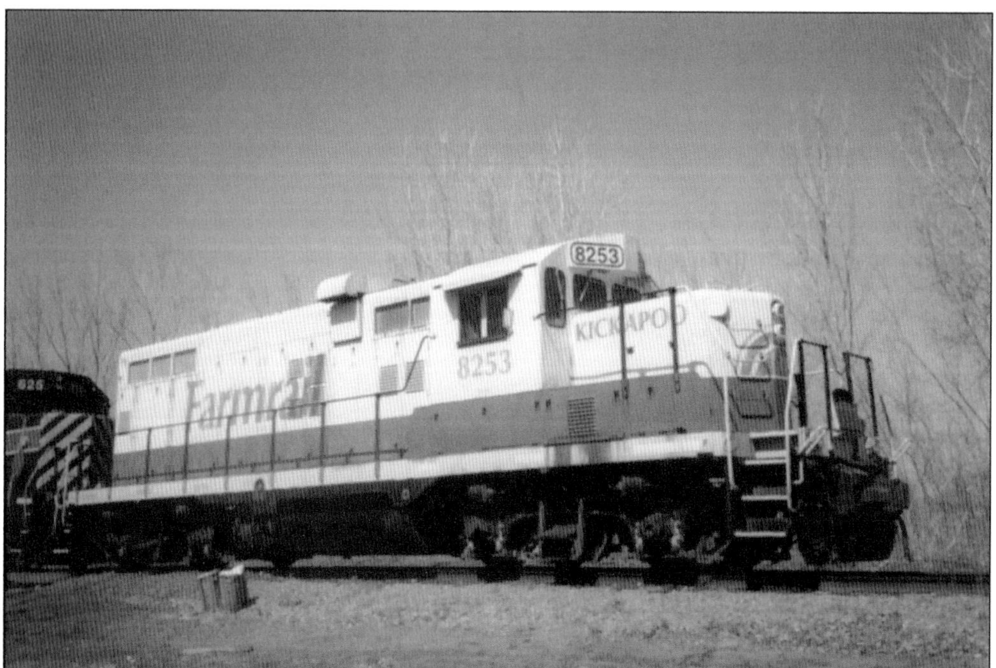

Farmrail named many of their engines after Native American tribes. Pictured here is *Kickapoo,* Farmrail engine no. 8253, in the train yard in Elk City, Oklahoma.

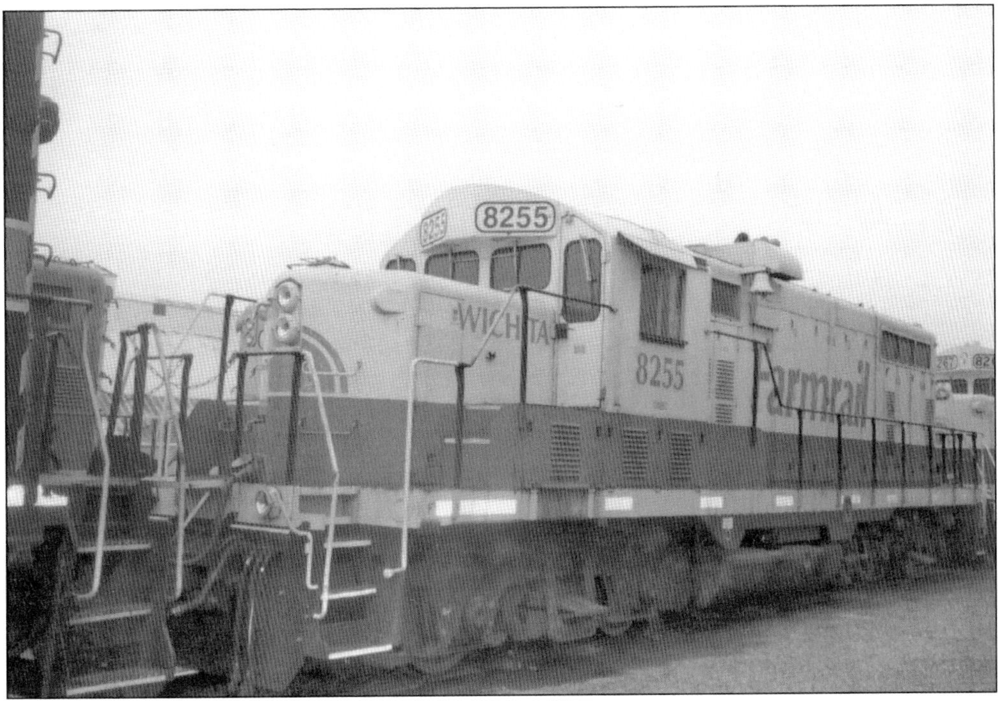

Wichita Farmrail engine no. 8255 is seen above parked for the weekend in the rail yard at Clinton. Below is the Tonkawa Farmrail diesel engine no. 8254 in the train yard at Clinton, with the warehouse in the background.

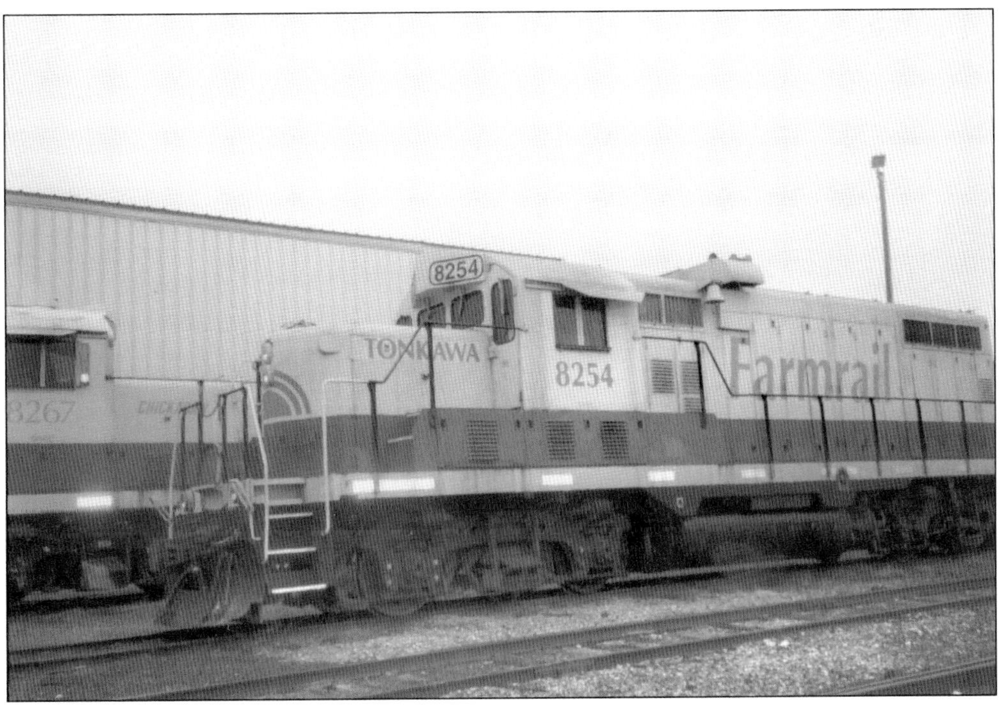

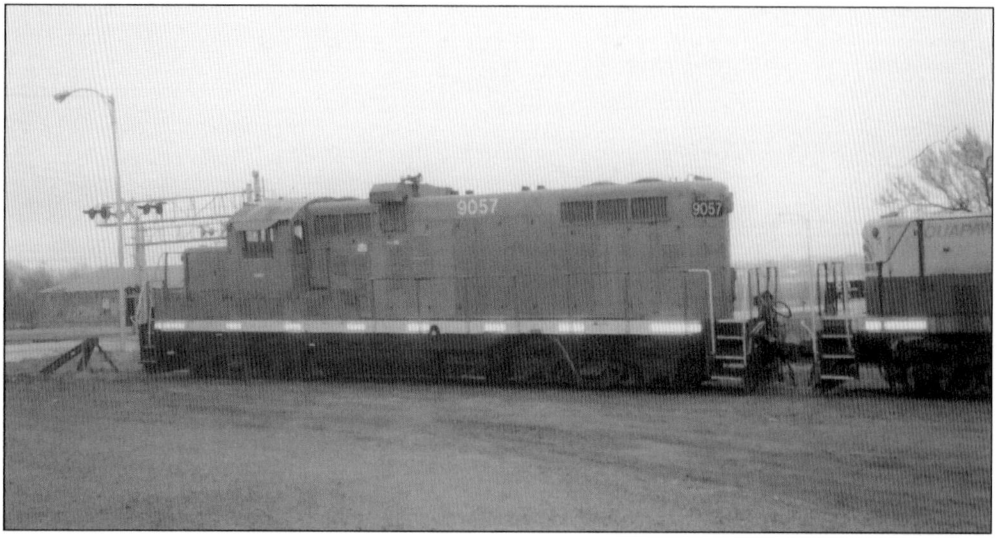

Above is blue engine no. 9057 sitting idle and waiting for another busy workday during a Monday morning at the Clinton rail yard; train signals are in the background. Below is Farmrail engine no. 8053 parked on the track in the rail yard in Clinton. The warehouse can be seen in the background, east of the Farmrail yard.

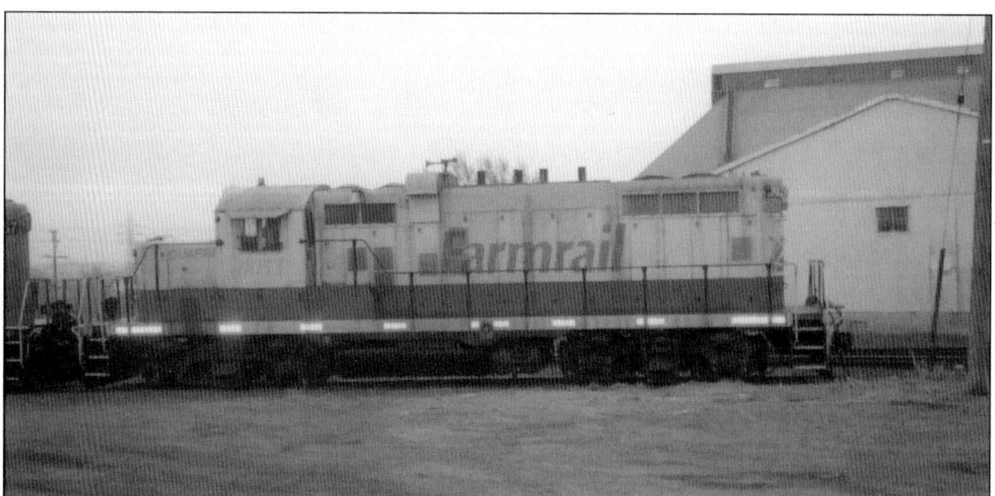

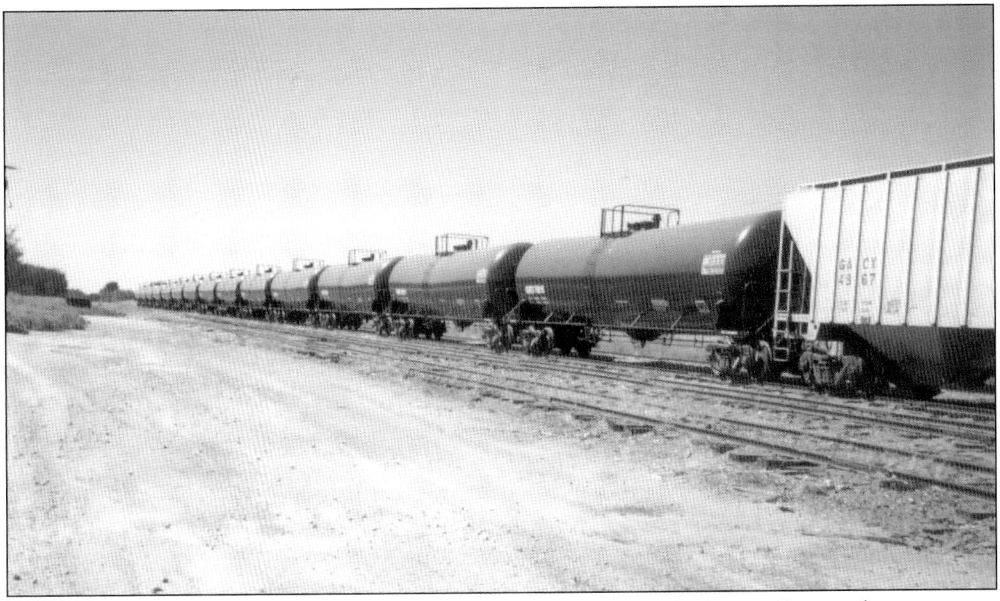

A number of tank cars are parked on the tracks on the west end of town. Farmrail stores many of their spare cars between Sayre and Erick, Oklahoma.

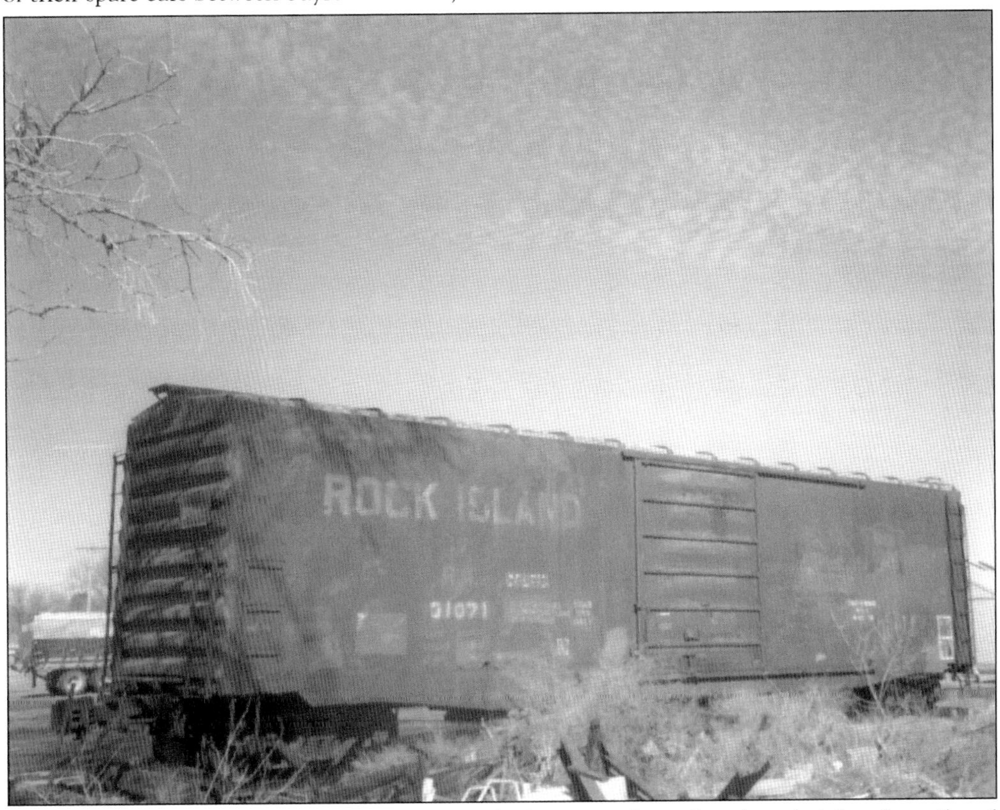

An old Rock Island boxcar sits on the west end of town in the railroad yard. After the railroad went out of business here, many farmers and businesspeople bought the cars and used them for storage.

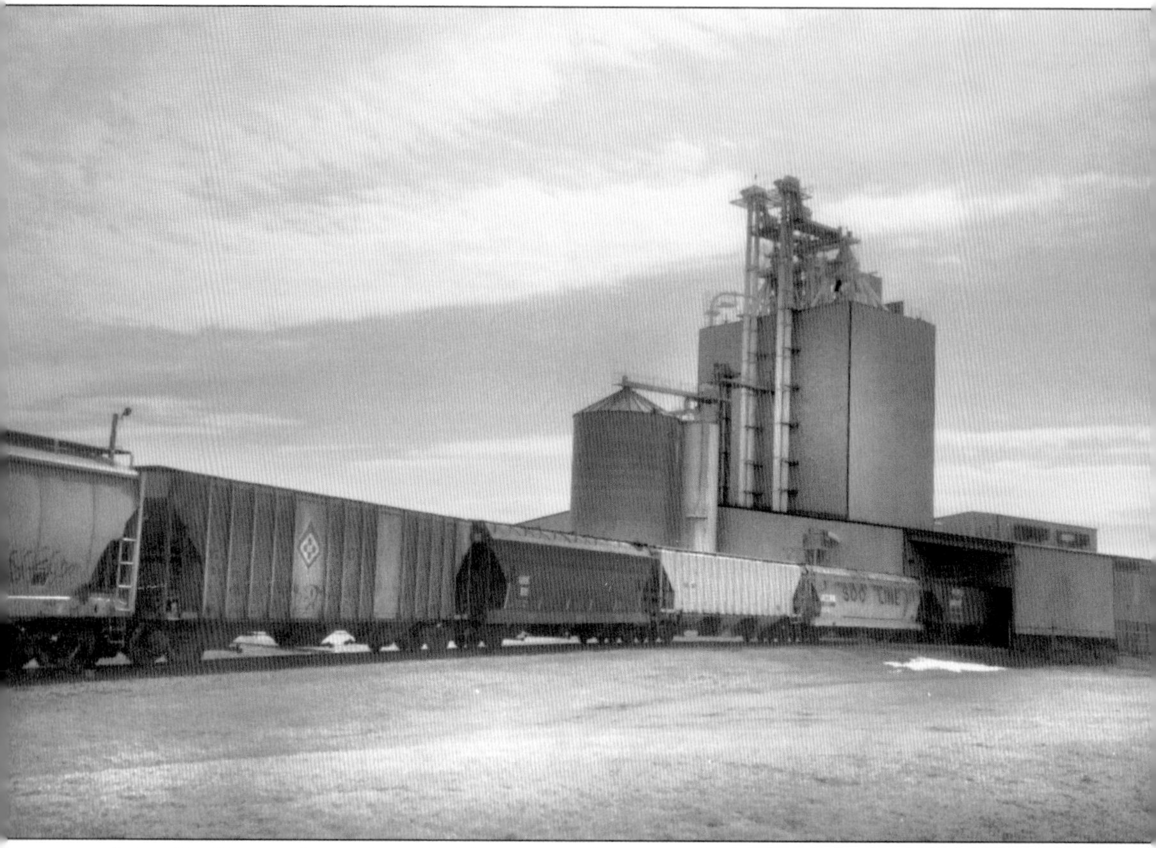

Mars Pet Care, a dog and cat food business, is located at One Doane Road in Clinton. Farmrail cars deliver corn and other grains, frozen fish, and chicken, which are then made into pet food. It ships a lot of pet food to many businesses west of the Mississippi River, including Walmart.

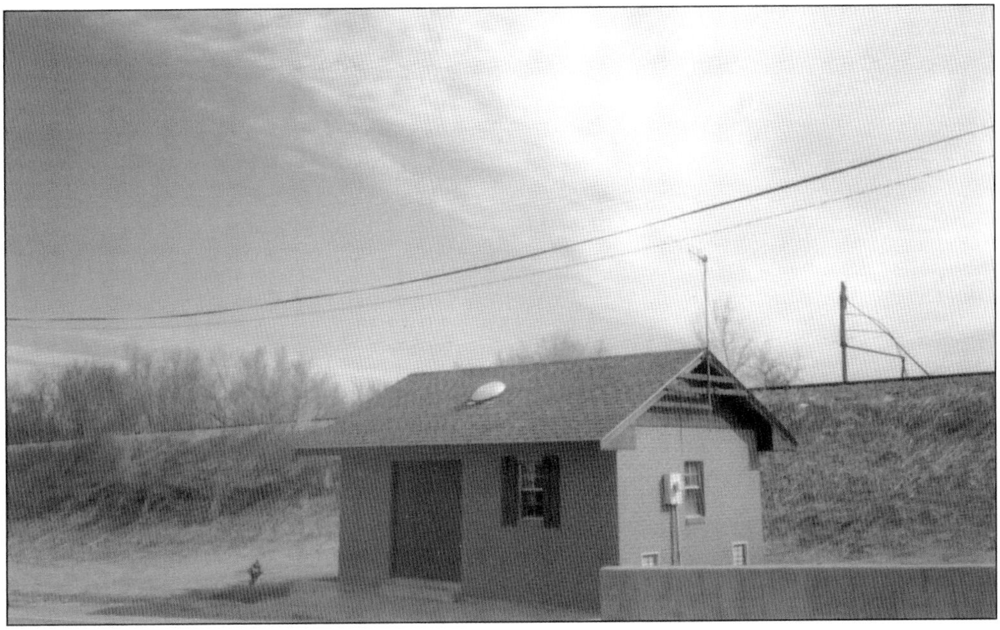

Above is a small ticket office alongside the railroad track on Neptune Road in Clinton, where train tickets used to be sold. Pictured below is Seneca diesel locomotive no. 8252 in the train yard at Clinton, Oklahoma.

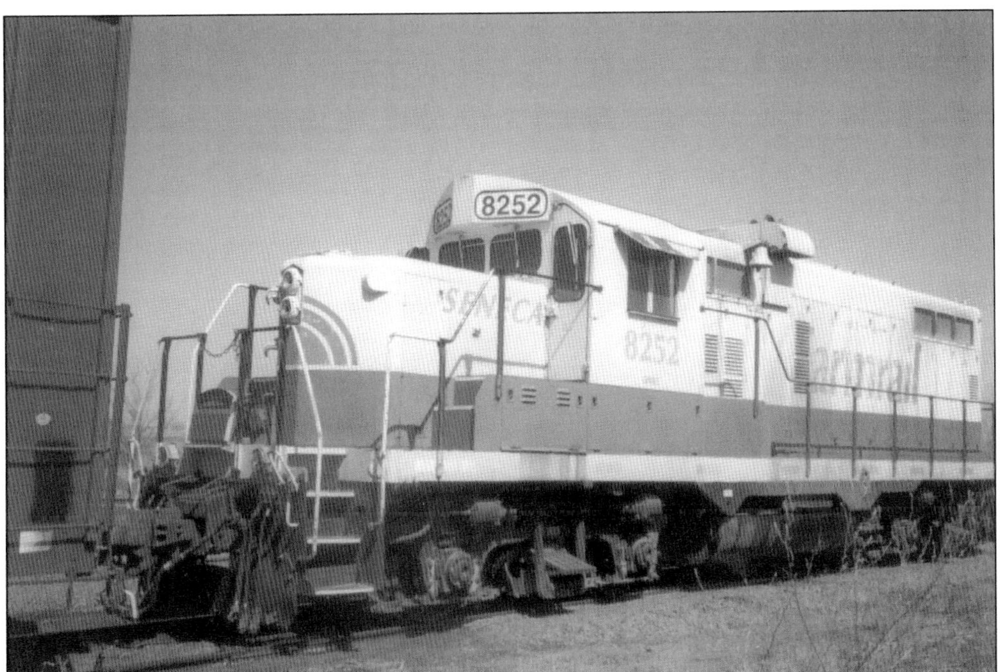

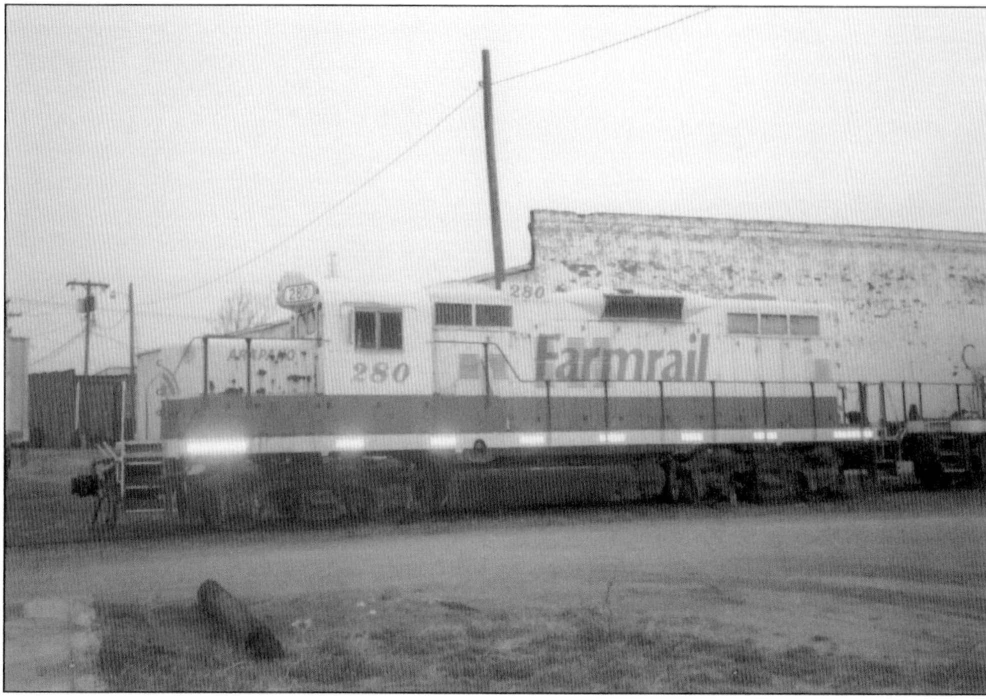

Above, Farmrail engine no. 280, named *Arapaho,* is parked in the train yard next to a warehouse while not in use in Clinton, Oklahoma. Pictured below, diesel engine no. 625 is being stored along the track at Elk City for use in the future.

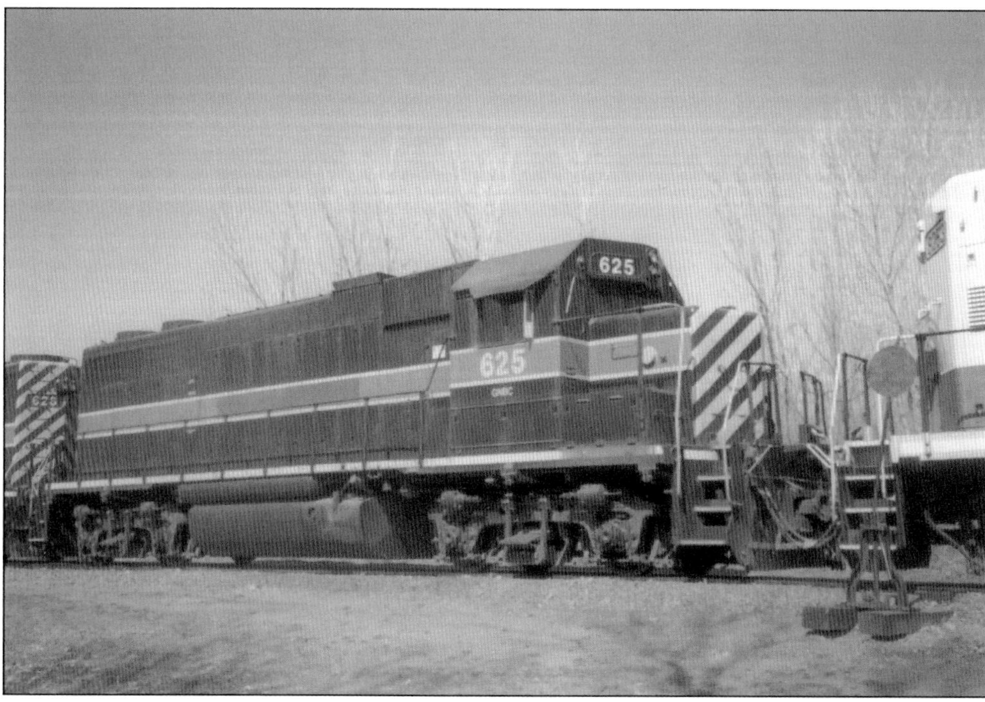

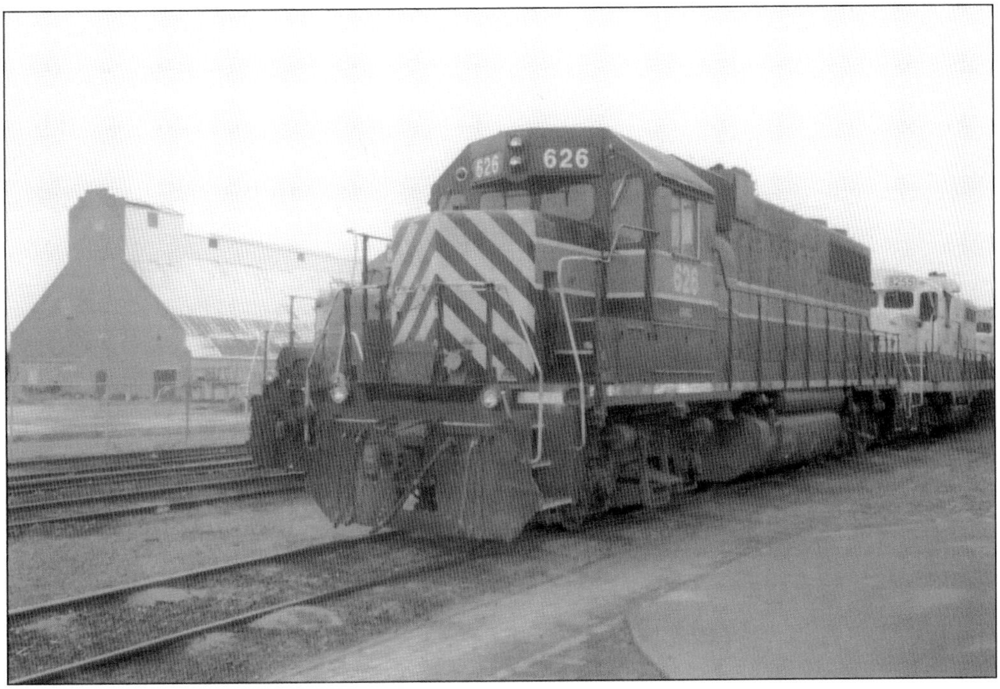

Diesel locomotive no. 626 sits above in the train yard at Clinton with the warehouse in the background. HLCX engine no. 3636, seen below, is idle on the track on East Seventh Street in Elk City. Farmrail would sometimes park its trains here until it was time to use them again.

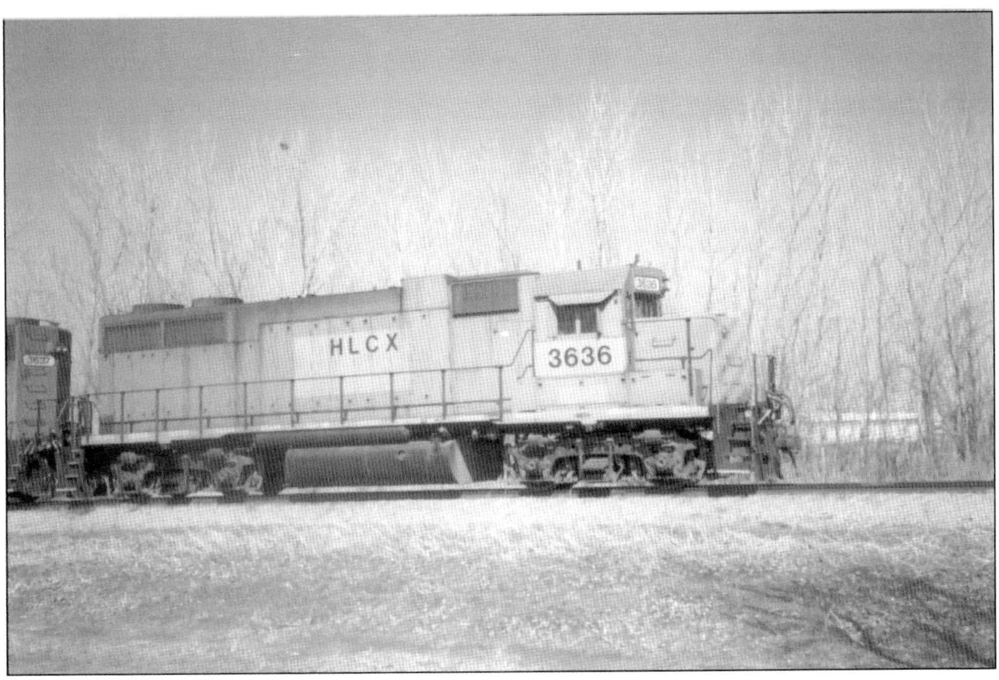

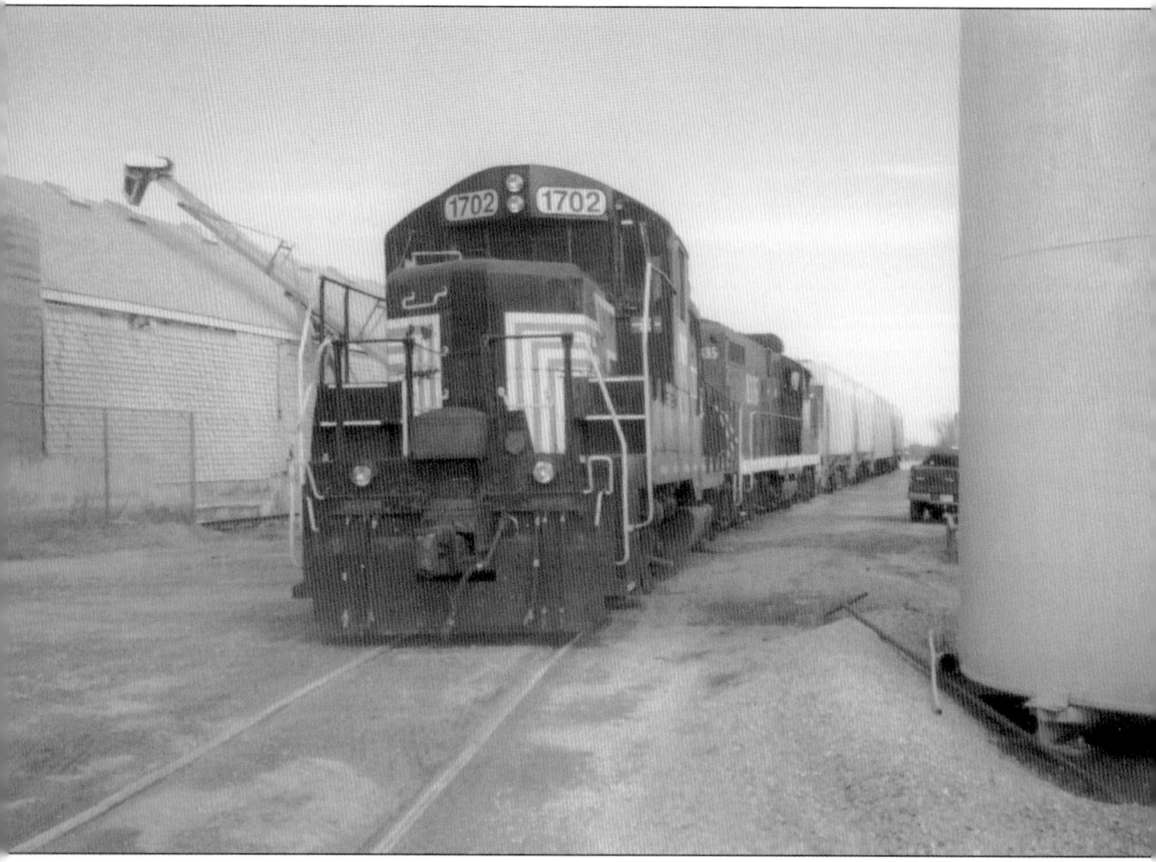

Engine no. 1702, a second engine, and a few freight cars are in the yard in Clinton near the elevators. The auger from the elevator to the cars is seen, and that is how the grain is transferred. These GP38 locomotives create 2,000 horsepower.

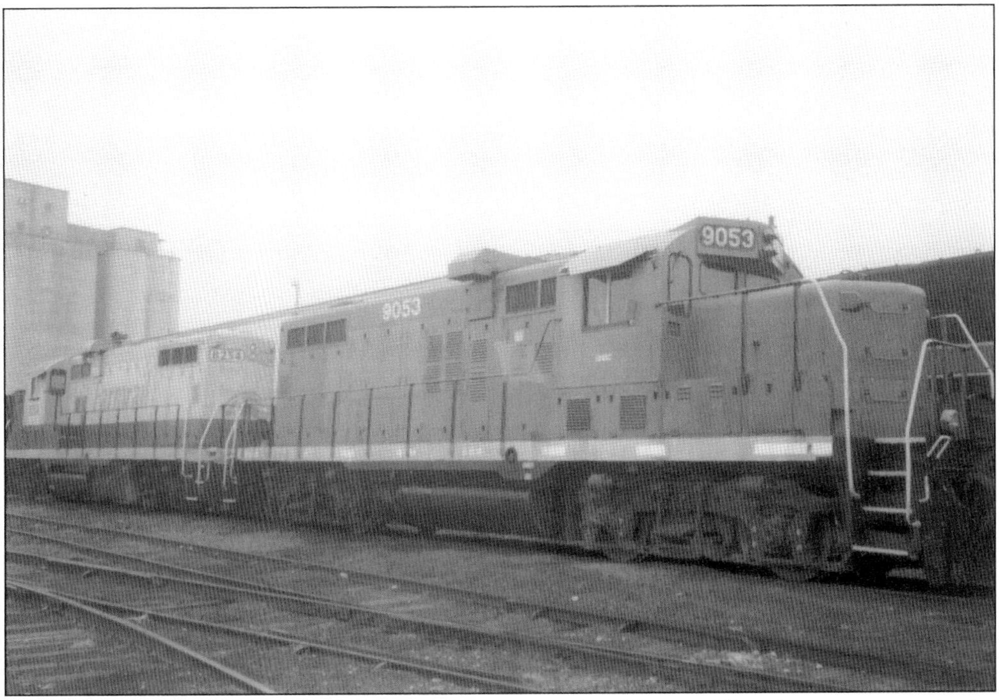

Above, diesel locomotive no. 9053 sits in the train yard at Clinton. The elevator in seen in the background to the left. Pictured below, Farmrail diesel engine no. 8267, called *Chickasaw*, is parked in the rail yard at Clinton.

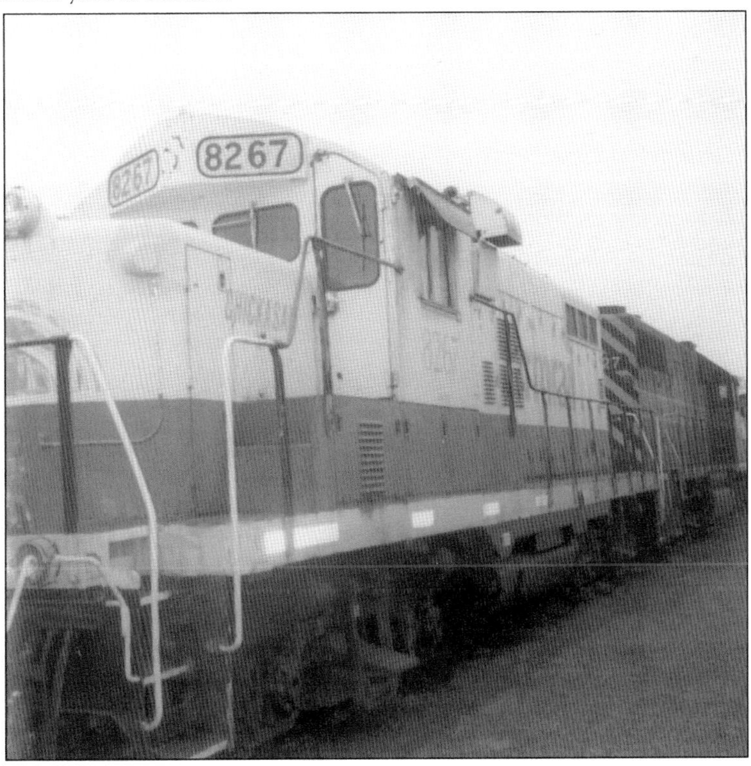

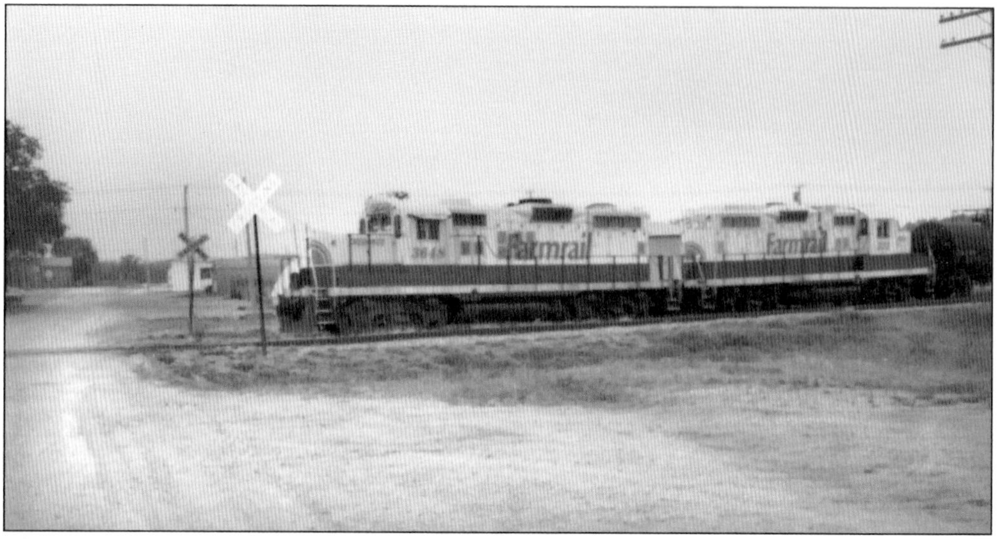

These are Farmrail locomotives, no. 3648, *Cherokee*, and no. 331, *Caddo*, are parked on the Rock Island track by Sixth Street pulling a line of tank cars.

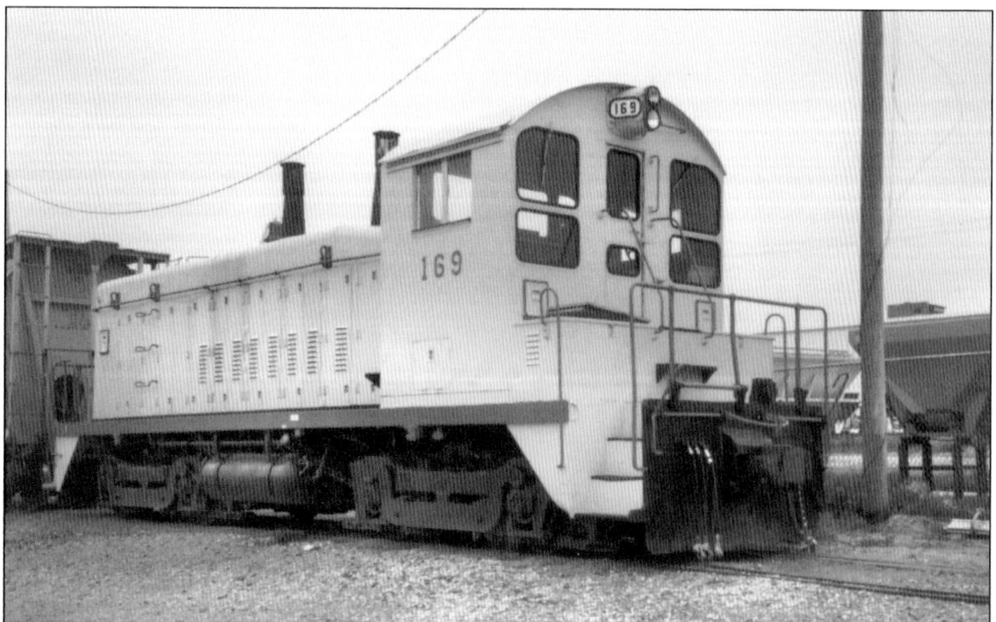

This is switcher engine no. 169 in the train yard in Clinton. Farmrail uses these engines to move its freight cars around in the yard.

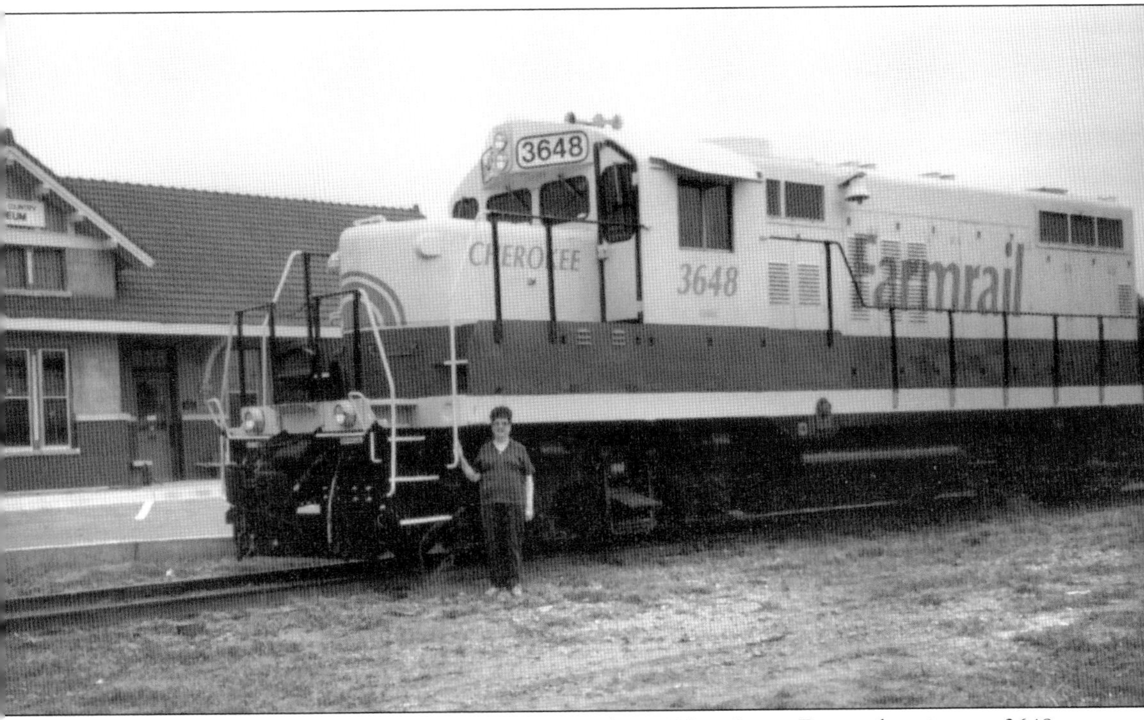

This is the Rock Island Depot, which was constructed in 1927 in Sayre. Farmrail engine no. 3648 is parked out front during the centennial celebration. The lady standing by the train is Shirley Killian, the author. After the Rock Island went out of business in 1979, the depot became the home of the Shortgrass County Museum. It has been placed in the National Register of Historic Places in 2000.

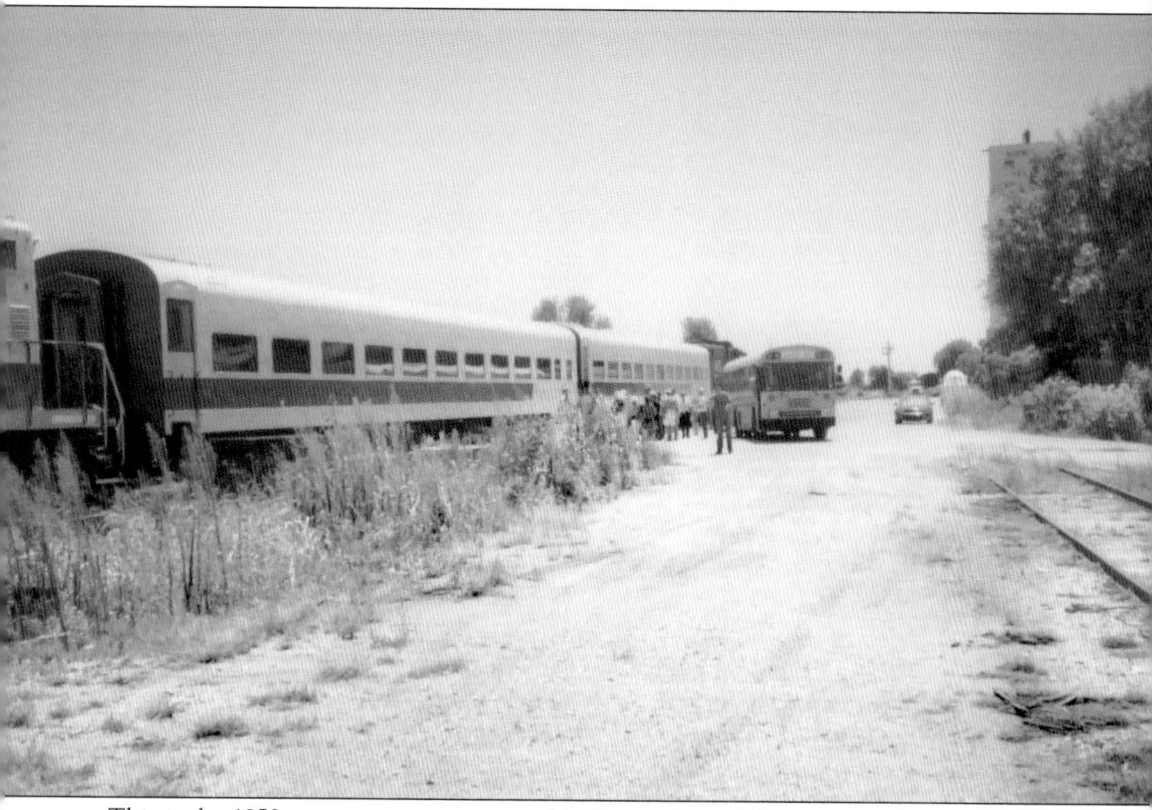

This is the 1950s passenger train, restored by Farmrail, in 2001. On that day, it was taking a tourist trip from Clinton to Okeema. It had arrived at Okeema, and school buses came out to take the train passengers to a nearby restaurant to eat lunch. One of the passenger cars was named *Cimarron*, and the train stopped on the bridge across the Cimarron River to let passengers take photographs.

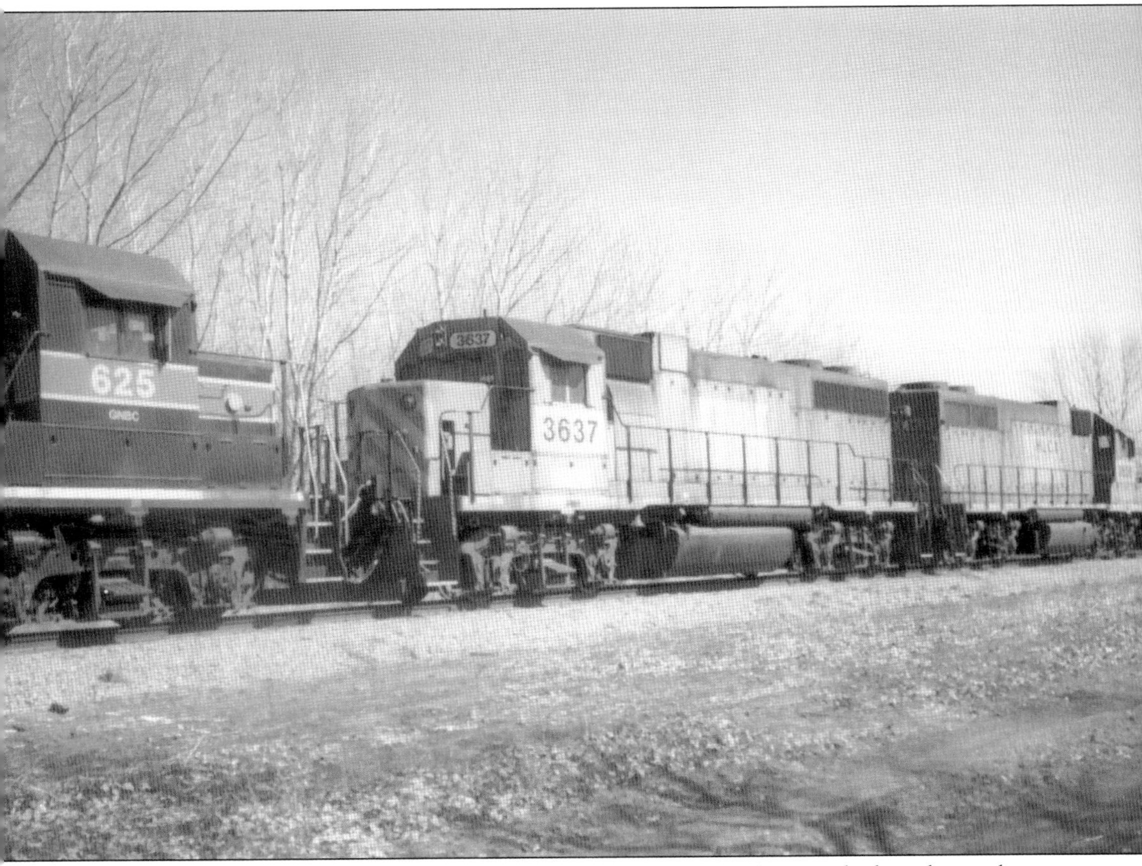

Gray locomotives no. 3637 and no. 3636, along with engine no. 625, are parked on the tracks on East Seventh Street in Elk City, Oklahoma, where Farmrail has a workshop for freight cars.

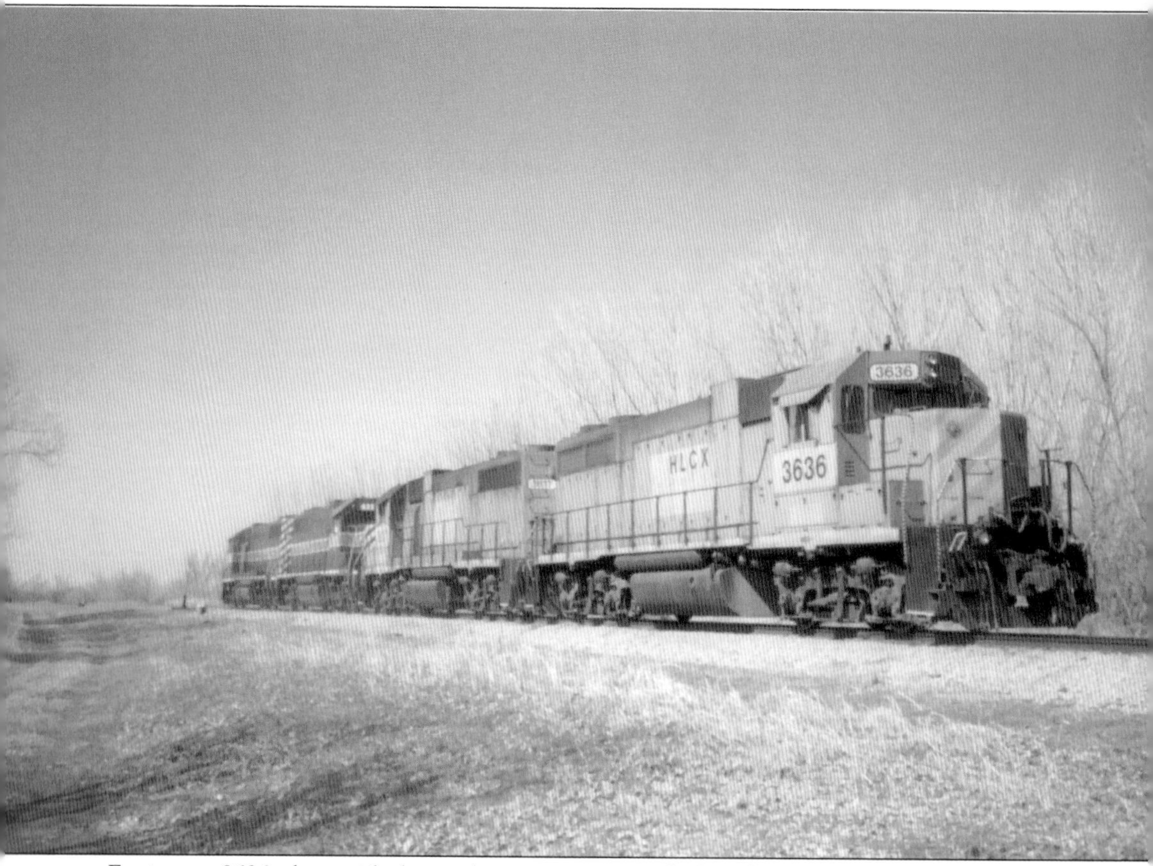

Engine no. 3636, along with three other engines, are parked on the railroad track near the Farmrail shop on East Seventh Street in Elk City.

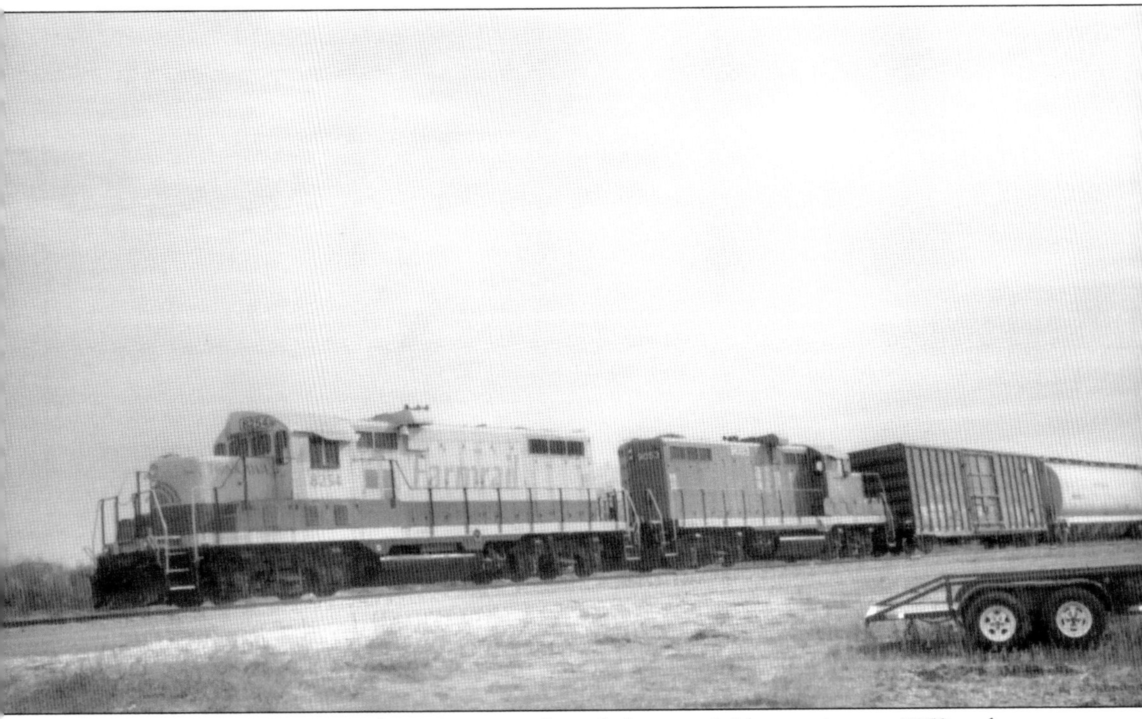

Farmrail engine no. 8254, *Tonkawa*, is at a rock yard along with blue engine no. 9053 and some railroad cars. The trains bring in rock that is ground up to make gravel and other products used on roads.

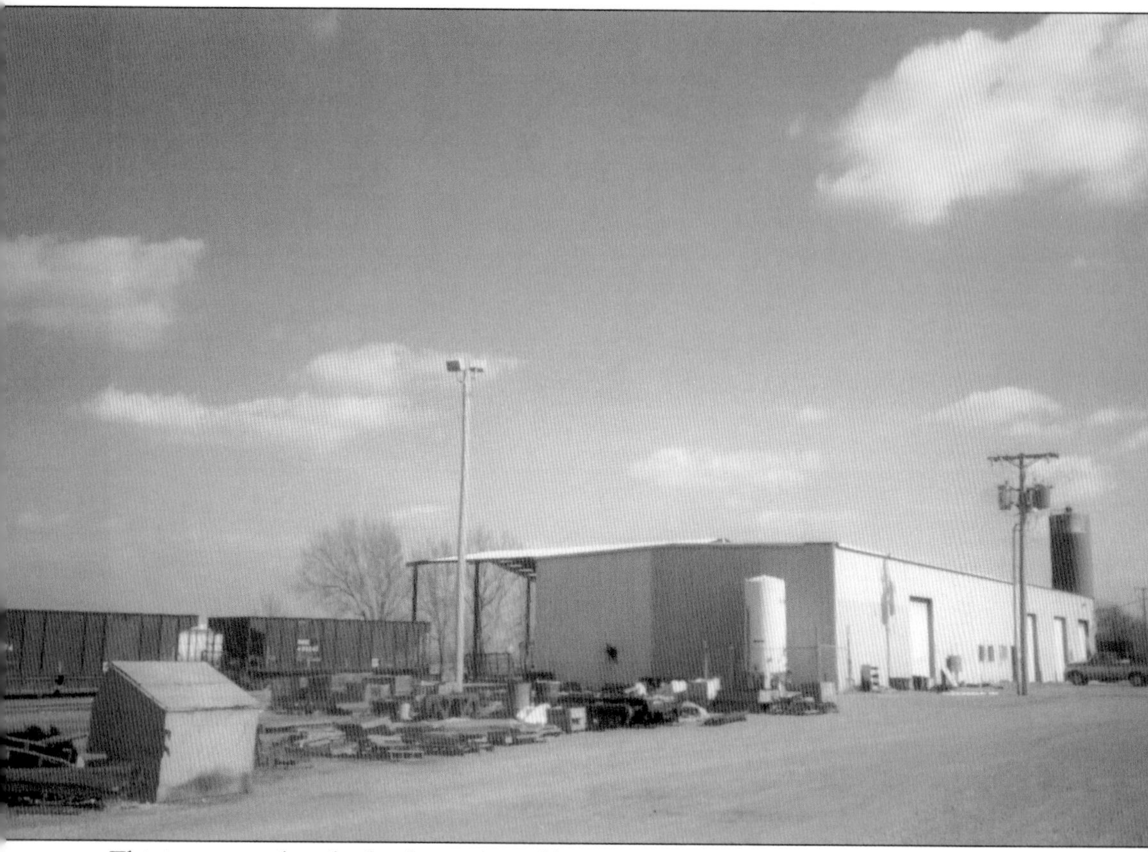

This is a repair shop for freight, tank, and hopper cars, and additional space is located on East Seventh Street in Elk City. Farmrail owns this building.

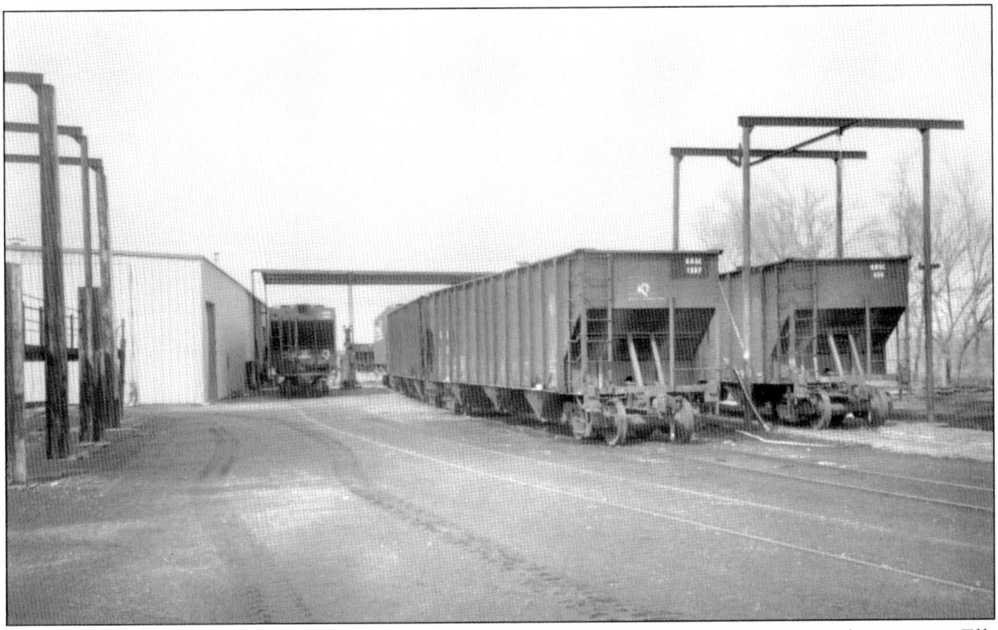

This building is owned by the Farmrail-Grainbelt Corporation on the East Seventh Street in Elk City. It is known as Rail Car Services, and freight cars are rebuilt here.

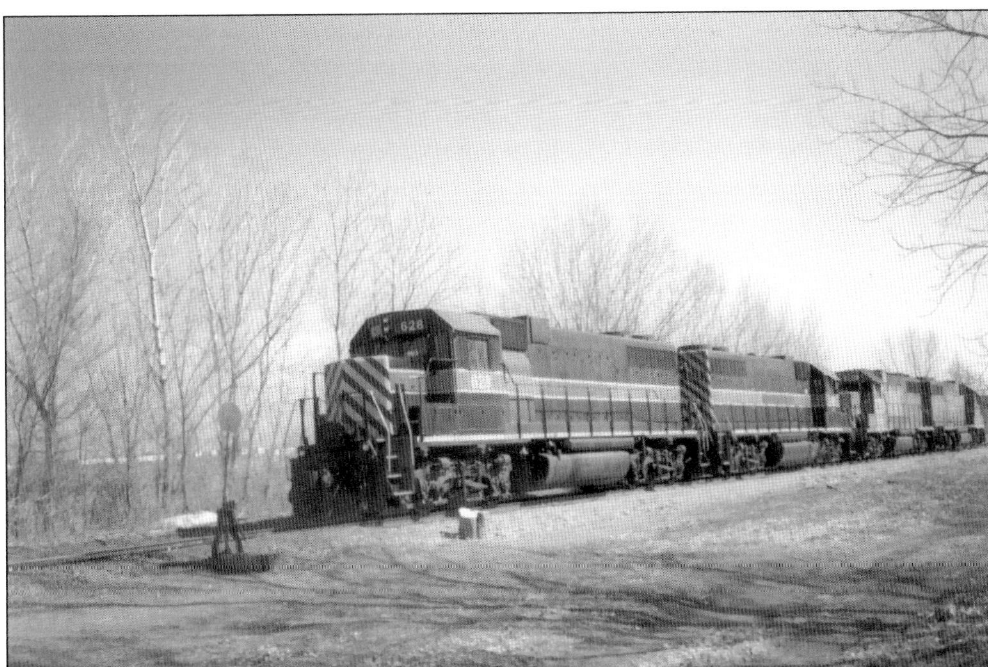

Engine no. 628 is at the Farmrail track yard in Elk City on East Seventh Street. Freight cars are brought here for repairs. Notice the switch stand in the foreground.

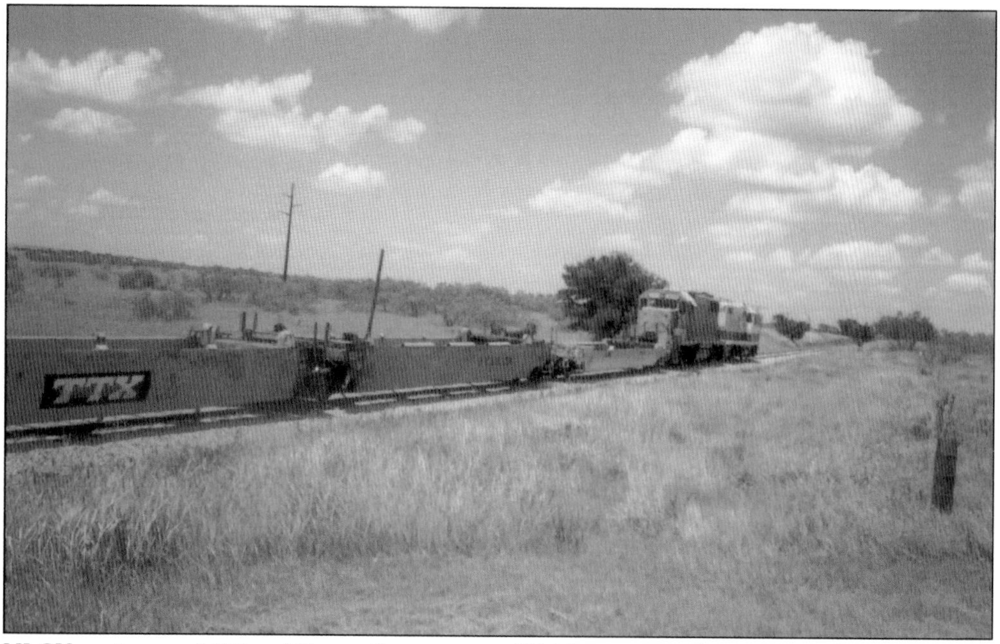

HLCX engine no. 3636 and Farmrail engine no. 8180 have stopped in Sayre and are waiting to pick up some double-stack well cars to stack pods on.

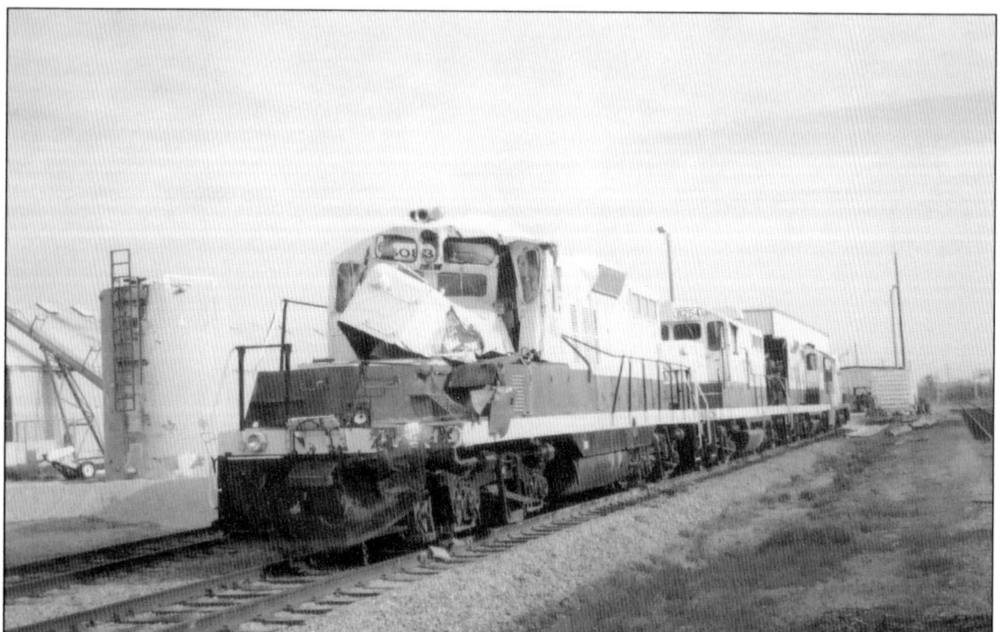

Farmrail engine no. 6083 was involved in a derailment in the yard at Clinton as it was waiting to be repaired in the workshop.

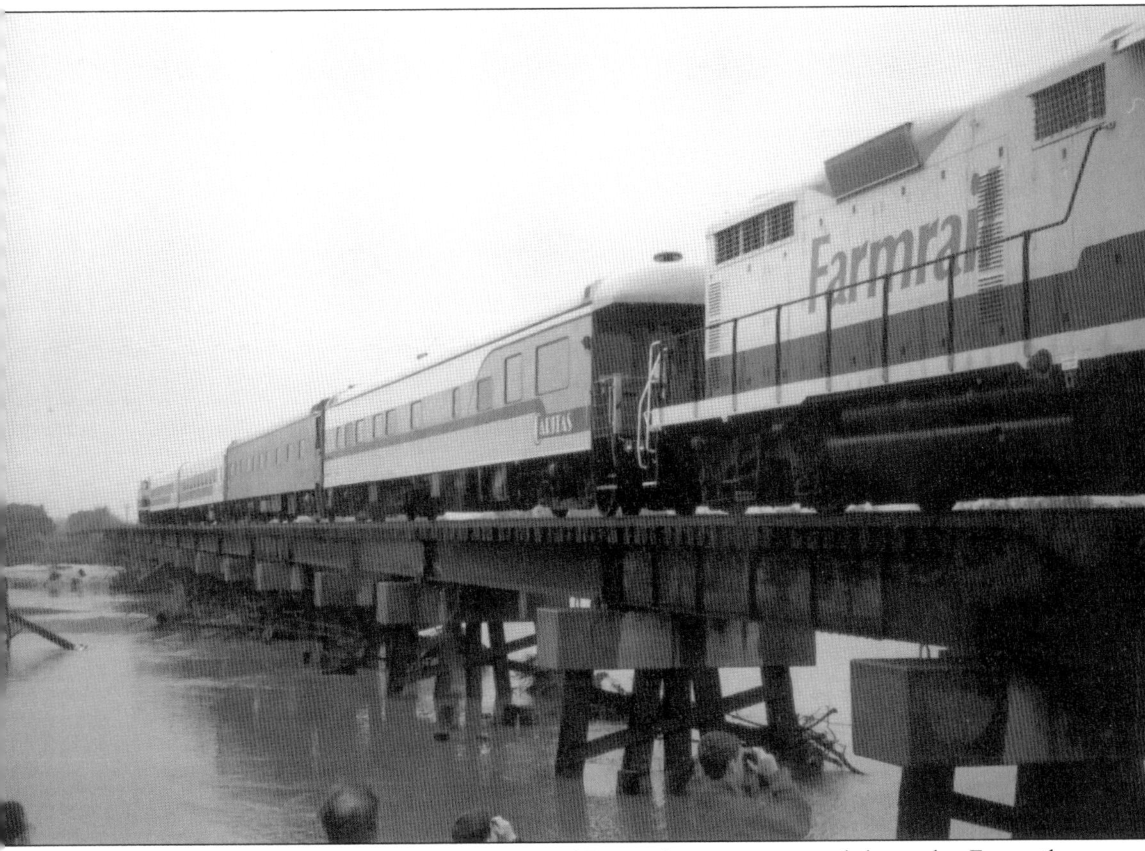

Farmrail engine no. 407 pulls Cimarron, Frisco, and Farmrail passenger cars, while another Farmrail engine is stopped on the Cimarron River Bridge on the way to Okeema. The train stopped here to allow passengers to take photographs.

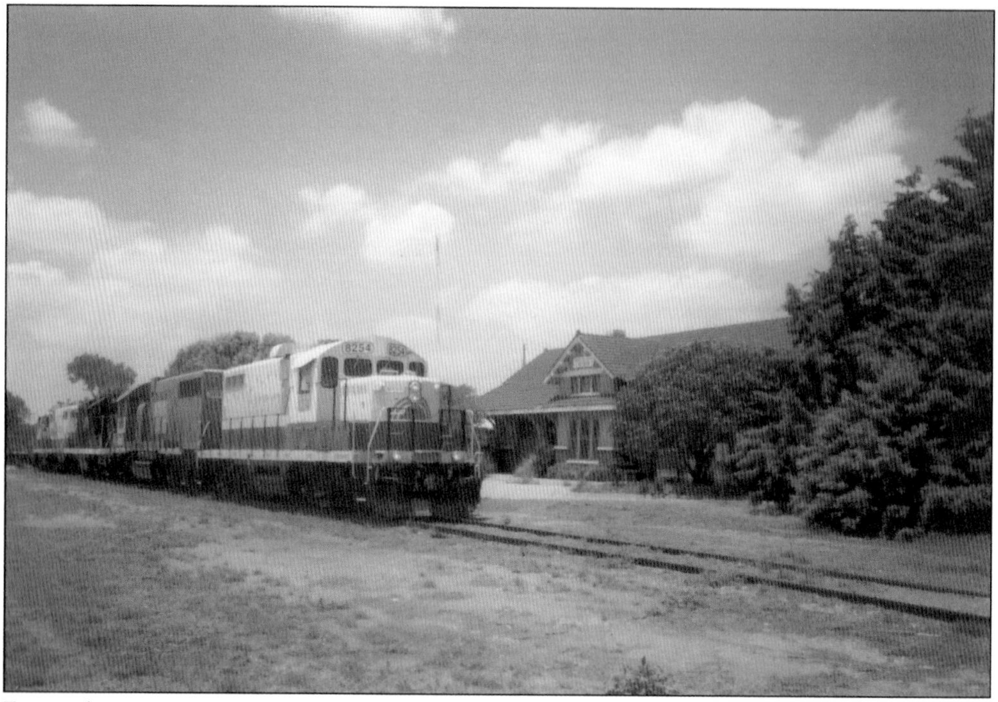

Farmrail engine no. 8254 and three other engines pass by the Rock Island Depot, which is now the home of the Shortgrass County Museum.

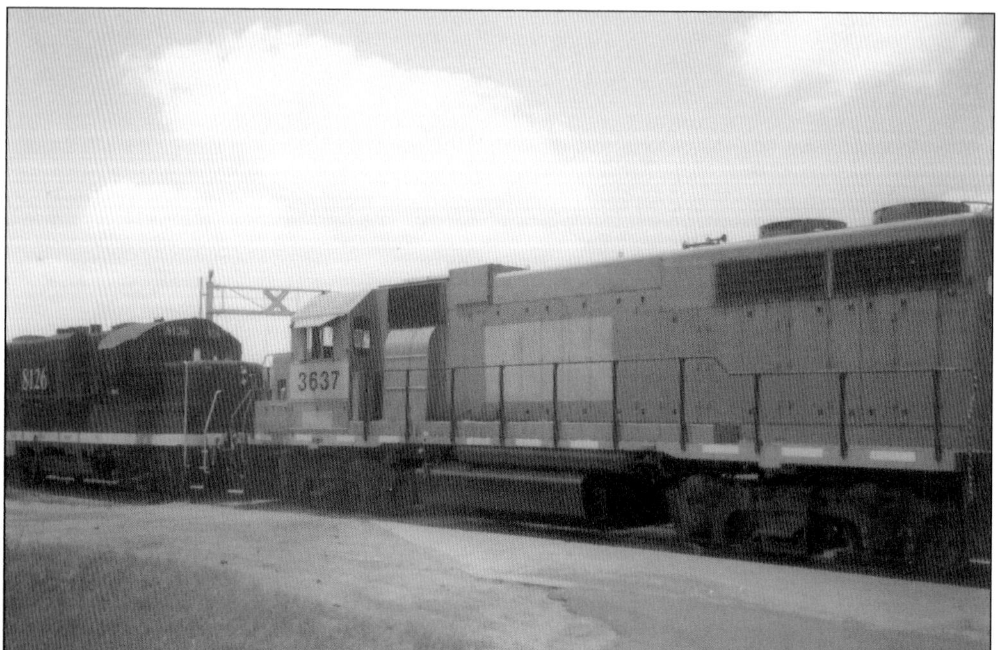

Gray engine no. 3637 and black engine no. 8126 go through the railroad crossing grade on the west end of town in Sayre near State Highway 152.

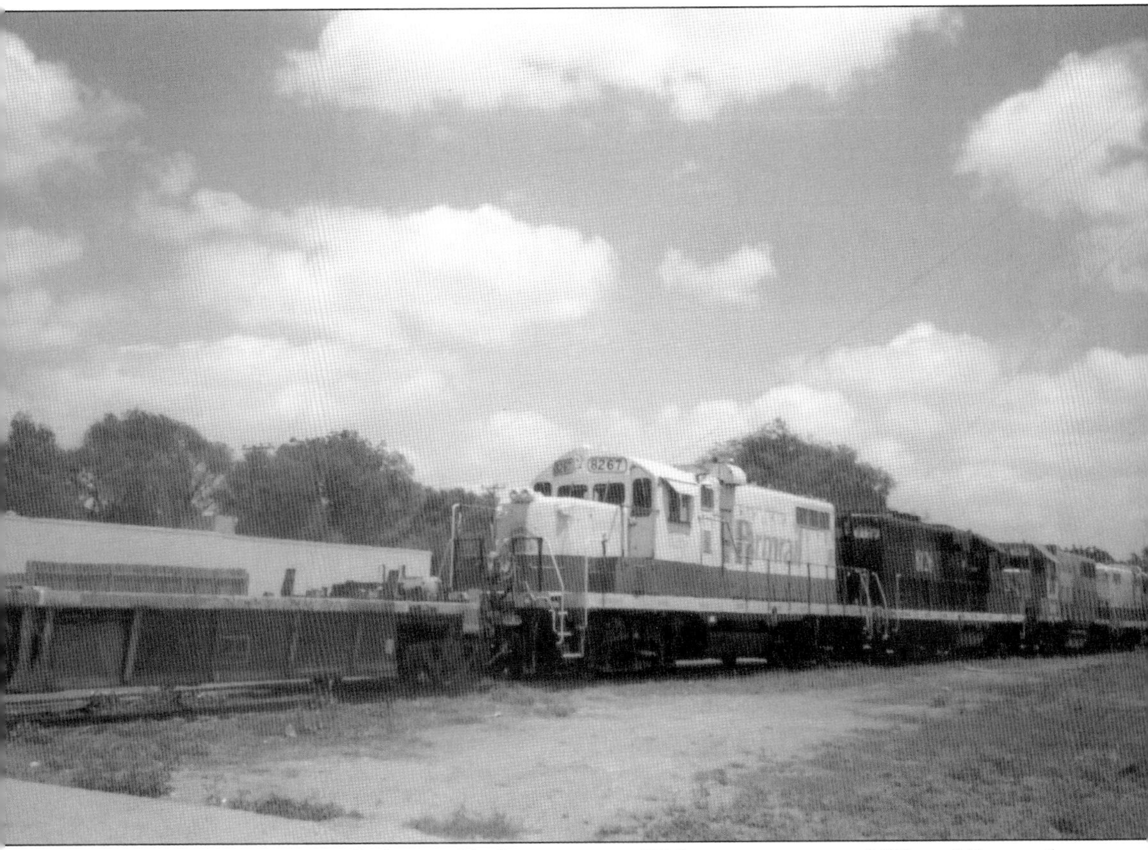

Farmrail engine no. 8267, *Chickasaw*; black engine no. 8126; gray engine no. 3637; and Farmrail engine no. 8254 are in the train yard on the west end of town in Sayre. They are picking up pod cars to take back to Clinton to be picked up by another railroad company.

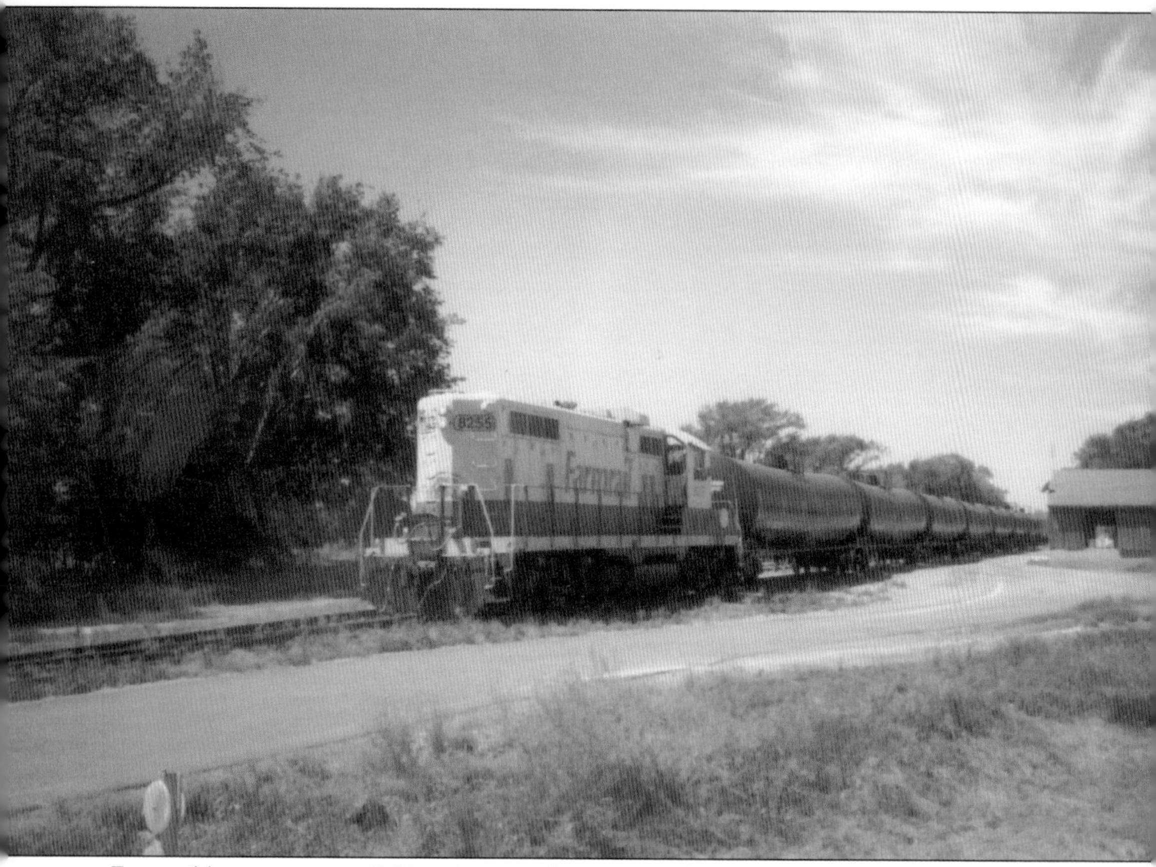

Farmrail locomotive no. 8255 picks up tank cars from the switch yard on the west end of town in Sayre. The building to the right is the Sayre Crop Service.

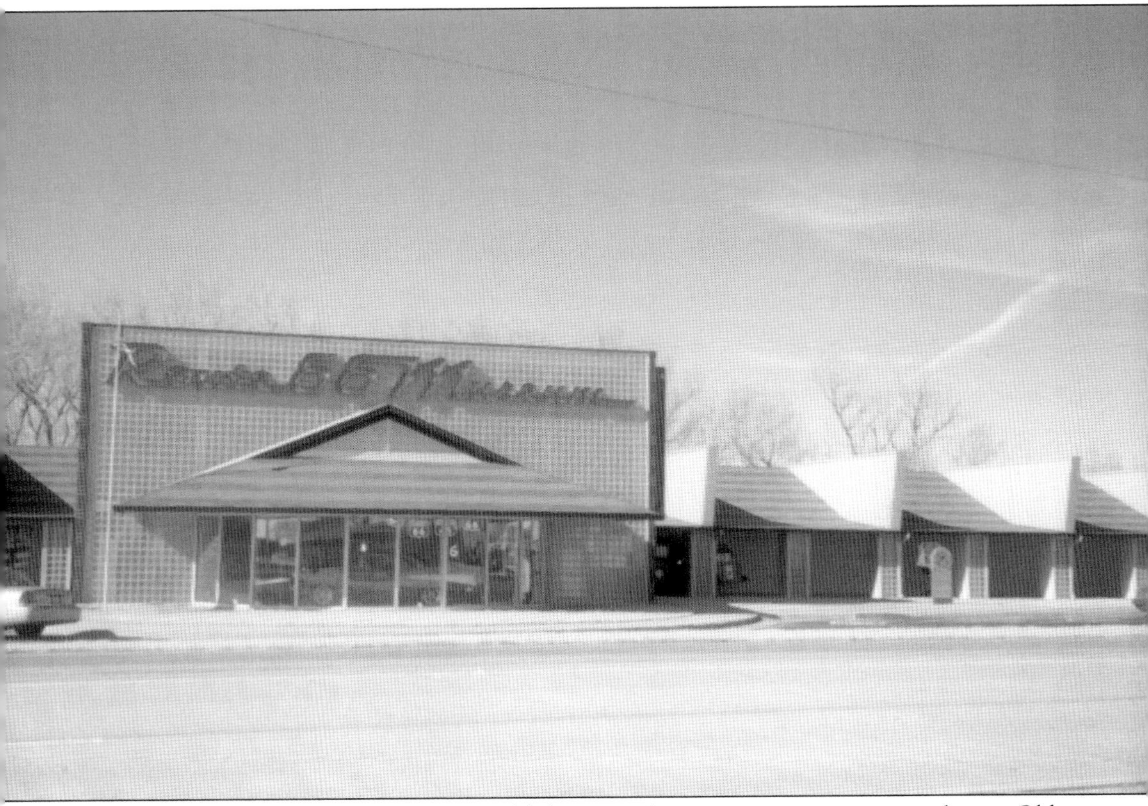

This is the Route 66 Museum in Clinton, Oklahoma, and it receives many visitors each year. Old cars, a large curio cabinet, neon signs, a drive-in theater, and a 1950s diner are part of its collection. It does a great job of showcasing the history of Route 66, and it is operated by the Oklahoma Historical Society. Michael Wallis narrates a recorded trip of the rise and fall of Route 66.

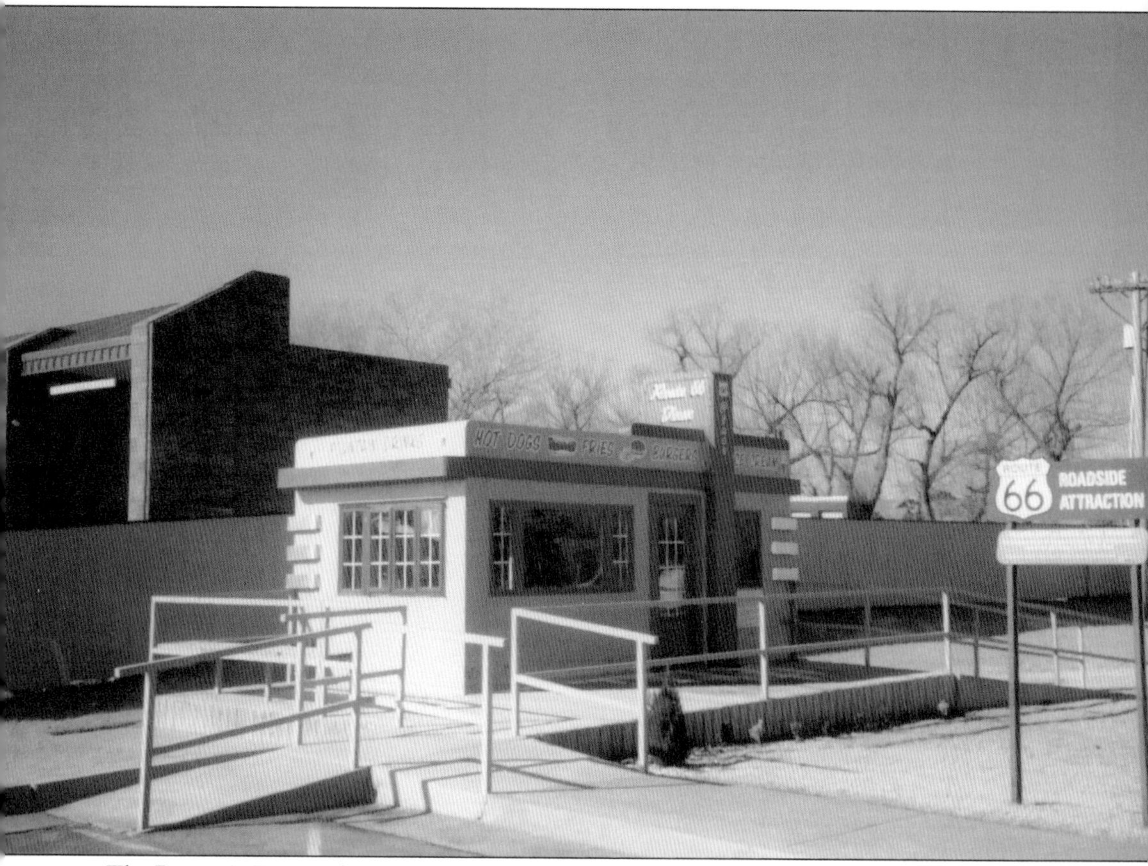

The Route 66 Diner is located near the Route 66 Museum and gift shop in Clinton. The railroad tracks run behind this building.

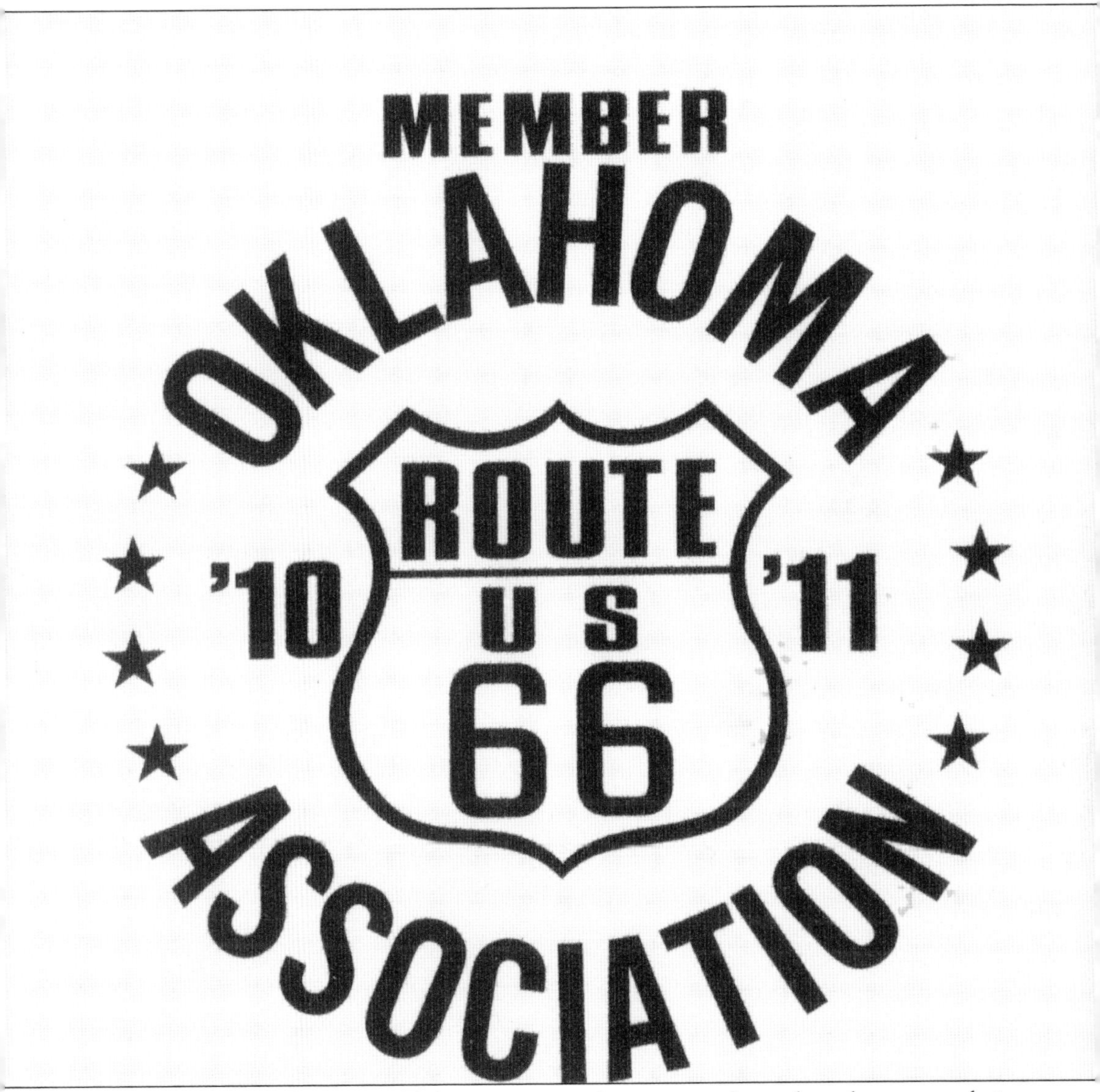

This is a sticker that the Route 66 Association sends to its members when they renew their membership each year.

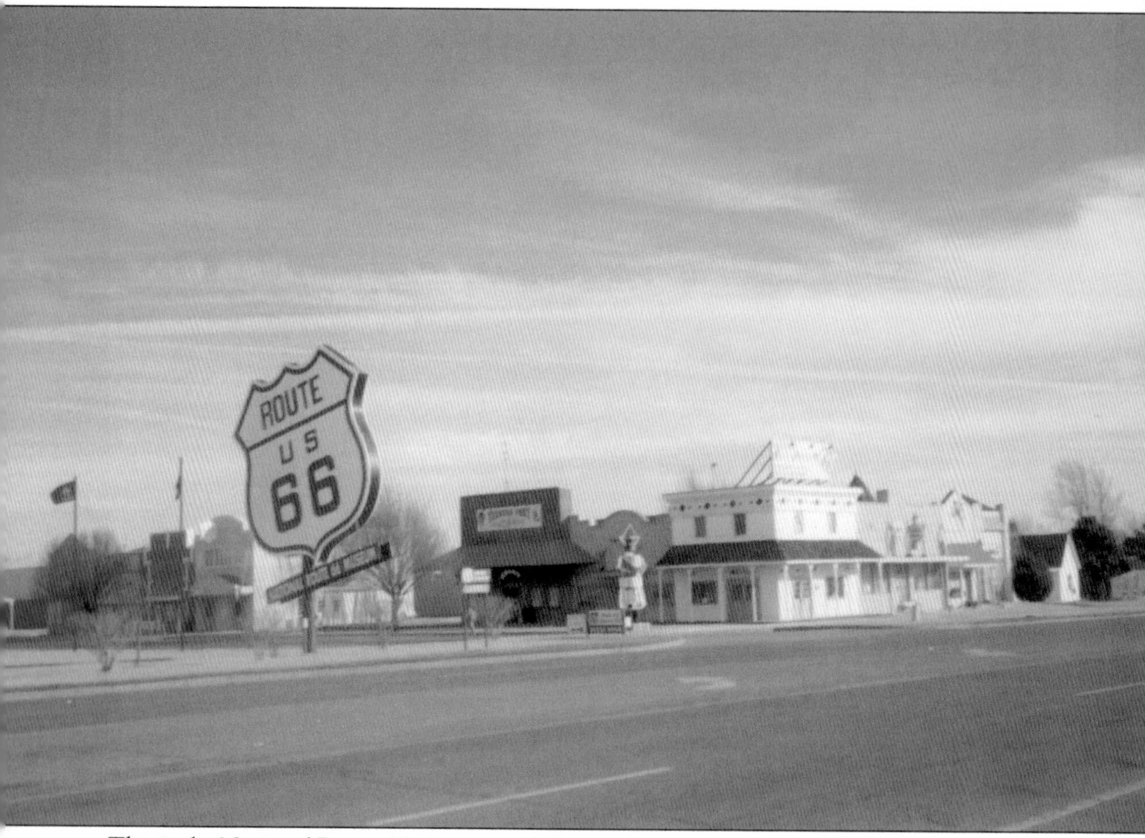

This is the National Route 66 Museum in Elk City. The author and her husband, Ray, helped one year by delivering a plaque from Sayre to this museum during the Bunion Derby.

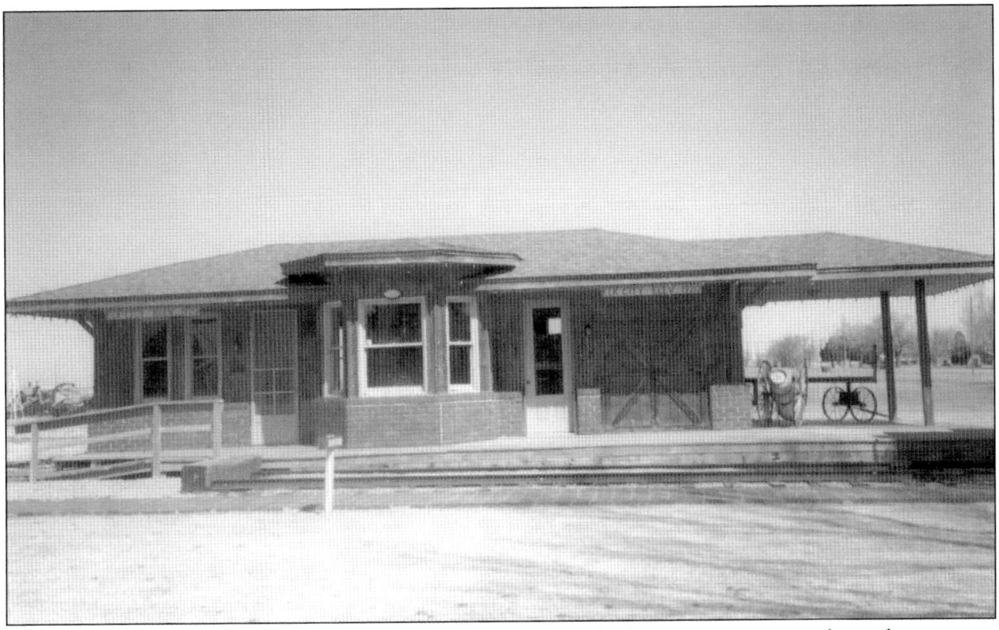

This is the depot in the museum yard at Elk City. Note the baggage wagon to the right.

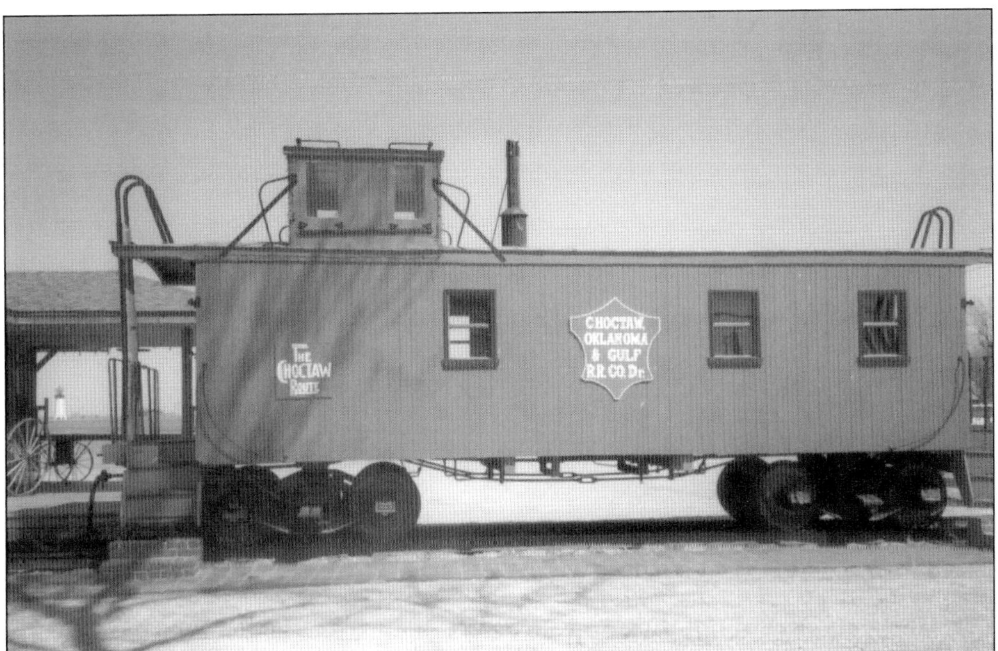

This is a Choctaw, Oklahoma and Gulf Railway Company caboose. Notice the sign that states it is part of the Choctaw Route. It is located in the museum yard at Elk City.

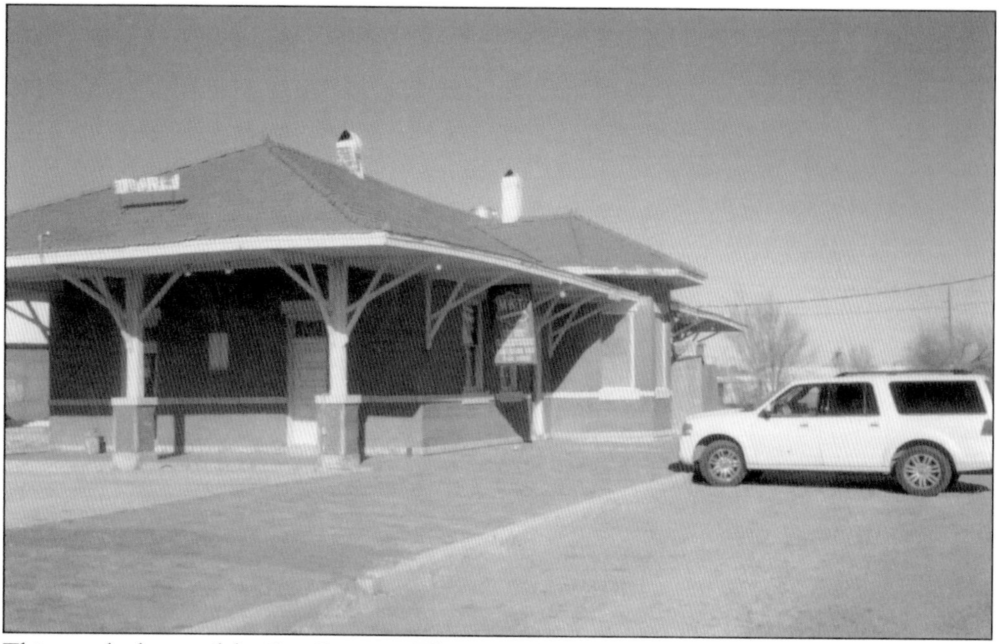

This was the home of the Katy Depot in Elk City. It has since been used as a restaurant for several years; the old baggage wagon was used for advertising purposes. A new restaurant in the Katy Depot will be opening in the fall of 2011.

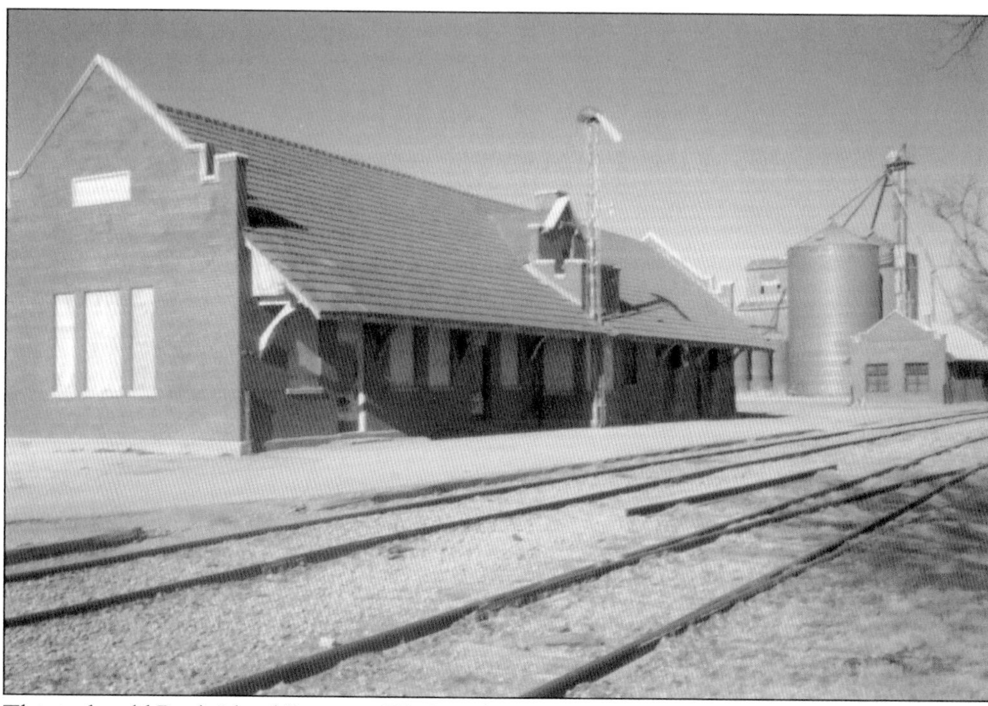

This is the old Rock Island Depot in Elk City that is now owned by the city. The office building is seen on the right with an elevator in the background.

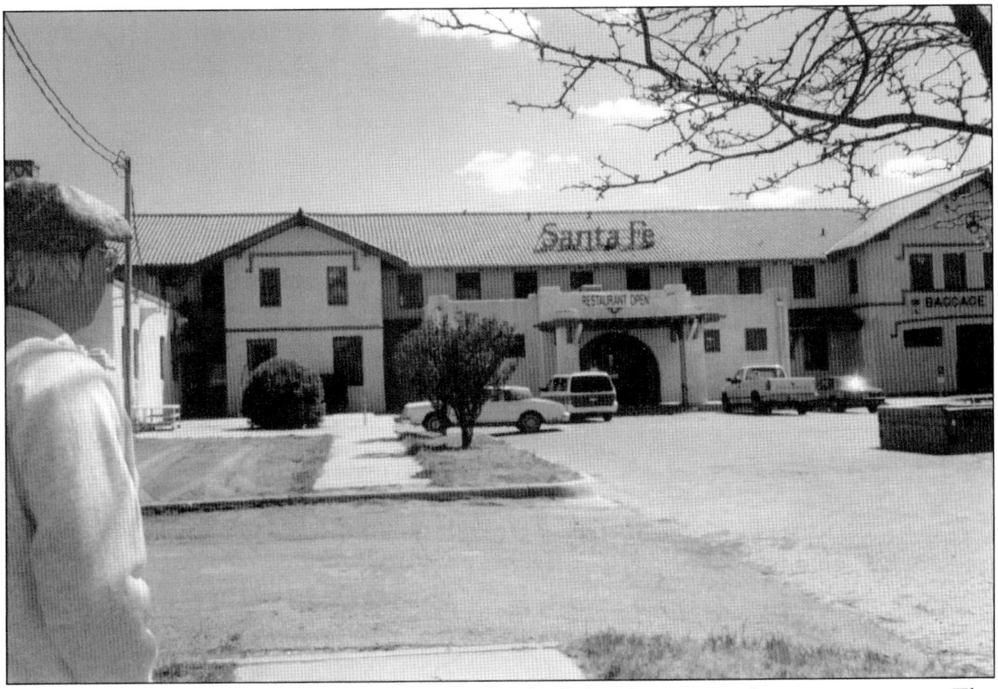

This is the Santa Fe Depot in Amarillo, Texas, which has been turned into a restaurant. The author and her husband ate at the restaurant a few years back.

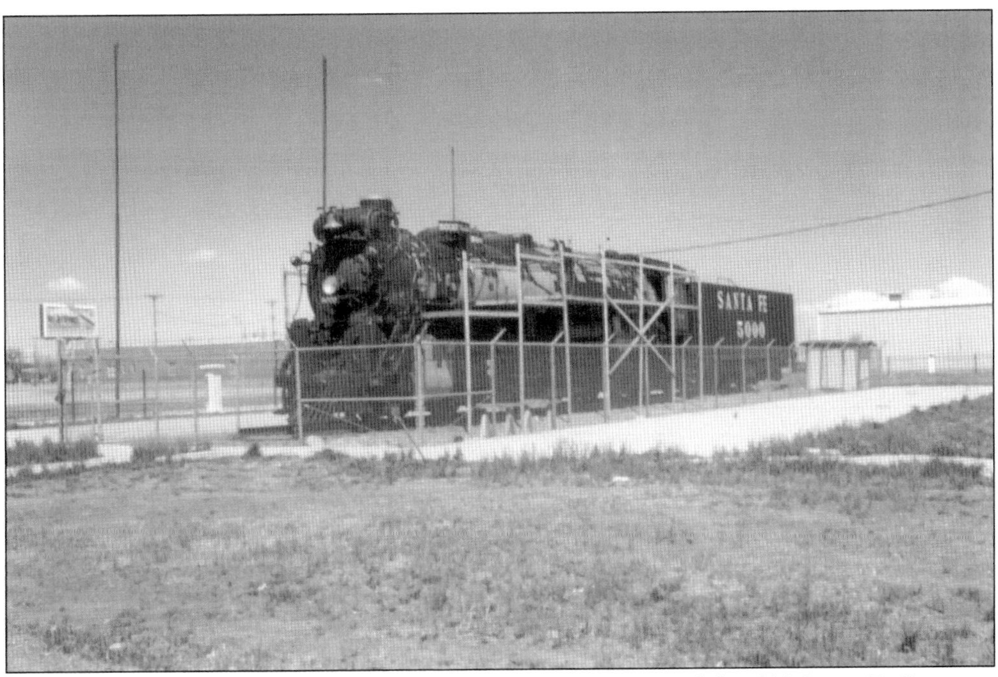

Santa Fe locomotive no. 5000 is seen here on display in front of the Old Santa Fe Depot in Amarillo, Texas.

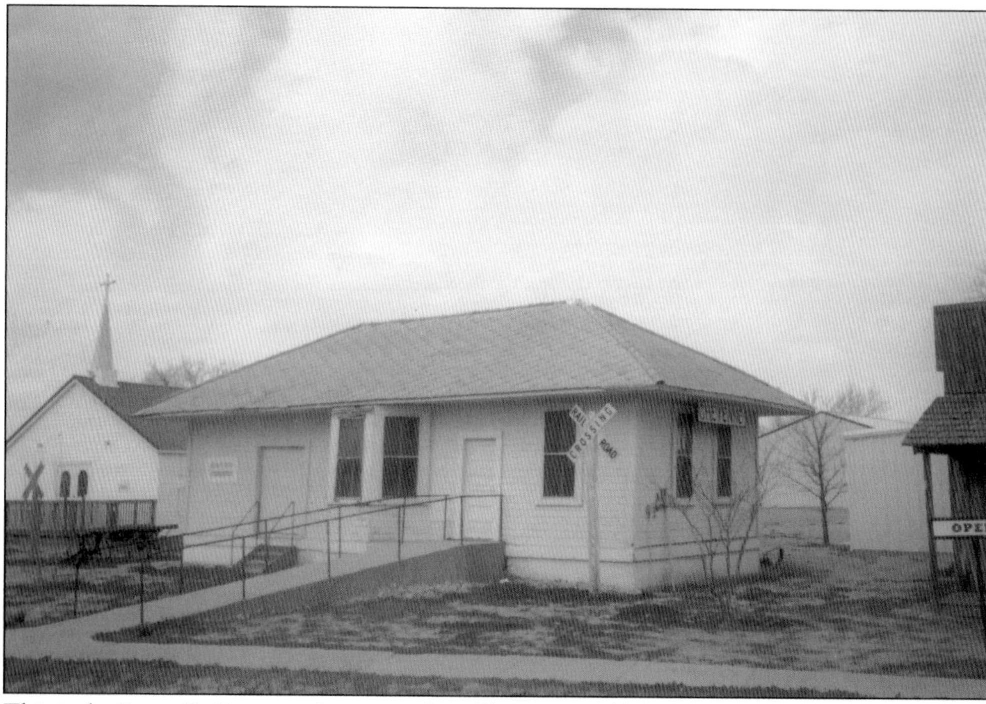

This is the Santa Fe Depot in the city park at Cheyenne, Oklahoma. Railroad crossing signs can be seen on each side, along with a baggage wagon on the left.

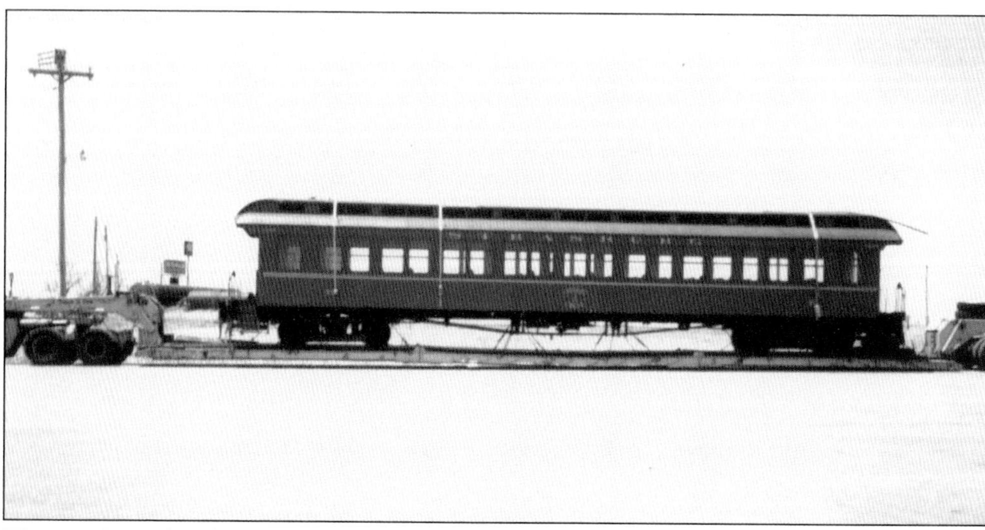
This is a Strawsburgh passenger car that was parked out near Simmons Truck Oasis a few years ago. It was quite a sight to see.

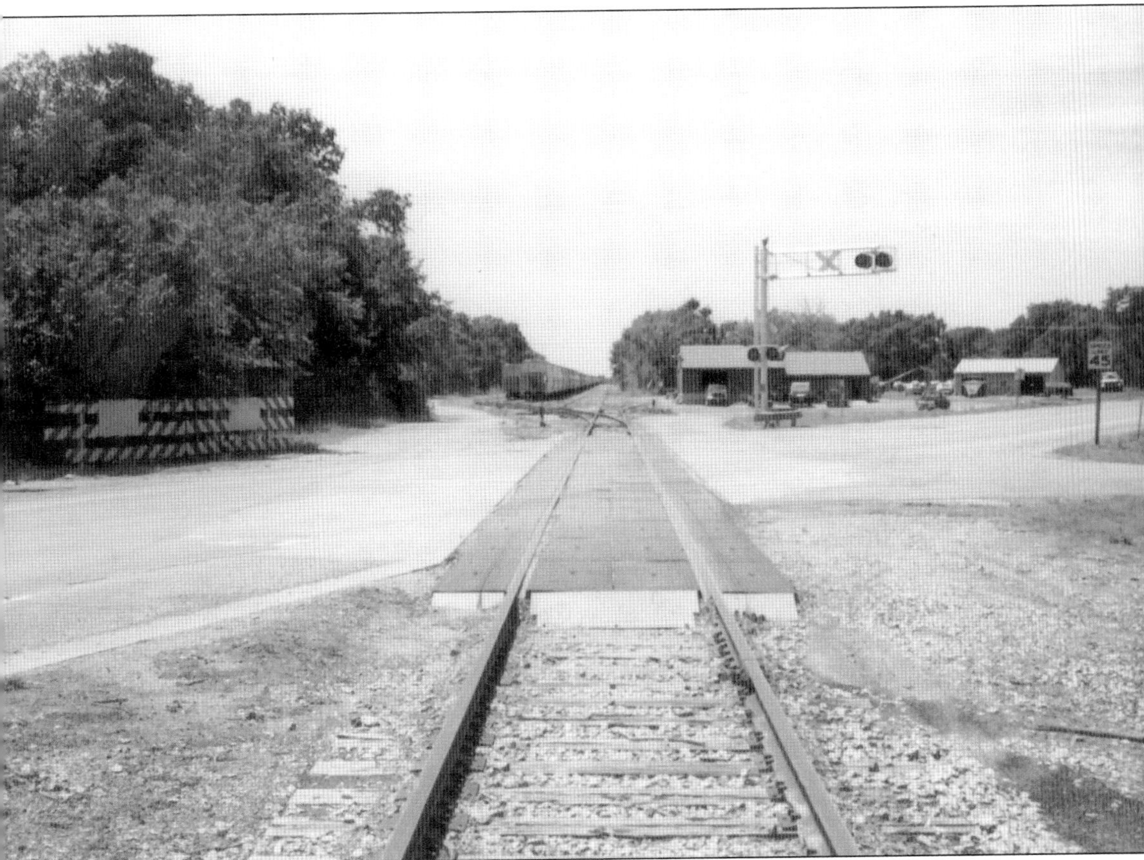

Seen here are rails that run west to the Sayre Crop Service. This is the area where the roundhouse, Harvey House, and the old depot used to be located. It has a more modern railroad crossing sign. Note the string of freight cars behind the engine on the tracks.

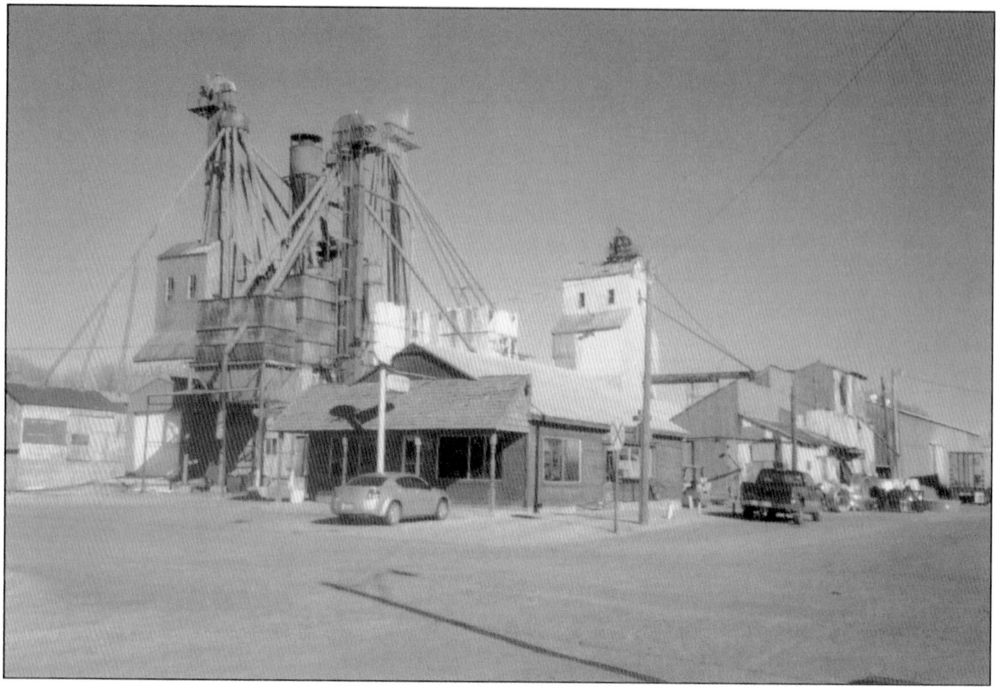

Pictured above is Puckett's Warehouse. In the image below are rails that run east to west past the storage elevators and across Third Street in Sayre; Puckett's Warehouse is seen on the left here. Notice the switch stand to the left of the track. The author's daughters used to love to run out and watch the trains pass when the family lived on Third Street. The building to the right in the background is the depot.

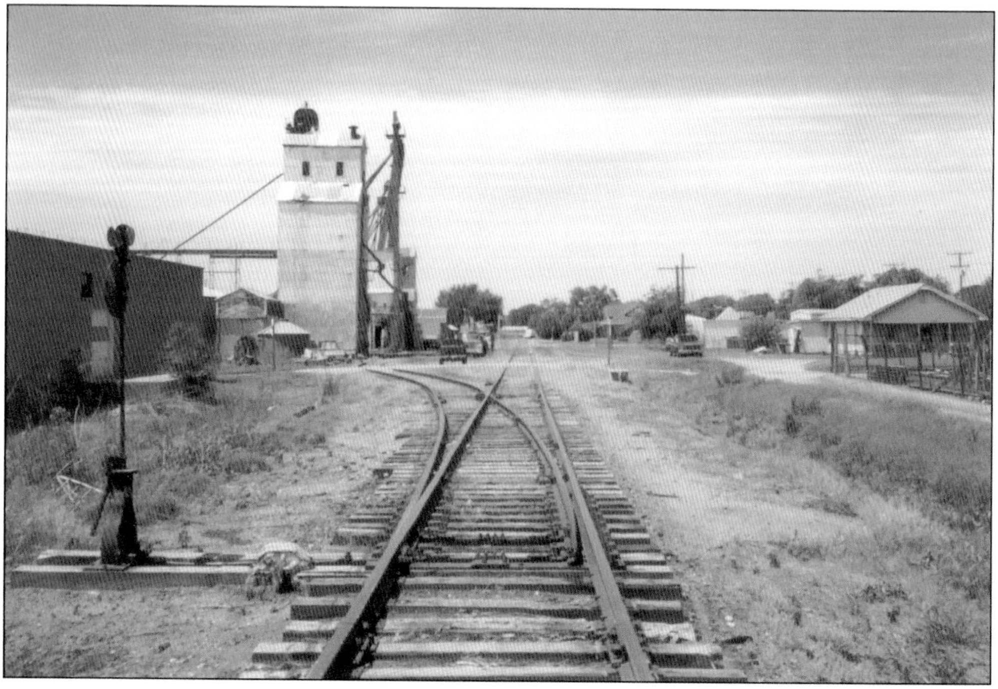

Four

R.S. and K. Railroad Museum

The R.S. and K. Railroad Museum (abbreviated for Ray, Shirley, and Killian) started in September 1990. Ray had retired from the postal service and wanted a little more to do in his spare time. Shirley suggested he get his six little trains out of the attic and set them up in his storage shed that joined the house. A giant garage sale took place, and the laying of track commenced. There are now more than 300 complete train sets, more than 400 tiny cars, 200-plus lighted porcelain houses, and more than 200 pieces of railroad memorabilia. The museum has had visitors from all 50 states and 21 foreign countries.

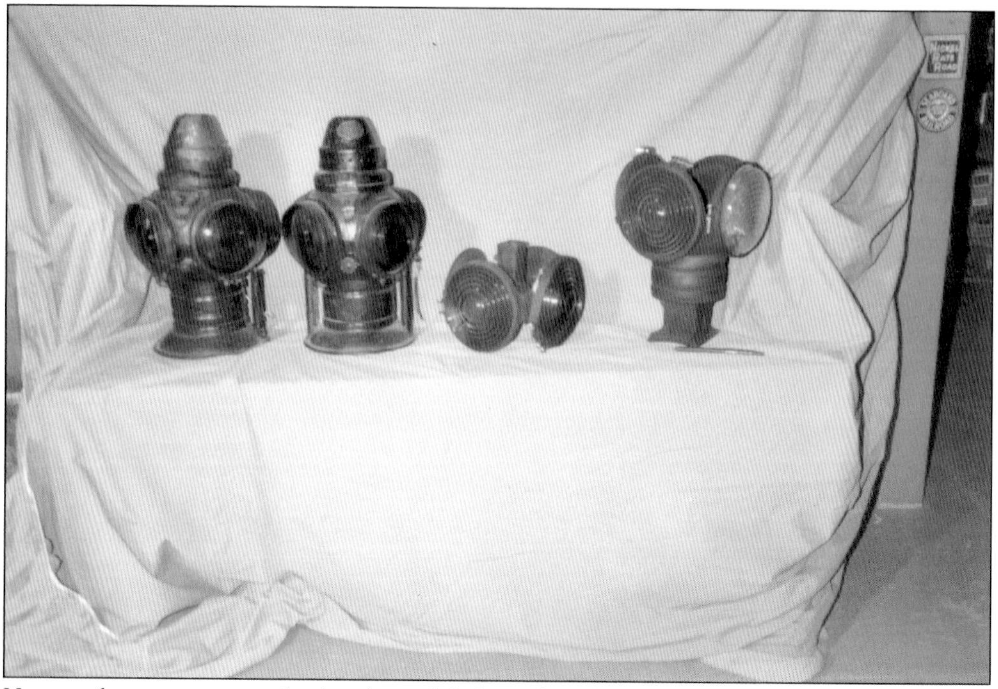

Here are four generations of railroad switch lights. They change them out around every 20 years. One set is made of cast iron, one set has a thick back, one set has a thin back, and one set has a big lens and a big bill.

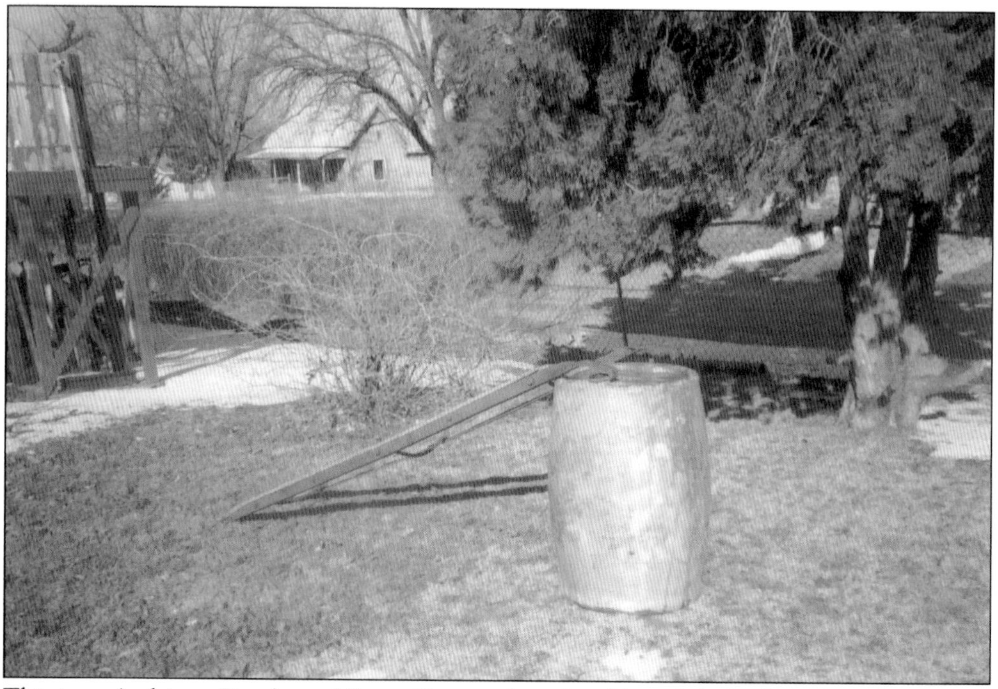

This is an Atchison, Topeka and Santa Fe water barrel and barrel skid. The railway used to roll barrels from the boxcars to the ground. Notice the homemade water tower on the left. This is PST 13-12 55-57 Galwater barrel.

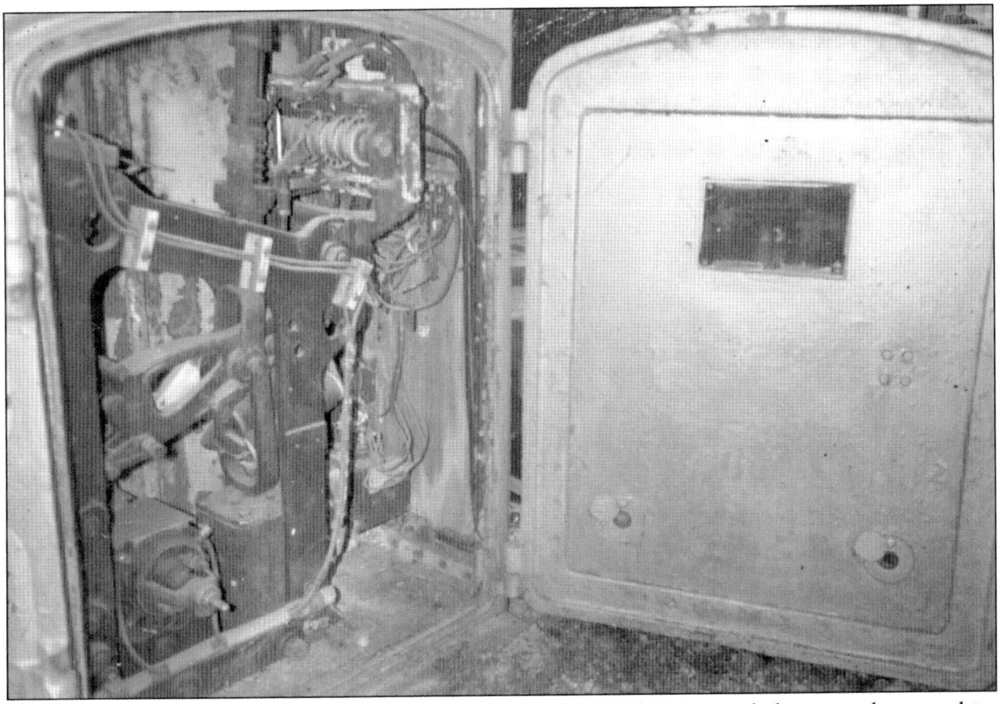

This is a chain-driven semaphore control box that was used to control the semaphore and its workings. It is located on the north side of the train museum next to the semaphore pole.

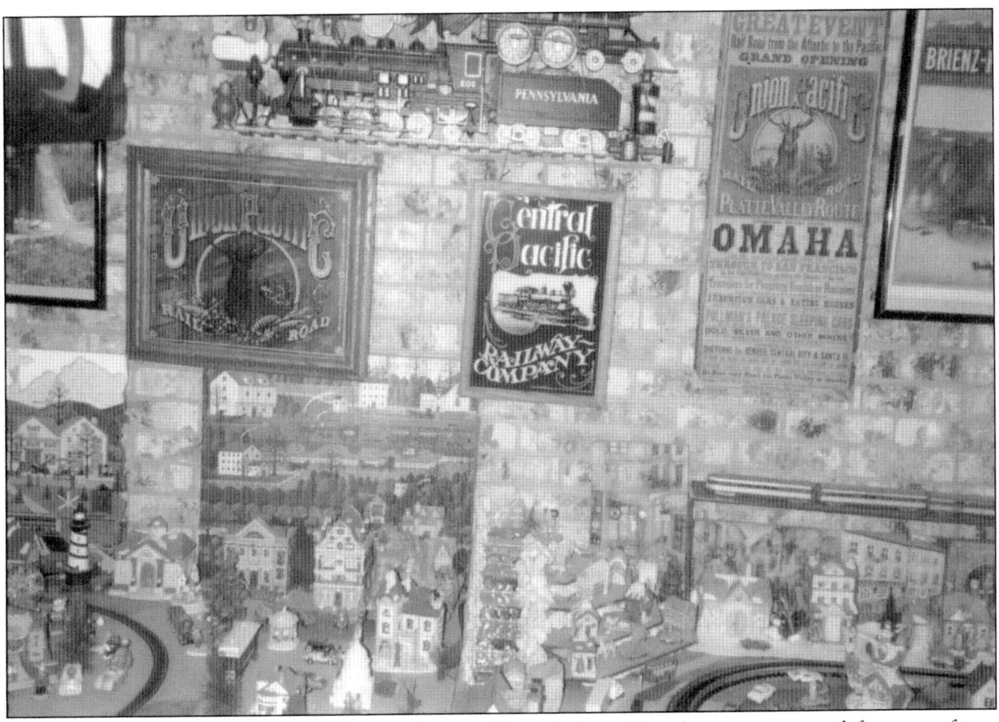

Railroads were an exciting way to see the world and also offered a way to travel far away from home. Their logos and insignias reflect the grandeur that surrounded them.

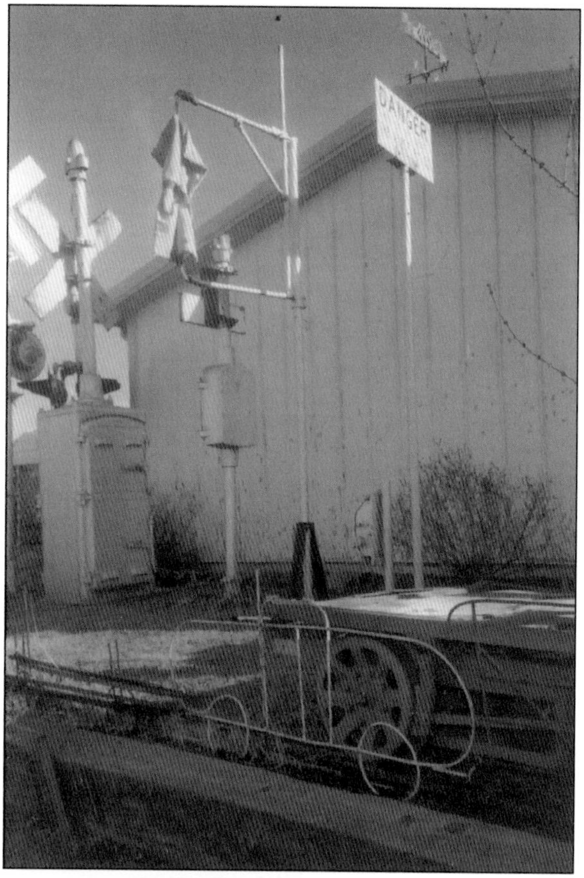

This is a railroad express mailbag post with the mailbag hanging, waiting to be picked up by the train at the R.S. and K. Railroad Museum in Sayre, Oklahoma.

Three Farmrail diesel engines sit in the yard in Clinton. Notice the elevators in the background where grain is stored.

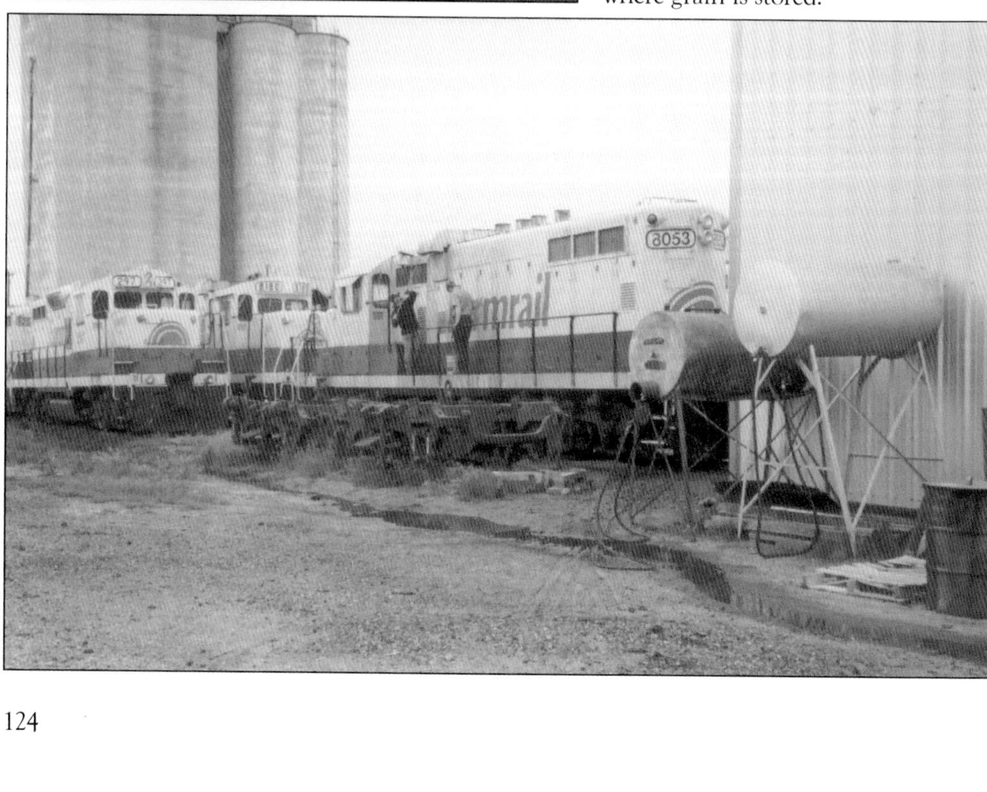

This is the last collector's calendar put out by Frisco Lines in 1990. It was in service from 1876 to 1990. At the top it reads 1876, its first year, with the name St. Louis and San Francisco Railway. It shows people waiting to catch a train at the depot.

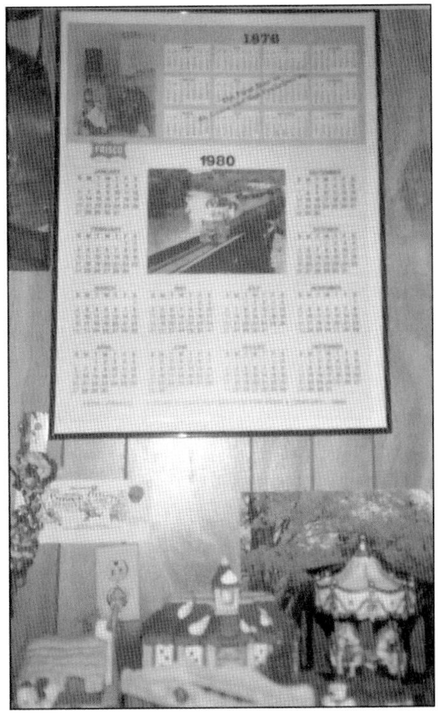

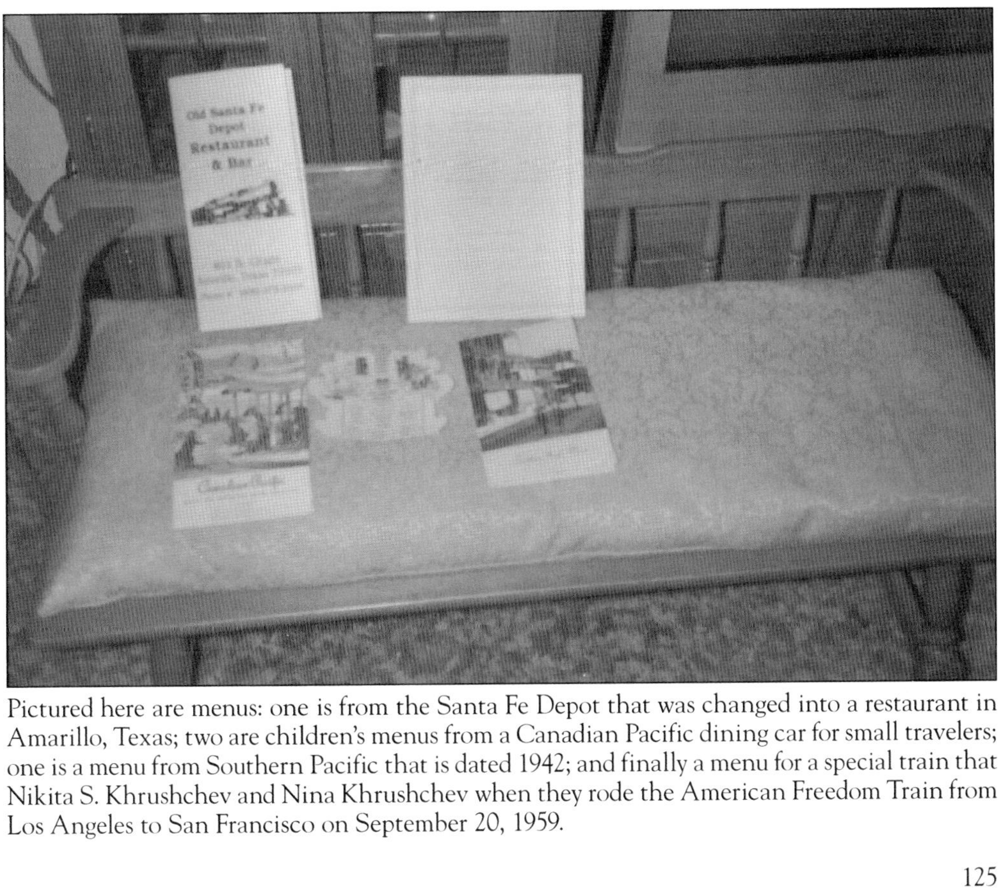

Pictured here are menus: one is from the Santa Fe Depot that was changed into a restaurant in Amarillo, Texas; two are children's menus from a Canadian Pacific dining car for small travelers; one is a menu from Southern Pacific that is dated 1942; and finally a menu for a special train that Nikita S. Khrushchev and Nina Khrushchev when they rode the American Freedom Train from Los Angeles to San Francisco on September 20, 1959.

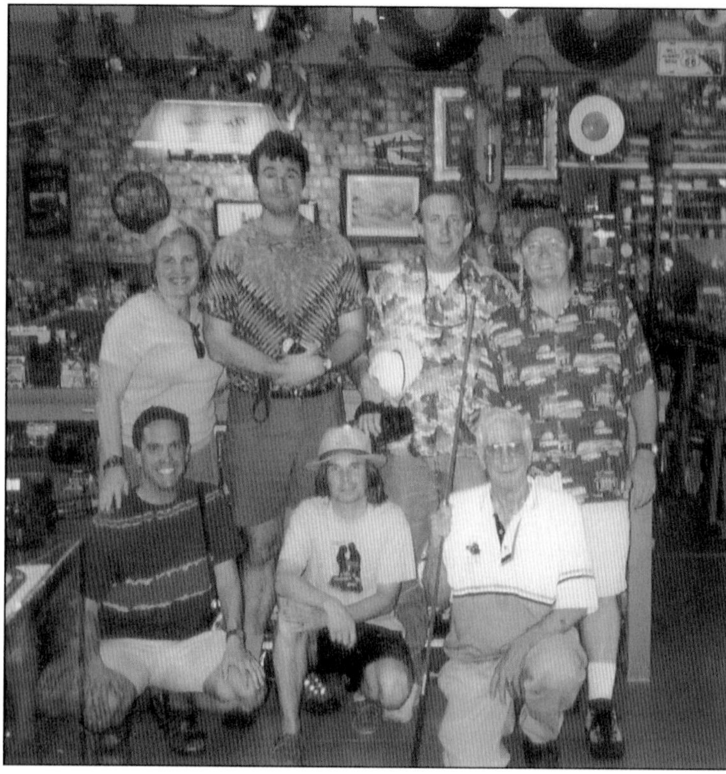

These are members of Pixar, who came to visit the R.S. and K. Railroad Museum on June 8, 2001. Michael Wallis, who writes about Route 66, was traveling with them. They were gathering information for the upcoming movie *Cars*, which was released five years later in 2005. Wallis was the voice of the sheriff's car in the movie. Pictured here are, from left to right, (first row) two unidentified men and Ray Killian; (second row) Darla Anderson, two unidentified men, and John Lasseter.

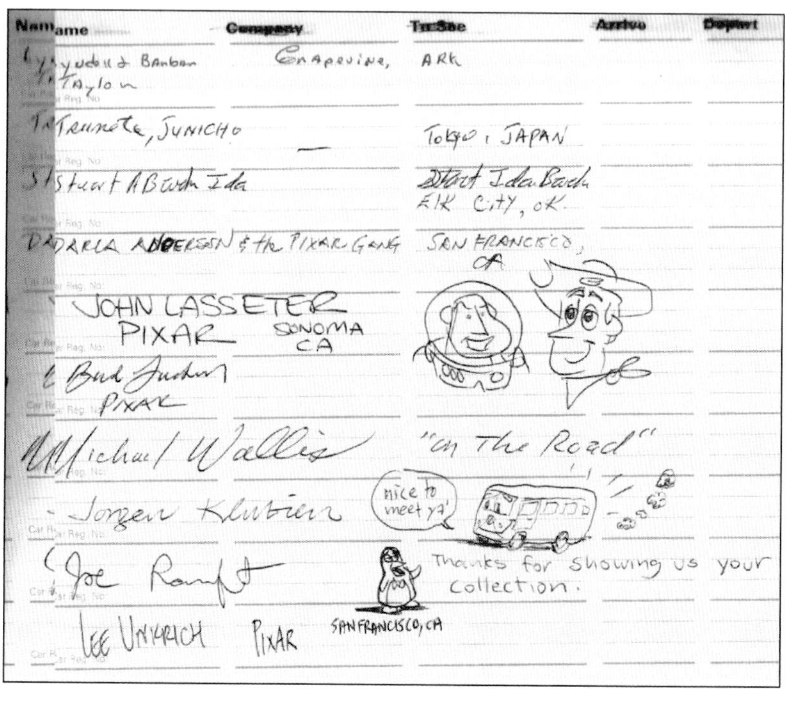

This is where members of Pixar signed in the R.S. and K. Railroad Museum guest book. They drew pictures of some of characters from previous movies after their names. Michael Wallis, who writes books about Route 66, was with them and signed the guest book as well.

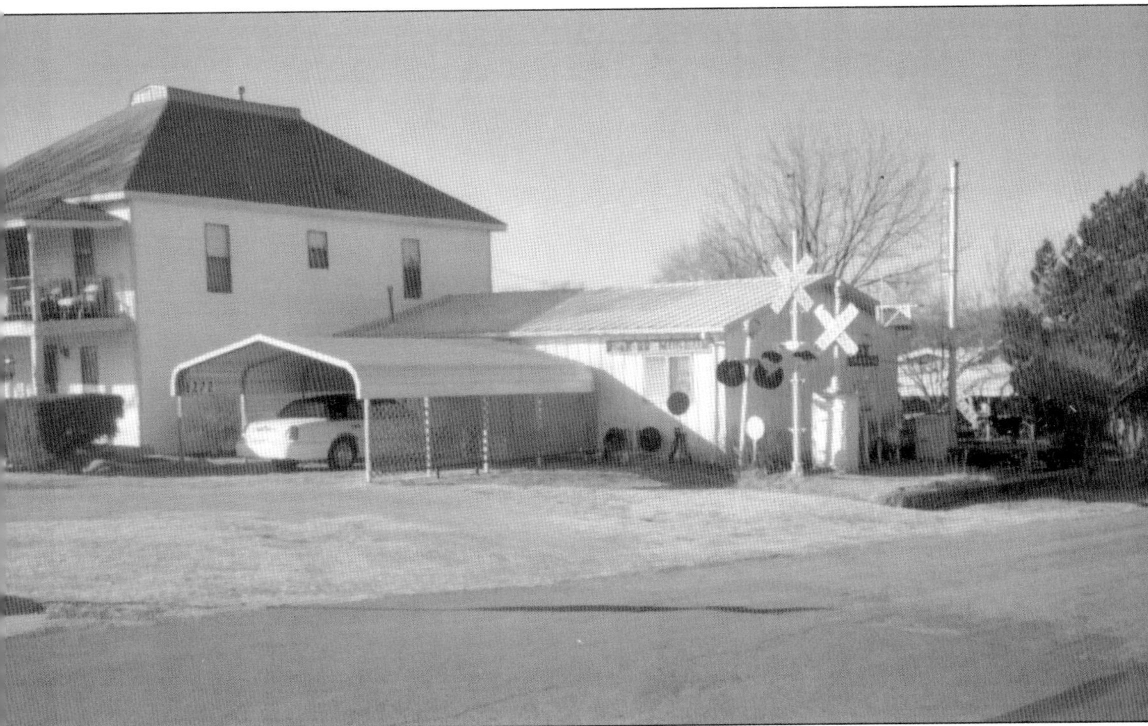

This is the home of the R.S. and K. Railroad Museum at 411 North Sixth Street in Sayre. The museum is on the north end of the property. The house was built in the early 1900s, and the author and her family have lived on this same corner since 1974.